DRAGONS
OR ANGELS?

D0294057

DRAGONS
OR ANGELS?

AN UNOFFICIAL GUIDE TO DRAGONS' DEN AND BUSINESS INVESTMENT

Modwenna Rees-Mogg

crimson

This edition first published in Great Britain in 2008 by
Crimson Publishing, a division of Crimson Business Ltd
Westminster House
Kew Road
Richmond
Surrey
TW9 2ND

A catalogue record for this book is available from the British library.

ISBN 978 1 85458 433 5

Printed and bound by T J International, Padstow, Cornwall

CONTENTS

PART 3   How to become an investor

Acknowledgements

Acknowledgements usually mean naming the many people who have helped the author in writing a book, but in this case, there are literally dozens of people who have helped who specifically asked to remain anonymous, so my task is only to saythat they know who they are and I will never be able to fully express my gratitude to them in making this book happen. Without them it would have been much less fun for me to write and for you to read.

There are some people who I can name. Thank you to Ali Vahdati at digital-I, Caroline Aldon at Octopus Intermediate Capital and John Lamerton for helping me with various charts and statistics.

Thank you also to David Lester for commissioning the book from me (what a chance you have given me!) and to my editorial team at Crimson, especially Holly Bennion, Lucy McLoughlin and Sally Rawlings. Back here at AngelNews, I would like to thank Sarah Abrahams and Jenny Colley for their invaluable contributions to this book. None of us will ever watch an episode of *Dragons' Den* again quite in the same way. A big thanks also to Debbie Dufour and Hatty Stafford Charles who kept the business going whilst we were busy writing. Thanks also to my amazingly tolerant partners who let me go underground to write it rather than spending time with them on other initiatives.

I would like to thank the many people over the years continue to behave angelically towards me as I have strike out on the entrepreneurial path, especially Henry, Kevin, Claire, David, Shaun, Norman, Simon, Philip, Peter, Chris, Jim, George, Brigitte, Grant, Jonathan and Stuart. This book would not have happened if you had not stuck your necks out for me over the years and helped me to get to where I am today. Finally thank-you to Thomas, William, Beatrice, David and Constance for allowing me either not to be there at all or, sometimes, being with you in body, but with my thoughts stuck up in the heavens.

PART 1

The *Dragons' Den* story

CHAPTER 1

What is *Dragons' Den?*

Match mad inventors with serious investors and watch sparks fly!
Alex Cameron (SERIAL ENTREPRENEUR)

Dragons' Den is quite simply a phenomenon. Easily the best programme about business in years, if not ever, it's still compelling well into its sixth series. Since the first episode was aired in Januray 2005, the programme has developed a regular audience of 3million viewers, around 770,000 search results on Google, 1,380 (and rising daily) videos on YouTube and its own entry on Wikipedia. It has made the 'Dragons' who have appeared on the show into national and even international celebrities; whilst many of the people who have pitched their business ideas on the show have found fame and riches, whether or not they were actually offered, or took, investment when they made their appearance. If nothing else, the entrepreneurs who featured on the show have had between five seconds and five minutes of free publicity on prime time UK television.

The show has entered that most important hall of broadcasting fame, one that has a life of its own. It has spawned not one, but numerous, spin-offs. Ricky Gervais, one of the most talented comedians of the day, made a spoof pitch to the Dragons as part of his *Extras* Christmas special in 2007; children have taken on the Dragons in a special show for *Children in Need* and repeats of the various series play regularly on cable TV channels such as Dave. The BBC has even extended the franchise of *Dragons' Den* with further shows called *Where are they now?* which also air on prime time television.

Alongside *The Apprentice* and to a lesser extent *The Restaurant*, *Dragons' Den* has turned business into a popular entertainment for the 21st century viewing public.

Perhaps the greatest symbol of the show's success is that the word 'dragon' now has a new meaning. It's no longer just the beast that breathes fire in many a children's story, or the creature that lives on in folklore as having been slain by St George, but for many it now also means a rich person who invests in perhaps crazy, but also brilliant business ideas. For every one they back the Dragons will miss another that goes on to become an amazing success, generating great riches for the person who thought up the idea in the first place.

Being a Dragon on *Dragons' Den* has helped the individuals to a new route to riches. The Dragons are now celebrities in their own right. Already multi-millionaires, they are now famous. With this fame they have been able to increase their personal fortunes, not because of the amazing investments they have made as a result of *Dragons' Den*, but because they have been able to publish books, get themselves onto the speakers' circuit charging £1,000s per hour so that people can hear 'their story' and even develop a spin-off TV series of their own.

Not bad for a TV concept borrowed from a similar show in Japan, which started showing just as the rest of the investment industry was beginning to recover from the woes of the dot-com crash.

To my knowledge, every book on the programme so far has been an official 'authorized' version of the show and/or the personalities on it. I felt it was about time that someone independent of the BBC, the Dragons and the people who have pitched on the show, took a good hard look at *Dragons' Den*, revealing the good and the ugly, the humour and the sadness that results from the programme and why its impact has been so great and sustaining. Of course, no such review would be worth its salt without comparing it to the real world upon which the show is based. So I decided to write *Dragons or Angels* to redress the balance. This book has three parts. First, is the unofficial guide to the show: I explain how the show began, analyse the Dragons and reveal what it is really like to appear on the show as a 'punter' trying to win investment for your idea. Second, I will explain how you can raise money for your business. Lastly, I will address a whole section on how to become a Dragon yourself and tell you about this very special breed of people who in the 'real world' are called 'angel investors'.

Why this show?

The concept of *Dragons' Den* was conceived in Japan, but was originally titled *Money no Tora* (Money Tiger). This original version was aired from 2001 to 2004 on Nippon Television and was the first entertainment programme in the history of Japanese television that dealt with the concept of business investment. During its three year run, as many as 16 business executives appeared in the programme as Tigers.

Following the success of *Money no Tora*, *Dragons' Den* was brought to broadcast on BBC2 in the UK in 2005. Currently well into its sixth series it appears the *Dragon's Den* is here to stay.

The concept has been so successful that in the UK alone, all over the country, in any month of the year, someone will be holding a '*Dragons' Den*' type event, often called 'Dragons' Den' with total disregard for any rights the BBC might hold to the name. These events provide the opportunity for investors to watch and listen to live pitches by entrepreneurs looking for investment for their businesses.

Dragons' Den – a global phenomenon

Dragons' Den in the UK

In the UK, *Dragons' Den* airs on BBC2; repeats from all series can be caught on BBC3 and Dave on digital and Sky television almost every day as well as being accessible on the online BBC website.

The UK show has seen six successful series across which nine well-known venture capitalists have taken a seat on the panel of Dragons. The table below illustrates which Dragons have been panellists in each series.

You can read all about the Dragons and what makes them tick in Chapter 2.

In contrast to the panel of fiery Dragons, Evan Davis, formerly the BBC's Economics Editor and now a presenter on Radio 4's *Today* programme, provides a mentoring role to the contestants behind the scenes of the Den. Evan has been congratulating and

Series 1	Series 2	Series 3	Series 4	Series 5	Series 6
Peter Jones					
Duncan Bannatyne					
Simon Woodroffe	Theo Paphitis				
Rachel Elnaugh		Deborah Meaden			
Doug Richard		Richard Farleigh		James Caan	

commiserating with entrepreneurs entering the Den for all six series of *Dragons' Den* in the UK and his motto remains the same: honesty pays. You can read a bit more about Evan's career and role in the Den in Chapters 2 and 5.

Dragons' Den beyond the UK

Sometimes TV producers hit on a format for a programme that ends up having global appeal. *Dragons' Den* is one of those formats. Each country will tweak the format a bit. In Australia the Evan Davis figure ran through the outline of the business and then the contestant negotiated with the Dragons. In New Zealand, they originally showed re-runs of the UK and Australian versions, but have now launched their own version. Over in Israel the show is called *Hakrishim* (which is Hebrew for 'The Sharks') and there are six Dragons who rotate their appearance weekly.

The Canadians have been pretty smart as they have picked up on the audience's interest in what happens to the companies after they pitch. Therefore, their first season included a final *Where are they now?* edition and in season two they included 'where are they now' segments inserted into the last few episodes of the show.

Dragons' Den in the Netherlands follows the same format as the UK, as does the show in Finland, although there it is called *Leijonan kita*, which translated means Lions' Den. In Arabia you can see a version – with only four Dragons – called *Al Aareen* (The Den), where entrepreneurs from across the different Arab countries get the chance to pitch.

The brilliant title of the show

The title of any TV show sets out what the audience should expect. Whether it is *Money no Tora* in Japan, *Dragons' Den* in the UK, *The Sharks* in Israel, *Lions' Den* in Finland and soon to be *The Shark Tank* in the United States, the title creates an immediate sense that this is not going to be a show for sentimental viewing.

Before watching a single programme, viewers are given a large clue that there will be clear winners and losers, the atmosphere will be electric and whatever happens, the results will be dramatic and there will be bloodletting.

The stars of the show

The investors

Clearly the biggest stars are the people who will be investing their funds. Whatever you call them – Lions, Tigers, Dragons or Sharks – the wealthy people who are willing to invest their own money in the best of the businesses are inspiring when you think about it. It is ironic, therefore, that the descriptions used on TV are so aggressive. In the real world of private investment, there was great surprise when people heard the show was going to be called *Dragons' Den*; investors are more commonly known as 'business angels', helpful rather than scary creatures.

The idea of an investor being a business angel is not a new idea. The term 'business angel' evolved from the concept of theatre angels who, for centuries, have invested in theatre productions on Broadway and the West End. I think the last laugh is with the angels; TV would not have been where it is today without all those theatre angels backing theatre, films and TV over the years.

The entrepreneurs

The other stars of the show are the people that present to the Dragons. They may be brilliant or disastrous, charming or rude, mad or just plain boring, but they act as the bait to raise the Dragons to action – and this is what makes the show so interesting.

The other stars of the show

Some glory should be attached to the amiable presenter of each show. In the UK this is Evan Davis, a presenter on BBC Radio 4's Today programme who takes on the role of narrator. Taking a neutral stance, Davis's commentary only heightens the tension of the other actors' roles, whilst his amiable debrief of each entrepreneur after they have pitched neatly wraps up everything.

Last, but not least, are the unseen stars of the show, the production team, headed by Producer Dominic Bird and Executive Producer, Helen Bullough and the theme tune composer, John Watt. From the set creators, to the people who select the entrepreneurs to present, and finally to the people in the cutting room who cut several hours of footage into a compelling one hour programme, it is my view that they deserve much of the credit for making the programme format such a success. Without such a great format, it would be hard for the Dragons, the entrepreneurs or Evan Davis to perform with such verve and excitement.

Ask the audience

Rather than asking who watches *Dragons' Den*, I feel I should ask the question, 'Who doesn't?' I don't think I met a single person while writing this book who is not familiar with the programme even if they claim never to watch it. And I don't just mean in the investment world. I recall popping into Marks & Spencer in Kings Road in London, just as I was starting to write the book. I was ordering a lot of food for a party and the manager helping me with the preparations asked why I was holding the event. When I explained that my day job was working in a world like *Dragons' Den* she replied, 'I love that programme, it makes me really want to start my own business.' Taxi drivers, office workers, babysitters, the lot, they all know about *Dragons' Den*. But it is not just ordinary people; celebrities such as Olympian, Dame Kelly Holmes, Radio One DJ, Chris Moyles, actress Pauline Quirke and yes, even the great Sir Alan Sugar himself, have appeared on TV extolling the virtues of the show.

Everyone has an opinion on the show. On the official BBC website there are comments that flash up from regular fans of the show, with remarks such as:

'A fantastic, inspiring programme', 'Love the show, I never miss an episode'; 'Compulsive viewing, more please!' They also have strong views about the Dragons. One of the best comments I heard was this:

'I wouldn't like to go on the show, they are so negative, and they all look really intimidating!'

But whatever people may or may not think about how they would feel about going on the show, they LOVE watching it.

Despite the British public having access to literally dozens of television channels, this one programme averaged 12.5% share of the viewing audience at the time it was broadcast. It appears that the figures are rising over time, not falling and that the audience ranges from shop workers to professionals.

There must be countless others who have also watched parts of the show on YouTube. If you search for *Dragons' Den* on YouTube you will find over 1,460 video clips. The favourite clips from the show regularly attract tens of thousands of views, whilst the clip of Ricky Gervais' spoof pitch has attracted over 400,000 views.

People have also put up hundreds of clips where parts of the show have been spliced with spoof presentations. Video clips have been made using *Dragons' Den* and *X-Factor*, *Dragons' Den* and *Dr Who* and even the Dragons' watching Bertie Ahern pitch to them. But some of the best are where people have made up their own spoof pitches. One of the very best you can see is Keith Hunter's Frigotron, www.youtube.com/watch?v=0y_8h3DqjCk and his Ye Olde Originale Pilot Episode, www.youtube.com/watch?v=PvLm2ybzt5U where the Dragons really are dragons!

The money is fake!

Nothing on *Dragons' Den* is quite what it seems. For a start the money piled up in front of the Dragons is fake. The set is also fake. Originally it was based in a warehouse on the edge of the City of London, but the current set is at Pinewood Studios. And the clips they put together to make the show are spliced from investment pitches that can last two to three hours and do not necessarily act as a 'true' summary of what went on. Some of them are cut to make good TV rather than representing a truly accurate account. However, as everyone who appears on the show has signed away their moral rights (their rights to have a say over how they are depicted), the producers can do what they like with what they film and how they use it!

I have looked into how many of the deals that appear to have been struck on TV actually result in money being handed over by the Dragons to the entrepreneurs. Information on the first four series suggests that out of 19 seeming investments, apparently only six really led to real investments being made. In a strange twist, several of the people who appeared on the show but were not offered investment told me that they had received calls from one or other of the Dragons after the show either offering help or telling them where they could find investment. Ironically, the fact that deals fall through and other deals happen where you least expect them to, is also a major factor in the real world of angel investment, so this is perhaps the one aspect of the TV show where you cannot cry 'fake!'

In the end *Dragons' Den* is about making great TV. Malcolm Burwell, an entrepreneur, sums it up.

> 'It does capture the essence of hope and crashing failure that we all experience fund-raising for one's precious idea. Of course, it is dumbed-down and made prurient so that it sells more air time with the average punter in the UK. The ideas seem generally of the type, 'I thought this up in my bathroom and gave it a go.' The kind of 'muddling through' type of idea that is prevalent in Britain. It doesn't seem to reflect the hurly-burly of fund-raising for technology start-ups. But all-in-all it's a good way to let the public see into this hidden process. I now avoid it. It's too painful to watch, without any particularly useful lessons. I learned what they are showing in my first six months of fund-raising and don't particularly want to be reminded of the agony of that time.'

What happened to that one?

As a rule, private businesses are terrible about staying in touch with people interested in them. I started my own business because private investors kept asking me, 'What happened to that company we both saw pitch a couple of years ago?' Fans of *Dragons' Den* are always asking the same question. The BBC has done some follow-up in a couple of shows, but they have got nowhere near to showing all the fascinating twists and turns that so many of the entrepreneurs have gone through after being on the show.

The *Dragons' Den* website

The BBC has a dedicated web page for the show: www.bbc.co.uk/dragonsdens, that is worth a visit for fans of the programme.

One key reason for going to the website is that you can apply to be on the show via an online form. Another reason is to sign-up to the BBC's mobile TV service where you can get the lastest news from the Den and see highlights from old shows and previews of new shows.

The website also has pages devoted to previous series of the show and profiles of Evan Davis and all the current Dragons. There is a 'Where are they now' section talking about some of the entrepreneurs and what has happened to them since they were on TV.

There is a good quality glossary explaining the business terms used in the Den and talking generally about enterprise and a couple of simple games to play based on the show.

There are also a few links to classic moments from the show and related *Dragons' Den* web pages.

Brilliant TV

Apart from the obvious great mix of wealthy successful people, some crazy and some genuinely brilliant young businesses, and a wide range of different types of people pitching, the thing that really makes the show great is the way it is put together and its atmosphere.

This quote from fan Sarah Abrahams captures the essence of the show:

> 'At the end of the day, I think it's the personality of the Dragons that makes the show, not the investments they make. And when it's not them, it's the crazy pitches and mad entrepreneurs who appear before them.'

CHAPTER 2

Meet the Dragons . . . and the teddy bear

The success of *Dragons' Den* is made by the performance of the Dragons. And *Dragons' Den* has now made them famous in the minds of the general public, whereas previously they were only well known in their own business worlds. Viewers have strong views about the Dragons – they either love them or hate them depending how they behave on the Show. No doubt their mothers would not always agree with what the viewers think and therefore, to set the record straight, here are some biographies of all the Dragons that have appeared on the UK series.

The current Dragons: Profiles

James Caan

Name – James Caan: The People's Investor

> 'Like all business people [the Dragons] have strengths and weaknesses but James Caan seems the most humble'.
>
> Iain Stewart (ENTREPRENEUR)

Nationality – British Asian
Family – Married with two children
Type of Investor – Offers to add real value to real businesses
Interests – Retail and services
Offers accepted on *Dragons' Den* – 4
Character on *Dragons' Den* – The humble investor and the mentor
Best quote from the show – 'You value your company at £1 million. What planet are you on?'
Telltale signs of scepticism – Always very polite and explains why he is backing out
Telltale signs of interest – Quick to put in an offer
Celebrity status – Celebrity speaker, own TV show planned, own website. His autobiography is to be published autumn 2008
Dress sense – Relaxed multi-millionaire
2008 *Sunday Times* Rich List ranking – 1,096th – £73m
Charitable works – The James Caan Foundation, The British Edutrust Foundation, The Educare Trust, The NSPCC and has built a school in Lahore, Pakistan, to educate local children

Before being a Dragon

Caan has been creating, building and selling businesses for over 20 years. In 1985, he set up the Alexander Mann Group, one of the UK's leading HR outsourcing companies, and achieved a turnover of £130 million before selling it to a private equity firm in 2002. He also co-founded an executive headhunting firm with partner Doug Bougie, which they successfully expanded globally through its Humana International brand, growing to over 147 offices across 30 countries before it was sold to a US company.

James is CEO of Hamilton Bradshaw the venture capital firm which he founded in 2004, to invest in sectors spanning from retail and property to finance, health clubs and technology.

How he shapes up on the show

James joined *Dragons' Den* for the fifth series and is known for his integrity, drive, and passion to succeed.

Famous deal

In series five, James Caan invested £60,000 for a 40% share in Laban Roome's gold plating company 'Midas Touch'.

Laban entered the Den very confidently with his gold plating machine, to give the Dragons an on-the-spot demonstration of his gold plating business. Laban outlined that he can gold plate anything, and had an impressive list of past clients such as Hindu temples, the Emmy music awards and bathroom fittings.

Throughout his pitch, Laban was self-assured and confident, expressing his passion and pride in the achievements he had made with Midas Touch.

However, Laban had trouble recalling his financial statistics and turnover, which caused most of the Dragons to back out of the investment. A last passionate pitch to the remaining Dragon, James Caan, proved beneficial to Laban, and James offered the full investment, but for double the equity Laban had hoped for.

Midas Touch is now renamed 'Goldgenie', and Laban has successfully expanded his business and has a wider and innovative range of products such as Apple iPods, mobile phones, roses and golf clubs.

Where is James now?

James returned to *Dragons' Den* for his second series on the panel in series six. He is launching his own television show to promote small businesses and the role they could play in the Olympics, and can often be found speaking at big entrepreneurial events. He also runs his own private equity investment firm.

What James thinks of his fellow Dragons

James Caan has told everyone what he thinks of the other Dragons on his website http://www.james-caan.com. Here are some of his comments:

Deborah Meaden 'A professional individual who does not suffer fools and definitely knows her stuff. She has an amazing attention to detail and can get to the core issue of an idea in an extremely short amount of time.'

Peter Jones 'Peter has a great sense of humour and is very good to work with. He has an incredible ability to think outside the box and see something that everybody else might have missed.'

Theo Paphitis 'A great character. I have a lot of respect for Theo – he's in the toughest end of the market because turning companies around requires tremendous ability and a deep understanding of how business works.'

Duncan Bannatyne 'A family man with a great business. He's had an amazing life, the ultimate rags-to-riches story. I admire Duncan for his achievements and his passion for the Bannatyne brand.'

Deborah Meaden

'Deborah Meaden gets the most into character as a "fierce dragon" – she's so good at acting ... or is she?'
Anne Thomas (ENTREPRENEUR)

Name – Deborah Meaden: The Marketeer
Nationality – British
Family – Married
Type of Investor – Highly logical investor. Only invests in what she understands and believes will make money.
Interests – Marketing, brands and tourism
Offers accepted on *Dragons' Den* – 7
Character on *Dragons' Den* – No-nonsense and fierce
Best quote from the show – 'You damn well ought to feel uncomfortable.'
Telltale signs of scepticism – Raises both eyebrows with wide eyes in disbelief and raises palms to show she is backing out
Telltale signs of interest – Smiling (rarely)
Celebrity status – TV appearances, own website
Dress sense – Hard-nosed business woman
2008 *Sunday Times* Rich List ranking – 1,794th – £40 million
Charitable works – The Princes Trust and Emmaus, a charity for the homeless
Website – www.deborahmeaden.com

Before being a Dragon

Deborah Meaden launched her own glass and ceramics export company straight out of business college, before setting up one of the first Stefanel fashion franchises in the UK. With several successful businesses in the leisure and retail sector under her belt, she became Managing Director of her family's holiday park business, Weststar Holidays. Deborah acquired the major shareholding in a management buyout and later sold the majority of the company in a deal worth £33 million whilst retaining a 23% stake.

She still retained an active role at Weststar but began to devote more time to finding good investment opportunities, including those she found on *Dragons' Den*, which she joined at series three.

Deborah is always on the lookout for good investment opportunities – her first was a market research company, reflecting her own interest in marketing.

In August 2007 she sold her remaining stake in Weststar Holidays to Parkdean Holidays as part of an £83 million deal.

How she shapes up on the show

In the *Dragons' Den*, Deborah's business style is formal and formidable with a 'no-nonsense' approach to the pitching entrepreneurs. However, once Deborah finds a company she wants to invest in, she actively offers her expertise in marketing and promises to transform its fortunes.

Famous deal

In series five, Deborah invested £35,000 in Sarah Lu's company 'Youdoodoll' for a 45% stake in the company.

Sarah entered the Den extremely confident and knowledgeable about her product, which was a make-your-own doll, which the owner can turn into a doll of anyone they like using transhers etc.

Sarah's figures were instantly impressive, and having sold 810 in three weeks simply by making them from her home, by hand. She also had some contracts from major high street stores that really caught the Dragons' attention.

Both Deborah and James decided to make Sarah an offer, but it was Deborah who made the deal, despite asking for 35% more of the company than Sarah had pitched for.

Since the investment, Youdoodoll is stocked in 43 various independent UK stores and 25 branches of Topshop.

Where is Deborah now?

Deborah also appeared in the sixth series of *Dragons' Den*. She currently has four businesses that she has investments in from being on the show; Youdoodoll, JPM Eco Logistics, SteriSpray, Prevention Device, misfuelling, mixalbum.com, and Reestore. All of her investments feature on her website where she has a 'What happened next' section showing the success they have experienced so far.

What Deborah thinks of her fellow Dragons

Deborah has never told anyone publicly what she thinks of the other Dragons.

Theo Paphitis

Name – Theo Paphitis: The Retail Expert
Nationality – Cypriot
Family – Wife, five children, two grandchildren
Type of Investor – Spontaneous and enthusiastic
Interests – Failing businesses
Offers accepted on *Dragons' Den* – 6+
Character on *Dragons' Den* – Master of the one-liner
Best quote' is from the show – 'I would rather stick pins in my eyes than invest in you,' 'Mrs P says . . .', 'Is this how you are going to spend my kids' inheritance?'

Telltale signs of scepticism – Mocks the contestants
Telltale signs of interest – Smirking
Celebrity status – Own website, autobiography, celebrity speaker
Dress sense – New world business magnate
2008 *Sunday Times* **Rich List ranking** – 581st – £135m
Charitable works – Theo has supported events such as the Cystic Fibrosis 'Liv' Charity Event
Website – www.theopaphitis.com

Before being a Dragon

Born in Cyprus, Theo came to England when he was six. Following his education at his local state school, he started his career at 16 as a tea boy/filing clerk with Lloyd's of London insurance brokers, before making his first foray into retail at the age of 18 at Watches of Switzerland. At the age of 20 he moved into finance – property and corporate, specializing in turnarounds, setting up his own company at the age of 23.

In the following years he purchased and turned around ailing companies like Movie Media Sports, Ryman the stationer, Contessa and La Senza lingerie chains, and Partners the stationer. He has turned these companies into successful, solid and profitable retail businesses.

Theo has several other business interests including a 50% share in the business that Rachel Elnaugh founded, Red Letter Days, which he bought with fellow Dragon Peter Jones from the administrators after it went bust.

Theo also spent eight years as Chairman of Milwall FC, taking it out of administration, into the Championship and to the FA Cup Final. He was also a Director of the Football League and an FA Councillor.

How he shapes up on the show

Theo replaced Simon Woodroffe on *Dragons' Den* for the second series and remains a firm favourite with the *Dragons' Den* audience. Theo offers wit and style to the programme, constantly asking the pitching entrepreneurs how they intend to spend his children's inheritance!

Famous deal

In series three, 29 year-old Imran Hakim brought the iTeddy into the Den. The teddy bear had an MP4 media player on his stomach which plays cartoons to children and reads them bedtime stories. He also has a website where you can download content. Imran wanted £140,000 and was offering 15% of iTeddy.

The only Dragon unmoved by the cuddly bear was Duncan Bannatyne. 'I'm so sad,' he said. 'Reading bedtime stories is a father's job. I don't want to be replaced by a teddy bear'. He was out.

Peter Jones saw huge potential profits through the whole distribution chain, and offered half the money for 22.5 %. Theo was quick to match Peter's offer but on condition that the patent would stand up.

Imran looked for a better deal from Deborah but her concerns about the patent forced her to drop out.

Richard said that, if Imran got the patent, iTeddy could be worth millions, but he didn't think he would get it. So he was out, too.

Imran went back to Peter and Theo and managed to negotiate them down to 20% each for £70,000. It meant he got the money he came for, the clout and expertise of two Dragons — and still kept 60% of iTeddy.

Since the show, the iTeddy has hit high street shelves and has been a huge success.

Where is Theo now?

Theo appeared in the sixth series of *Dragons' Den* and continues to run a number of successful British businesses.

What Theo thinks of his fellow Dragons

When asked which of the Dragons he would share a desert island with, he said that he would only share with all of them, not one in particular. He describes Duncan Bannatyne as 'an archetypal Scotsman who plays the part very well'. He also says of Duncan 'he is a very good businessman, but you [get] the feeling that he [is] looking for his own space and hasn't quite found it'. He says Peter Jones is very charismatic, but that didn't come across on the show because 'I think he had adopted the demeanour of everyone else'. He feels Rachel Elnaugh was very cold towards him though she helped him with his TV wardrobe. Doug 'certainly knew his stuff'. 'He is a very analytical guy and very intellectual, but not the sort of person I would normally be rubbing shoulders with'. . . and 'he frightened me'. Theo thinks James Caan has 'no dress sense whatsoever'. When he first met Deborah he thought one look from her could turn you to stone, but now thinks she has become one of the boys.

Duncan Bannatyne

Name — Duncan Bannatyne, OBE. The genuine self-made man
Nationality — Scottish
Family — Wife and six children
Type of Investor — Hard man who has done it for himself and expects the same from others
Interests — Health and fitness
Offers accepted on *Dragons' Den* — 4
Character on *Dragon's Den* — Rock star of the business world
Best quote from the show — 'You are barking mad; it's as simple as that'
Celebrity status — Own website husely successful autobiography fronted the 2008 TV show about the *Sunday Times* Rich List, famous for his leisure centres
Telltale signs of scepticism — Wide-mouthed dumbfounded
Telltale signs of interest — One hand on chin, sat back in chair, very relaxed
Dress sense — Relaxed businessman
2008 *Sunday Times* Rich List ranking — 267th — £310m
Charitable works — As a fervent charity fundraiser Duncan supports a number of key charities including the United Nations Children's Fund (UNICEF) and Scottish International Relief. He was named as an Honorary Fellow of UNICEF and, through his work with Scottish International Relief, has helped fund two orphanages in Romania and Colombia. Duncan was awarded an OBE in the 2004 Queen's Birthday Honours for his services to charity.
Website — www.duncanbannatyne.co.uk

Before being a Dragon

At the young age of fifteen, Duncan volunteered for eleven years with the Royal Navy. After which, he served several years before receiving a dishonourable discharge for disobedience and attempting to throw an officer off a boat landing jetty in Scotland. In his autobiography he claims this was in part a reaction to this officer's abuse of his authority, in part a dare by his drunken shipmates, and in part a way of getting out of the Navy, with which he had become disillusioned. Bannatyne was only nineteen years old when this happened. After the incident he had to serve nine months in a military detention centre before being discharged.

He began his entrepreneurial life by trading in cars, but it was with an ice cream van that he changed the course of his life – setting out to become the king of the '99'.

He then switched to nursing homes, becoming a multi-millionaire in the process. Since then Duncan has built up a chain of health clubs called Bannatyne's and also owns Bannatyne's Casino, Bar and Hotels.

Duncan was recently awarded an honorary Doctor of Science (D.Sc.) from Glasgow Caledonian University for services to business and charity.

He was also North Region Entrepreneur of the Year 2003 and Master Entrepreneur of the Year 2003 for the North Region.

How he shapes up on the show

Duncan has been a panellist on *Dragons' Den* since series one and is renowned for his 'to the point' approach with pitching entrepreneurs. He is always keen to jump up and try the products brought to 'the Den' and has a sharp eye for the individual behind the product.

Duncan is famous for saying exactly what he thinks and for declaring himself out quickly.

Famous deal

Duncan Bannatyne and James Caan entered a joint investment of £150,000 for 36% of the equity in Peter Moule's 'Chocbox' invention.

The Chocbox protects and insulates standard electrical connector blocks, negating the need to cover them with tape. Due to new electrical regulations, Peter invented the Chocbox, which immediately had a market if all UK homes were to meet these new regulations.

Chocbox has become a great *Dragon's Den* success story after landing a £25 million deal with one of the world's biggest electrical distributors only a few months after appearing on the show.

Where is Duncan now?

Duncan appeared in the sixth series of *Dragons' Den*, and still runs his successful Bannatyne brand. Spending more and more time on charity now and has become very hands off with his businesses.

What Duncan thinks of the other Dragons

Duncan has said he thinks Peter Jones is extremely knowledgeable about technology and he, Peter, likes the idea that anyone with a good idea can make it. He has said of Doug that he is always very focused on looking for a quick return on his investment. He thinks Simon Woodroffe is one of the nicest, entrepreneurs he has ever met and looks at investment opportunities differently, keeping an eye out for companies that he could add his Yo! magic to. He says Theo is an incredibly witty guy, who aggressively purchases investments and really turns up the heat in the Den.

On Richard Farleigh he said he's clearly interested in a broad range of companies, and for him it also comes down to the people ... and is on the lookout for companies he can take towards a stock market flotation. He is enormously likeable and good fun to have around.

On Deborah he says she is incredibly down to earth, strong-willed and sensible and that she wants to add value and is quite prepared to do this by getting her hands dirty.

Peter Jones

Name – Peter Jones: The Visionary
Nationality – British
Family – Divorced, new partner, five children
Type of Investor – Invests for interest and pleasure as well as money
Interests – Telecoms, media, leisure and publishing
Offers accepted on *Dragons' Den* – 6
Character on *Dragons' Den* – The hard worker/Simon Cowell Figure/Genuine High Achiever
Best quote from the show – 'You're in Disneyland.'
Telltale signs of scepticism – Outright laughing after a period of silence
Telltales signs of interest – Remains silent until the last moment, giving nothing away but wearing a smug grin
Dress sense – Serious businessman and expects the same from entrepreneurs who pitch to him, but with a light touch (his socks!)
Celebrity status – Autobiography, celebrity speaker, own website, board game, own TV shows and appearances on US TV shows
2008 *Sunday Times* Rich List Ranking – 513th – £157m
Charitable works – The Peter Jones Foundation which provides support and funding for children in the UK. The foundation hosts the Forgotten Children charity and The National Enterprise Academy
Website – www.peterjones.tv

Before being a Dragon

Peter's entrepreneurial journey started early when, at the age of 16, he founded a tennis academy. He then set up a computer business and had various other business interests.

At the age of 28, Peter joined corporate giant Siemens Nixdorf and ran its computer business in the UK. In the mid-1990s his first major business collapsed when a creditor went bust. He picked himself up and in 1998 he founded Phones International Group, a telecommunications firm that now generates revenues in excess of £200m.

His business interests range from telecoms; leisure and publishing as well as TV and media. Peter has won many national awards, including Emerging Entrepreneur of the Year in 2001.

Now in his early forties, Peter is considered to be one of the UK's leading businessmen.

How he shapes up on the show

Peter has been in all six series of *Dragons' Den*. Peter is also known for his sharp mind, quick wit and quirky one liners. When appearing on the programme, Peter likes to wear extravagant socks with his elegant suit, as he feels this prevents him from completely showing up the other Dragons.

In the summer of 2005, Jones teamed up with another *Dragons' Den* star, Theo Paphitis, to buy the gift experience company Red Letter Days from fellow panellist Rachel Elnaugh, under whose ownership it had collapsed.

Peter also created Wines4Business.com, an online retailer specializing in the sale of wine and champagne to corporate clients, as well as Celcius.co.uk, a specialist recruitment business. He has many investments from the show *Dragons' Den* including *Wonderland* (a new luxury lifestyle magazine), Square Mile International (providing data services for marinas), The Generating Company (a contemporary circus company), iTeddy and Reggae Reggae Sauce among others.

Famous deal

Peter invested £50,000 for 30% of Celia Norowzian and Ian Forshew's concept 'Beach Break Live'.

Celia and Ian had run the three-day student music festival for a year and initially had some good figures in their pitch. However, a grilling from the Dragons revealed that although they had a high number of attendees, only 50% of them were paying, and the rest were mainly festival workers.

It was also revealed that the couple had made a loss of £30,000 the previous year, and these figures alone were enough for Duncan Bannatyne and James Caan to back out, by stating angrily that they should use volunteers to work at their festival.

Despite Duncan and James having issues with the low ticket prices and other statistics, the other three made the couple offers. Deborah initially offered all the money for 40% before reducing to 35% after Theo and Peter matched the money for 30% of the company.

After a lengthy battle between the Dragons, Peter said he would accept a 25% share in the company for all the money, and the deal was done.

Since Peter's investment, Beach Break Live is much more professional and has the support of many universities across the UK. The festival looks set to be an annual success in years to come.

Where is Peter now?

Peter appeared in the sixth series of *Dragons' Den* and is enjoying television success in America on *The American Investor*, which works on a similar concept to *Dragons' Den*.

He owns a TV production company called Peter Jones TV, and his business portfolio also includes a range of property investments.

What Peter thinks of the other Dragons

Peter is known for his regular conflicts of interest in the Den with fellow Dragon Duncan Bannatyne, who has also been in every series. On one occasion, he was so disgusted with Duncan for undercutting his bid that he responded with 'You've just completely been a sly little s**t'. He has also said that in the first episode everyone was very polite but clearly eyeing each other up and jostling for position, especially when the cameras started to roll.

The previous Dragons: Profiles

Four people have been dragons in previous series. They are:

Richard Farleigh

Name – Richard Farleigh
Nationality – Australian
Family – Wife and two children
Type of Investor – A real business angel
Interests – Focuses on the person, not a type of company
Offers accepted on *Dragons' Den* – 4
Character on *Dragons' Den* – Mr Nice
Telltale signs of scepticism: Keeps quiet
Telltales signs of interest: Sensible questioning
Dress sense: Cool dude entrepreneur
Celebrity status: Autobiography, website
2008 *Sunday Times* Rich List ranking: 1,446th – £50m
Charitable works: Involved in Wikiproject Australia

Before being a Dragon

Richard Farleigh was one of eleven siblings. His father, who moved around Australia with his wife and children, was reported to be a violent alcoholic. When Farleigh was aged two, he and his siblings were taken into care and sent to foster homes.

Despite this he went on to excel later in life at mathematics and chess, winning a scholarship to read economics at the University of New South Wales. After graduating with honours, he joined Bankers Trust Australia in Sydney when 23 as a trader and stayed there for ten years. He was hired to run a hedge fund (an investment vehicle that explicitly pursues an absolute return on its underlying investment) in the tax haven of Bermuda and moved there with his first wife and baby son. There, he became friends with David Norwood, a chess grand master, and three years later, he had earned enough to retire, aged 34, and moved to Monte Carlo. It was at this point that he spent much time with Norwood investigating research from Oxford University in the UK that had potential commercial applications. IndexIT was the company formed to fund some of these ventures; it was later sold to Beeson Gregory for £20m.

He has made millions of dollars after investing his own capital in British technology companies and his personal wealth is estimated at around AU$160,000,000.

As well as many technology investments, Farleigh also invested £2m in the renovation of the old French Embassy in London, turning it into a private members club, Home House, which was later sold at a profit.

How he shaped up on the show

Farleigh was selected in 2006 to appear as an investor on *Dragons' Den* for the show's third series. His appearances on the show echo those of former dragon Doug Richard in standing out by always trying to offer constructive advice to contestants, even when not interested in investing, as opposed to negative comments often offered by some of his fellow Dragons. He gradually became a popular Dragon on the show, mainly due to the fact he had the reputation for making the most offers compared with the other Dragons throughout his time on the show.

Despite being a financial expert, Richard did not prioritize 'numbers', but believes the key to finding an investor is simply a good idea.

Famous deal

Reggae singer and chef Levi Roots strummed his way into the Den asking for £50,000 to manufacture his spicy Reggae Reggae Sauce. In return Levi (real name Keith) was offering 20% of the equity in the business.

The sauce is a secret recipe from Levi's grandmother and must be hot stuff because even Peter Jones raised a sweat after trying it.

Not everyone was impressed. Duncan Bannatyne thought it wouldn't make much money, Deborah Meaden considered it might make just enough to provide a lifestyle business, and Theo Paphitis said that the orders Levi already had meant that he didn't need the investment at all. So they all declared themselves out.

In the end Levi warmed two of the Dragons' hearts though; Peter Jones offered half the amount for 20% of the equity, and Richard Farleigh chipped in with the remaining £25,000 for another 20%.

So he left the Den with £50,000 and 60% of his business and gave the Dragons a reprise of his song, disappearing to warm applause.

Since securing investment from Richard and Peter, Reggae Reggae Sauce has really taken off with a contract with Sainsbury's and is on supermarket shelves across the UK.

Leaving the show

Richard was axed after the fourth series of *Dragons' Den* for investor James Caan. There has been a great deal of controversy over his exit from the show, with many viewers believing the directors of the show wanted to portray a multi-cultural panel of experts.

Being one of the public's favourite Dragons, there was a huge amount of backlash after he was axed. There is even an online petition to bring him back: www.bring-backrichardfarleigh.com

Commenting on his departure from the show, Richard said,

'It would be disappointing if that was the reason – rather than anything fundamental – if it was because I was the wrong colour. I don't know why this has happened and I am very disappointed and bemused – I wasn't expecting it because all the feedback I got was very positive. I had even moved back to the UK to focus on commitments for the show. I am gutted that I have not been invited back.'

Where is Richard now?

Since leaving *Dragons' Den* Richard has returned to being a business angel investor and has kept a low profile.

What Richard thinks of the other Dragons

Richard has not given his opinion on any of the Dragons in particular, but had mentioned that he did not like their harsh attitude to the entrepreneurs.

Doug Richard

> 'I did pitch my own company to Doug Richard, and found it a very pleasant
> and useful [if ultimately unsuccessful] discussion'.
> Patrick Benham-Croswell

Name – Doug Richard
Nationality – American
Family – Wife and three children
Type of Investor – Tech-focused
Interests – Technology transfer, commercialization, and business incubation.
Offers accepted on *Dragon's Den* – 1
Character on *Dragons' Den* – Hawk, Predator
Best quote from the show – 'If I invested, I can't afford to have you run the business'.
Telltale sign of scepticism – Raises one eyebrow and looks amazed
Telltale sign of serious interest – Asks a lot of questions about Intellectual Property (IP) Protection
Dress sense – International banker
Celebrity status – Celebrity speaker, advises the UK Conservative Party on its enterprise policy, Queen's Award for Enterprise, columnist in *Growing Business* magazine
2008 *Sunday Times* Rich List ranking – Does not appear
Charitable works – Works alongside 'Red Balloon', a local educational charity in Cambridge. Doug has also been involved in schemes such as The Big Green Challenge which aims at reducing carbon imprints
Website – www.thedougrichardproject.com

Before being a Dragon

Doug is a successful entrepreneur with 20 years' experience in the development and leadership of technology and software ventures, both in the US and in the UK. His qualifications include a BA in Psychology from University of California at Berkeley and a Juris Doctor at the School of Law, University of California at Los Angeles.

Between 1996 and 2000 he was President and CEO of Micrografx, a US publicly quoted software company, which he sold to Corel Corporation in 2000. Prior to that he also founded and subsequently sold two other companies: Visual Software and ITAL Computers.

How he shaped up on the show

During his time on *Dragons' Den*, Doug was renowned for his 'hawk'-like persona, where he rarely invested, once swore at an entrepreneur and reduced one to tears. He was marked from the other investors on the programme by a straightforward, no-nonsense style.

With his strong views and opinions he was picked up for ridicule on the BBC TV comedy impressions show *Dead Ringers* for a short time.

Famous deal

Doug offered with Rachel Elnaugh, to jointly invest a total of £120,000 for a return of 20% each in the equity of Tracey Graily's business Grails.

Grails creates beautifully made, individually tailored, hand-finished women's suits with a choice of design, fabrics, lining and buttons for professional, high-earning business women.

Tracey entered the Den in series one with two other ladies, all three of them modelling the tailored suits she intended on developing. She outlined that her customers pay around £700 for a suit that is entirely made to measure from the exact materials of their choice.

Despite most of the Dragons showing a blatant disinterest in her business and stating she would have a limited market for the suits, Doug and Rachel saw otherwise.

Reflecting on the show, Tracey describes that

> 'the impact has been pretty amazing, I've seen a 50% increase in customers, and what was particularly interesting was the number of additional website hits – 7,000 visits in the week after the show. Being on Dragons' Den certainly was nerve-wracking, and it is great drama'.

Following the investment, Grails quickly ran out of money and was closed down.

Leaving the show

Doug left the show after series two of *Dragons' Den* to concentrate on adding to his already significant wealth by developing his own ideas. He is currently heading up a new mobile social networking business called TruTap, which offers a free global messaging service which lets you take your social life everywhere you go on your phone.

Where is Doug now?

Doug is the Chairman and CEO of hot mobile social networking business TruTap and Chairman of the Conservative Party Small Business Task Force. He is also Founder and Vice-Chairman of Cambridge Angels.

In 2006 Doug was an Honorary Recipient of The Queen's Award for Enterprise Promotion. In 2007 Doug became a fellow of the Royal Society of Arts.

What Doug thinks of his fellow Dragons

Doug does not comment on the Dragons with whom he appeared on TV, but he has been publicly critical of at least one of the current dragons. At a recent conference at which they were both speaking he said of James Caan,

> 'I think he's really condescending, actually. I cudda sworn that there's a room full of adults here.'

Simon Woodroffe

Name – Simon Woodroffe, OBE
Nationality – English
Family – Partner, one daughter
Type of Investor – Looked for the unusual
Interests – Entertainment
Offers accepted on *Dragons' Den* – 1
Character on *Dragons' Den* – The people's person/Ordinary Bloke
Best quote from the show – 'My advice to you is to get real.'
Telltale sign of scepticism – Looks very interested/bored
Telltale sign of serious interest – Becomes very talkative, in contrast to his usual quiet self
Dress sense – Rock star manager
Celebrity status – Several appearances on other TV shows, celebrity speaker, author of The book of YO! and Yo! Sushi, company website based on his Yo brand
2008 *Sunday Times* Rich List ranking – Does not appear
Charitable works – Helped to design the stage for Live Aid. Part of the CBI Ambassador for Entrepreneurship programme and advises the government's Small Business Service and Enterprise Insight and NFTE (Nifty), a programme supporting entrepreneurship in schools
Website – www.yocompany.biz

Before being a Dragon

After leaving school at 16, Simon spent almost 30 years in the entertainment business. Through the 1970s and 1980s his production companies, based in London and Los Angeles, designed rock n' roll stages for artistes like Rod Stewart, The Moody Blues and Stevie Wonder, and events like Live Aid.

A natural progression led Simon into television at the start of the 1990s. He spearheaded the development of television deals to show huge international rock concerts worldwide, organizing the financing and distribution of the Nelson Mandela concerts, shows for Amnesty International and the Prince's Trust concerts. His television production deals included Japan's number one pop show, Hit Studio International.

In 1997, Simon founded YO! Sushi, a conveyor belt sushi bar. The concept was to make eating a complete entertainment experience and featured call buttons, robot drinks trolleys and Japanese TV. The first restaurant opened on London's Poland Street and became an overnight phenomenon. Today it continues to expand both at home and abroad: 45 sites by the end of 2007 in the UK, France, Ireland and the Middle East and a forecast turnover of £30m.

In 1999 Simon won the Ernst & Young Entrepreneur of the Year Award and became part of the CBI/BCC Ambassador of Entrepreneurism campaign. In 2001 he was awarded the accolade of Best Venue at the Retailer of the Year Awards.

How he shaped up on the show

Simon was one of the original Dragons on *Dragons' Den*. He had a reputation for plain speaking and being interested in unusual deals. None of the offers he made completed after the show. He left after one series. He was very popular with the other Dragons.

Best deal

Simon did not close on any of the deals from *Dragons' Den*. He said 'I made more money than anyone else out of that first series and that was zero. I never ended up making an investment to tell you the truth.'

Leaving the show

Simon left *Dragons' Den* after just one series. He said of the show, 'The trouble with *Dragons' Den* and one of the reasons I left, is that the BBC wanted to get crap people on so that I could kick the sh*t out of them, and I didn't really want to do that. I think it's always been about encouraging. I always thought we should get better people on and I actually think it would be a better programme long-term because you could then have seen more follow-ups.'

> 'When people come to me and say they're going on Dragons' Den I always say to them "the thing to remember is that when you walk up the stairs and into the Den just remember it's a TV show"' It's not five people thinking "how am I going to be able to make an investment here?" they're actually thinking "am I going to be the star of this next little piece?"'

Where is Simon now?

In recognition of his contribution to hospitality, Simon was awarded an OBE in the Queen's Birthday Honours 2006.

The YO! story continues to develop. As well as Yotel, Simon continues to develop new YO! brands including YO! Zone: part spa, part café, part bar and part nightclub; and YO! Home, which will provide a futuristic take on the traditional home.

What Simon thinks of his fellow Dragons

Simon gets on well with the Dragons he appeared with on TV and does not comment on the others by name, although he has commented that in his view the Dragons do try to be the star of the piece after each pitch rather than treating it as another investment opportunity.

Rachel Elnaugh

Nationality – English
Family – Husband and five children
Type of Investor – Small, but active
Interests – Marketing, entertainment
Offers accepted on *Dragons' Den* – 4
Character on *Dragons' Den* – The phoenix
Best quote from the show – 'I don't like you.'

Telltale sign of scepticism – Sniggers and subtly shakes head
Telltale sign of interest – Genuine smile and wide eyes
Dress sense – Serious business woman
Celebrity status – Celebrity speaker, one book *Business Nightmares*, website
2008 *Sunday Times* Rich List ranking – None
Charitable works – From an early age Rachel ran charity events at her father's electrical store, where she set up a little charity table in the shop, selling homemade crackers and gift-tags made from old Christmas cards
Website – www.rachelelnaugh.com

Before being a Dragon

Having started her working life at an accounting firm, at the age of 24 she created the market-leading experiences brand Red Letter Days on a shoestring budget from the front room of her home. Red Letter Days went on to generate over £100million in turnover in the 16 years that she ran it, and in doing so pioneered the UK's £250 million experiences sector. This earned her an Ernst & Young Entrepreneur of the Year award in 2002, as well as being shortlisted for the 2001 Veuve Clicquot Businesswoman of the Year award and the Growing Business Entrepreneur of the Year award in 2002.

How she shaped up on *Dragons' Den*

During her time on *Dragons' Den*, Rachel became notorious for waiting until all the other Dragons had declared their hands before indicating how interested she was in a deal.

Best deal

Rachel invested £54,000 in Tracie Herrtage's company Le Beanock for 49% of a share in the equity.

The suspendable Le Beanock is a bean bag/hammock suspended from high ceilings and lofts to replace your sofa and costs around £900.

The male dominion of Dragons mocked the idea and thought that the prices swung too high, the concept was ungrounded and it wasn't an interesting proposition for their equity.

Rachel Elnaugh, however, wasn't put off and agreed that Tracie's vision hit a niche market. Yet business is business; unflinching Rachel seized her opportunity and cut the tightest deal yet, buying 49% of Tracie's company as sole investor.

Since the show Tracie says everything has been 'mad'. She added, 'The way they film the show is brilliant for the audience, but really daunting for the entrants…Since the show I've had hundreds of emails, and now have the money to start an advertising campaign. I've even secured distribution contracts for Italy and the Channel Isles.'

Leaving the show

After Red Letter Days investors went into administration in 2005, the remaining assets and goodwill were bought by fellow *Dragons' Den* investors Peter Jones and Theo Paphitis.

Since leaving the show, Rachel has branded *Dragon's Den* as being 'entertainment for the masses', and has understandably mixed feelings about the show. However, when asked if she regrets agreeing to do the show, Rachel said 'Oh, not at all. It's a very rare opportunity, isn't it, being on a TV series, and although it is a double-edged sword, and maybe I wouldn't have lost the company if I hadn't been in the spotlight and hadn't been so media-worthy, it's led to so many opportunities and taken my life in a completely new direction. So many positive things have come out of it I can't possibly regret it at all.'

Where is Rachel now?

Rachel is now involved in a number of new business projects and is a prolific business speaker and conference chairman. She was a member of the judging panel of the Grazia Businesswoman of the Year Awards 2006 as well as the Accountancy Age Awards 2006. She was voted IAB 'UK Champion of Entrepreneurship' in 2008.

Rachel launched her own unique Entrepreneurial Profiling system at the Business Start Up Show at London's Excel in April 2008. She has just published Business Nightmares, which is part autobiography and part a review of famous business people who have faced and overcome disasters in their businesses.

She is now known and respected for using the lessons she has learned from her own business experience to motivate and inspire other entrepreneurs.

What Rachel thinks of her fellow Dragons

Rachael is always very complimentary about Simon Woodroffe and Doug Richard, but keeps quiet about the other dragons.

And Finally Evan Davis – the 'teddy bear'.

Evan Davis

Name – Evan Davis
Nationality – British
Role on Show – Presenter
Character on *Dragons' Den* – Guardian Angel
Motto of show – Honesty pays

Before *Dragons' Den*

Evan attended Dorking County Grammar School, and later studied Philosophy, Politics and Economics at St John's College, Oxford from 1981 to 1984, before obtaining an MPA at the Kennedy School of Government at Harvard University. While at Oxford University, Evan edited Cherwell the student newspaper.

Before joining the BBC as an Economics correspondent in 1993, he worked as an economist at the Institute for Fiscal Studies from 1986 to 1988 and again from 1992 to 1993. Between 1988 and 1992 he worked at the London Business School. Evan also worked as Economics Editor on BBC Two's Newsnight programme from 1997 to 2001. Since becoming the BBC's Economics Editor, Evan has been responsible for reporting and analysing economic developments on a range of programmes on BBC radio and television, particularly the Ten O'Clock News. He also has a role in shaping the extensive BBC coverage of Economics across all the corporation's outputs, including online.

In 1998, Evan released a book called Public Spending, published by Penguin. In it he argued for the privatization of public services as a means to increase efficiency.

How he shapes up in the Den

Evan Davis is the presenter of *Dragons' Den* and has the unenviable task of welcoming the would-be entrepreneurs into the Den and then debriefing them as they emerge either triumphant, or more often than not, with their tails between their legs. It is a role that demands diplomatic skill, as Evan must deal with the bruised egos of the contestants whilst acknowledging the reasons why the Dragons have turned them down. Because of this and his round, almost cartoon-like features, he was described by Charlie Brooker as 'the world's biggest teddy bear'.

Where is Evan now

Evan continues to be the presenter of *Dragons' Den* and *Where are they now?* and other spin-offs. In November 2007 it was announced that he was standing down as BBC Economics Editor for 12 months to join the *Today* programme as a full-time presenter, replacing Carolyn Quinn.

He also writes a blog for the BBC website entitled 'Evanomics' in which he 'attempts to understand the real world, using the tool kit of Economics'. Subjects he has discussed include road pricing, care for the elderly, Gordon Brown's Budget and how to choose wine.

Evan has won several awards including the Work Foundation's Broadcast Journalist of the Year award in 1998, 2001 and 2003, and the Harold Wincott Business Broadcaster of the Year award in 2002.

He has also made several appearances on the quiz show, *Have I Got News For You* and has written a book based on *Dragons' Den* called *Your Idea can Make you Rich* and co-authored *Dragons' Den: Success from Pitch to Profit*.

Dragons' Den – free publicity or real life?

'Dragons are disrespectful and paint angels in a very bad light. . . a successful investor
does not abuse entrepreneurs and make them look foolish (even if they are!)'
Rowena Ironside (INVESTOR)

Many people watch *Dragons' Den* to enjoy the Dragons tearing apart the visions of hopeful entrepreneurs. While this clearly makes good television, is it actually valuable to an entrepreneur with serious hopes of attaining funding? The show has great merits as it summarizes the real issues that arise when entrepreneurs pitch for investment; the trouble is that it does it in such a harsh way. Some kindlier private investors, known as business angels, admit that it is having a bad effect in the real world, with their fellow angels becoming increasingly aggressive in their approach to entrepreneurs. 'Real investors are just as harsh,' said a business adviser. 'The problem is the Dragons are forced to reject propositions on air, while in real life they just don't return phone calls.'

There are always two viewpoints in this world and another charming investor, Chris Arnold, believes that in real life business investors are not as harsh as the show indicates. '[In real life] they are more pragmatic and less aggressive, they look for opportunities, not to knock things down!' Many others confirm that they would never humiliate an entrepreneur in the way the Dragons do.

The entrepreneurs who have been on *Dragons' Den* have interesting opinions on the Dragons. Danny Bamping, who appeared on the show to gain investment for a puzzle game, claims that during his pitch the Dragons completely turned on each other. He said, 'They just couldn't stand each other.' But there are plenty of other tales to suggest that the current team of Dragons get on perfectly well with each other. I suspect it is just like the real world. Most business people tend to get on quite well with each other, even if they would not dream of becoming proper friends.

There is no doubt though that becoming a Dragon will make you famous and Gary Taylor, who pitched his truck valeting company, made a good point. He said '*Dragons' Den* is an ego boost show for the judges to hype their profiles.' Andrew Gordon who was also on the show thinks, 'The Dragons are on the show for their own self-interests, to promote themselves as a brand . . . their motives to invest are secondary in my opinion.'

What do the Dragons themselves think about it? And more interestingly, what do they think of their fellow Dragons? The current Dragons are pretty discrete and, if asked, usually go out of their way to say nice things about each other. Even comments from past Dragons do not tend to get personal about the other Dragons; they may criticize the show's format and accuse the Dragons of using it to get famous, but they do not name the individual Dragons they dislike or disapprove of.

After leaving the show, Richard Farleigh outlined,

> '*When I first went on Dragons' Den I was shocked by how tough they were.*
> *I even had to talk to one guy after filming because he was so upset*
> *by what had been said to him.*'

While on the show, Richard was notorious for being the 'friendly' Dragon, and he has made no secret of the fact that he disliked the other Dragons' unnecessarily harsh approach.

Simon Woodroffe left the show after just one series. He has complained about the BBC's approach and has said of the other Dragons,

> '*It's not five people thinking: "How am I going to be able to make an*
> *investment here." They're actually thinking: "Am I going to*
> *be the star of this next piece?"*'

Rachel Elnaugh's views are interesting. Whilst on the show she was clearly very engaged with it, and following being axed as a Dragon she has described the show as,

> '*Coliseum TV created exclusively for the torture of those who manage to get*
> *featured on the show, and entertainment for the masses.*'

She sometimes still introduces herself as

> '*I am Rachel Elnaugh and I was a Dragon.*'

Perhaps it is original Dragon, Doug Richard, who should have the last word on what the Dragons really think about the show. He has said,

> 'They approached me, and being American, I just said, "Me on TV, free publicity. Great, bring it on!"'

CHAPTER 3

The real *Dragons' Den* experience

Have you ever wondered what really happens behind the camera on the set of *Dragons' Den*? Are the Dragons actually as nasty and 'diva-like' as the camera portrays? Is the process all very high profile, with the contestants being treated as respectable entrepreneurs? Here, people who have been on the show reveal what it is really like. Some entrepreneurs thoroughly enjoyed themselves and felt it was a great experience, others are pretty neutral and some really hated it. It is clear though that there is far more to the whole experience than you might imagine from the slick TV show that we see. Let's take the whole experience step by step.

> *'Complete Rubbish!'*
> Andrew Burton (VENTURE CAPITALIST)

The application process

To apply to be on *Dragons' Den* apparently just requires you to download an application form from the official BBC website or to fill in the form online. In fact, many people apply direct to the producers of the show via someone who knows someone on the production team and recommends they apply. Of course not everyone who does apply will appear on the show. Only the BBC would be able to tell us exactly how the people who get filmed actually get to be on the show.

Assuming you do fill in the form you have to provide lots of information about your business and yourself, such as whether you have a criminal record.

Entrepreneurs who have been on the show have told me that you do not automatically get called to appear on the show just because you have submitted a form. In fact, it is quite likely that you will have to ring and badger the production team to give you a test screening. Successful contestants report they persistently nagged the team to get given a screen test. This can lead to getting a chance at the last minute, and finding themselves being actually filmed for the show three days later.

At the screen test, the producers are not just looking at whether you are a great entrepreneur or whether your business is the next Google. They are also looking to see if your pitch will make good TV, even if your idea is absolutely rubbish. This might explain why some really dud business opportunities get to appear on TV. And we should not forget that the producers are tasked with making good TV, not with finding good businesses.

Real investors confirm that they believe the pitches aired on *Dragons' Den* are definitely chosen for their entertainment value rather than just because they are worthy of real life investment. Dave Auger, a real investor, agrees that the quality of those pitching on the show is unrealistic. 'The pitches are entertaining, but in real life they wouldn't get far enough through the process to present to angels...' In fact, an insider who is involved in selecting business ideas to appear revealed that the BBC only chooses the ones that he argues will be good for entertainment value rather than those he thinks are good investment propositions. So the message is clear: if you want to appear on the show, you need to prove to the BBC that your pitch will be entertaining as well as good for investment.

'The Process is Ridiculous!'
Martin Rigby (VENTURE CAPITALIST)

Before you are allowed into the Den

Before you even get a chance to prove you will be entertaining on TV, you must hand over your business plan and many other documents about your business. People who have been on the show talk about this being an awful lot of information. You cannot just send in your business plan – you have to send them all the background papers behind your business plan, including documents such as your patents. All of this information is sent into the BBC so that the Dragons can see it on the day.

You must also sign a document agreeing that you waive your moral rights to the BBC. This is standard practice if you are being filmed for TV and sounds innocuous. After all it means the BBC can safely use anything they film referring to you and your business. It would be impossible for them if they had to come back to get approval from everyone they film. The bad news for the person being filmed is that in signing the document you give up the right to have any say in how they portray you. So right up until the show airs you will not be sure how they are going to make you look.

Assuming you get past this stage you need to go for a screen shooting, where you are filmed to see if you look good on TV. You can take comfort from the fact that each of the Dragons has had to have a similar trial too.

Get through this and you will be invited to turn up to pitch to the Dragons. Originally the filming took place at a warehouse near Tower Bridge, but these days a proper set has been created at Pinewood Studios in West London, which looks identical to the original location.

The day of filming

Did you know that when it comes to the filming of the show you may have to wait days to get in front of the Dragons? *Dragons' Den* is currently filmed twice each year for a show that will be aired later that year. It takes several days of filming for the producers to get enough good footage to make into one show lasting for an hour. Therefore, the people pitching have to turn up and wait for their slot.

Reports suggest that this can take up to three days. And all that time you have to wait in the 'green room' at the studio. You are ordered not to exchange business cards with anyone else in the room, with the threat that you will be evicted from the line-up if you do so. There are BBC staff everywhere keeping you distracted. Some entrepreneurs loved the staff, but others told me that they are as unnerving as they are supportive. The staff have been known to suggest, at this last minute stage, that entrepreneurs change their pitch – and even their hair styles. Tales of people getting so nervous that they are sick or collapse and then cannot actually pitch to the Dragons circulate amongst the entrepreneurs who have got to this stage.

So be prepared to find yourself hanging around for nerve-wracking hours before you are called to appear before the Dragons.

'A Long Way from Reality'. . .
James Finlayson (ENTREPRENEUR)

The big shoot

One entrepreneur told me that despite all the other distractions, the first thing they noticed when they walked up the stairs into the Den was that the money was fake! Then they noticed the blaring lights over the Dragons' heads and then they noticed the 20-odd-strong film crew huddled to one side of the room out of shot from the cameras.

As they enter, they become aware that the room is boiling hot and weirdly quiet, despite there being so many people in such a small space. They have to walk over to the pitching place, which is marked with a big cross. Almost before they have had a chance to catch breath (they are out of breath because of nerves and the walk up the stairs and across the room) the filming starts and off they go.

On the TV show it is sometimes fairly obvious that the clip is just that, a clip of something much longer. What it does not show is that you might well be pitching for a good two hours or more. Some of this time will be spent on the pitch itself and a lot of it will be while you answer the Dragons' questions. But you may also find that the cameras run out of film, meaning you have to break and then start again, or you may have to reshoot bits. Once again stories abound that appear to prove that this is all about great TV, rather than great investment. One I heard was an entrepreneur, who had been successful in getting money, being asked to walk up the stairs several times so that the film crew could get just the right shot of them walking into the Den!

In this context certain things seem a bit odd. For example, the shots you see on TV of product demonstrations not working. Most of us will never know whether the demo was only tried once and failed to work, or whether it failed to work several times, or whether it was the shot of it failing to work which stayed off the cutting room floor.

The entrepreneurs told me that if they brought a colleague with them, he or she was kept downstairs out of sight and hearing, with no idea of what was going on. If they were then called up to the Den to meet the Dragons, they were not briefed at all as to what to expect when they got into the room, so they had to think on their feet about what to say, with no idea what had already been discussed – exactly as it appears when you watch.

When you are the last person to be filmed in a day, it quickly becomes clear that both the film crew and the Dragons want to finish on time, pack up and go home. On these occasions the need to call for a wrap (i.e. an end to filming) becomes very urgent. One entrepreneur told me that when he was filmed they forgot to film all the Dragons declaring themselves out because they were in such a hurry. Everyone started getting up to leave when they realized this and so the production crew made all the Dragons sit down again so they could film just one of them saying, 'I'm out.'

The Dragons are only human

In the Den the Dragons are not like they appear on TV. They are much more human and run through the range of emotions and opinions that you might expect from such strong and clever people. Entrepreneurs told me of laughter as well as tears, especially when they managed to score a point over one or more of the Dragons. Also the Dragons are clearly quite friendly to each other. They have been overheard talking about arrangements to socialize together outside the show.

After the filming

Following on from the filming with the Dragons, the entrepreneurs are debriefed by Evan Davis and no-one had a bad word to say about this part of the experience. Perhaps they hardly have time to think, as immediately afterwards, the BBC puts you in a cab and sends you home, without being given a chance to talk to any of the other entrepreneurs who you had met earlier in the day.

Between filming and the TV programme being aired

Depending on whether you accepted money from the Dragons or not apparently affects the degree of influence you have over how you are portrayed on the TV programme. If you did accept money, the BBC does let you see the rushes (the draft versions of the show), but if you are not offered or do not take the money offered, that is it. The only thing you will be told is whether or not you are going to appear on the show. You may only be told this the night before. The BBC also decides the dates and running order of the episodes in each series. They will fit this to their wider scheduling on BBC2. Although you will probably by told when you are likely to appear, remember that the BBC may change this at any time. The recently happened to many entrepreneurs when Series Six was brought forward in the schedule by about six weeks. So, don't plan your product launch around the time you expect to appear on the Show. If you do, the chances are you will find that you timed it wrong. For many people I talked to this was felt to be one of the most unfair things that could happen to an entrepreneur running a young business. After all if you appear on the Show before you product is launched it is a great invitation for your competitors to rush off and bring out a competing product before you can get yours selling to customers. Unlike other reality shows, this aspect of *Dragons' Den* is unique. An episode being screened when the entrepreneur is not ready for the publicity risks having a really serious negative impact on their business.

Between filming and the airing of the show, the entrepreneurs just have to sit and wait. They told me the way they coped with the suspense was to force themselves to forget about the whole experience and get on with life, until, that is, the night the show was aired, when they were typically sitting at home with only family and close friends around them, gritting their teeth or biting their nails as they waited to see what the BBC had made of them.

'Perhaps as high as 10% accurate.'
James Davies (ENTREPRENEUR)

The days following the show

Entrepreneurs tell me amazing stories of phones never stopping ringing, email inboxes bursting at the seams and discussions with pretty famous and interesting people taking place in the days after they appeared on one of the *Dragons' Den* episodes. Some of them told me that one of the Dragons, even though they were not investing, had rung up and offered advice or made recommendations about where else they could get investment.

No doubt for the people whom the show made to look like idiots, the situation is very different, but I know of no cases where any entrepreneurs have made a public fuss. Perhaps the fact that they waived their moral rights has something to do with it?

What happens afterwards – is it the deal real?

An investigation in 2006 revealed that, up to that date, 13 of the 19 contestants who had appeared on the show AND had been promised investment had not received any money, and probably never would. Clearly others have done so, including the ones described in this book, but anyone who believes that a deal agreed on a handshake on TV is the same as a real deal is mistaken.

Contestants that are successful in securing the money told me they expect to meet with their relevant Dragon(s) after the show to discuss the deal further and form a contractual agreement, but very often contestants leave the venue without this happening and are left waiting for a phone call. They find it difficult to contact the Dragons themselves and there are times when the conversation goes no further, or the outcome was not the same as they thought had been agreed.

Of course there are the times when it all works out, and the most famous example of all is Levi Roots with his Reggae Reggae Sauce. Levi appeared in the first episode of the fourth series, and offered a 20% stake of his business in return for £50,000. He entered the Den singing a song about his product that he had written himself, and even tried to get the Dragons to sing along! He was offered the £50,000 for a 40% stake in his business by Peter Jones and Richard Farleigh. Leading from the success of his spicy sauce, Roots released an extended version of his song *Reggae Reggae Sauce* that he had performed during his pitch. Shortly after his appearance on the programme, Sainsbury's started stocking the sauce in their stores. Today, not only is Levi running a successful manufacturing business, but he is also a long way to becoming a cult figure in the world of enterprise in his own right.

Another great case study for a successful result is Igloo Thermo Logistics founded by Alistair Turner and Anthony Coates-Smith.

Igloo Thermo Logistics is a refrigerated delivery service owned by a very cool duo: Anthony Coates-Smith and Alistair Turner. They calmly walked into the Den and asked for £160,000 in return for only 8% of equity in the business.

When entering the Den, it was obvious that Anthony and Alistair were well prepared for their pitch. Both wearing smart suits and cleanly shaved, they looked well-presented, and with their flip-chart presentation prepared, they both looked every inch the professional entrepreneur. After a convincing, well-prepared and smooth pitch, they opened up the floor to the Dragons to ask them any questions about their business.

During this question time, Peter Jones became slightly heated and accused them of having frozen brains as their pitch valued their business at nearly £2 million. They stood firm, though, and the Dragons' resistance melted, showing that sometimes having confidence in your business idea when others try to criticize it can pay off!

Their strong confidence and well-organized business plan, which they rigorously stuck to, clearly impressed the Dragons. In the end the pitch turned into a bidding war, with all of the Dragons wanting a piece of the business. So they are in the rare group of entrepreneurs who have received interest from all of the Dragons.

Duncan went in first with an offer of half of the money for 20%, swiftly matched by Richard, who then reduced their combined equity demand to 30%.

Deborah and Theo tried to undercut them with a combined bid for all the money for 25%.

Finally Peter Jones weighed in with two bids – all the money for 16% or half the money for 12.5% if he went into a deal with Deborah or Theo. Determined to clinch the deal, Richard Farleigh and Duncan made their final offer, all the investment for 22.5%.

There was a nerve-wrenching wait as the Igloo duo walked to the back of the Den to decide whether or not to accept any of the deals. In the end they did, and went with the offer from Richard and Duncan despite this not being the most generous offer.

Alistair Turner and Anthony Coates-Smith became some of the first entrepreneurs to appear on *Dragons' Den* and then become paper millionaires. Igloo Thermo Logistics was valued at around £4 million a matter of months after their investment on the show.

Their business now delivers chilled and frozen foods for the likes of Marks & Spencer and pharmaceutical firms and they are currently in the middle of negotiating some very big contracts. They have opened a new centre in Leeds and are significantly expanding their original Watford base. Having beaten thousands of applicants, Igloo has been named South East Regional Winner of a big award.

Commenting on the benefits of appearing on *Dragons' Den*, Anthony said,

'The media attention – the PR has been very good for us. We were the highest valued company to go into the Den. But Duncan and Richard don't interfere with what we do. Going on Dragons' Den was the single most frightening experience of my life. The public see 15 minutes, but we were actually in front of them for two hours!!'

In terms of what the future holds for Igloo, Anthony has explained,

'We are looking to double turnover on an annual basis. We have already trebled it this year. By 2010 we want it to reach £20 million. At that point we will look at potentia suitors to possibly take it off our hands. We have lready spoken to the BBC and let them know that we want to be the first contestants on Dragons' Den to become Dragons!'

Real experiences in the Den

Dragons' Den is a reality TV show, so no-one should get too hung up on the whole thing. Some people win investment who clearly thought they were never going to; others don't, who feel they should have. No doubt the majority come away with an experience they anticipated whilst the most sophisticated recognize that whether they got the money or not, five to ten minutes of free publicity on prime time UK TV in one of the most popular television programmes screened today, was worth every ounce of agony, embarrassment or distortion. If nothing else, all of them will have learnt far more about pitching for investment and also about being filmed that they probably could ever have got any other way.

But how do the entrepreneurs feel: here are the stories of three people who have been on the show and come out the other side.

Andrew Gordon (Creator of StableTable)

'When I arrived, I turned up way too early and mistakenly entered the set. I spoke to some people for a while until they realized I was on the show! I was then escorted to a small room for a number of hours, but the production staff were really nice and supportive. There were six other business people in the room seeking investment, and I think I was third to go on to the set. Following a make-up session, I was then thrust upstairs and asked to pitch. After being rejected I was whisked away in a cab, and was home within the hour. I ended up in the pub that night, celebrating my success. Didn't get any investment, but it was a great experience.'

James Seddon – (Creator of EggXactly)

'I heard about the show through a friend that works at the BBC who thought I would be interested in going on. I arrived at the venue at 8.30am for three consecutive days as there were about eight different businesses waiting to pitch, which could not all be seen in one day. I must say, the staff at the BBC are delightful, we were given coffee and biscuits and the most wonderful lunch every day. Each pitch varies in length depending on how interested the Dragons are and so none of us had any idea when we would be called to the Den, and those who went to pitch did not return to the room, but left through a separate exit. While we were waiting, we were allowed to practise our pitches, which actually served to increase our nervousness. On the third day I was tapped on the shoulder and called into the Den. Prior to this moment, none of the contestants see any of the Dragons; they are kept very much separate from us.

'Walking into the Den was very surreal; I felt I was being led like a condemned man! The walk up the stairs to the room also means you get slightly out of breath before even starting the pitch. The Dragons are also a lot closer than they appear on the television, and there are around

20 camera and sound crew standing along one side of the room, so it is easy to see why many people can be easily put off during their pitch. I honestly could not think of a less suitable environment! Although around 12 minutes of my pitch was shown, I was actually grilled by the Dragons for around 2 hours, and because I was offered investment I was asked to run my entrance and exit a few times so they could get sufficient footage of me for the show. After the pitch I left through a separate door and went to speak with Evan Davis briefly, before going home.

'I had done many pitches before going on the show, but I can openly say that Dragons' Den was the most difficult of all! If you mess up during a normal pitch, you would look stupid in front of about 12 people, but if I had messed up on Dragons' Den, I would have looked stupid in front of millions of viewers! Although my investment fell through I would definitely encourage people to go on Dragons' Den. It really is an eye-opener, and is great to get some good feedback on your business idea. Since appearing on Dragons' Den, EggXactly is going very well, and I have been awarded the Energy Lab Prize for the most energy efficient product of the year.'

Andy Harmer – 'Double Dates' (Now known as Celebrity Experience Ltd.)

'I had heard about the programme and watched it a few times, and felt I could do with some advice from someone with business experience. I thought about applying for the show when just by coincidence I was working at an exhibition in London where they had a stand. I told them about my idea and they liked it, and knew that I would be great entertainment value for the show.

'Prior to the show I felt prepared and confident as I had worked really hard to get my business plan done in a month. I also had my pitch pretty much nailed. At the very start while in front of the Dragons I messed up my first line, which I dwelled on, and therefore ended up on a blubbering downward spiral and mind of blankness! I actually tried to walk off to do another take but they wouldn't let me. So, I strolled back to the piece of sticky tape where I was meant to stand to be stared at by the Dragons and the rest of the nation while sweating profusely. The first thing that went through my mind was "pretend to faint"!! Thank God I didn't, but it was close! It would have got me some great publicity but I thought that the public humiliation had gone far enough as it was, and somehow I managed to find some composure. In the question time I got a mixture of positive and negative comments from the Dragons; they liked my idea but they thought that above anything else I just needed some business advice and not the amount of money I was asking for. James Caan offered me half the money for 25%, and I needed to convince Peter Jones to match the offer if

I was to make a deal. In the end he didn't, and I felt gutted, but also slightly relieved. I could have been on the verge of giving away half my business, thank God I didn't do that either.

'As I was leaving the show Peter Jones said for me to call him, which was a good sign. I called his company and they gave me some excellent advice which I have taken and I am now starting to trade. Although I was disappointed after the show, I got good coverage, they liked my idea, I was advised I didn't need the money and walked away still with 100% of my business and now I finally feel that it couldn't have gone better.

'The advantages to the show were the publicity and amount of knowledge and experience that I gained. There were no downs for me really apart from sweating a bit on TV! I am glad I went on the programme as it was a massive learning curve for me. I believe in my product and love the challenge of trying to turn my vision into reality, and I will persevere until it does. The Dragons only made me more determined to succeed. The programme gave me great coverage and I had a lot of good feedback and outside investors who contacted me. But I suppose the most valuable thing to me was the advice I got, and that it came for free!'

CHAPTER 4

Dragons' Den versus the real world of private investment

'I think Dragons' Den is a very successful commercial enterprise; I don't think it reflects how angels operate, and I think it gives a poor impression to the public... but it is successful entertainment... my children watch it.'
(INVESTOR)

Dragons' Den clearly shows one side of the investment world where private individuals back exciting young businesses with great potential. This is a world that, until Dragons' Den, was shrouded in mystery with everything acted out behind closed doors. But the show is not an accurate reflection of the normal world of business angel investing. Everything from the sort of businesses that present to real investors, to the implied time it takes to close a deal, is far different in the real world compared with how it appears to be on the show.

Some of the key differences are:

- investors usually take much longer to consider an investment before making an offer to invest
- investors tend to do their due diligence before making a final offer, not afterwards as the Dragons appear to
- investors treat the debate about the amount of money needed and the valuation much more seriously than the Dragons appear to
- investors are much less arrogant about their own abilities to add value through their experience and contacts
- occasionally investors will invest on a handshake, but this is VERY rare indeed.
- Investors are much more interested in exit and how and when it will happen, something the Dragons rarely mention.

Some of the key similarities are:

- Dragons and investors alike quick to spot a good commercial opportunity
- Both will base their investment decisions mostly on whether they respect and get on with the entrepreneur

Both prioritise key issues such as the size of opportunity, the intellectual property protection inside the business, the profit margins and whether the entrepreneur will actually be able to achieve not only what he or she has promised but also what it takes to grow the business and then sell out.

Here is a typical successfull investment story told to me by one entrepreneur.

> 'We received our initial round of investment in Aug[ust] 2006 with The Claret Club (an Angel investment group) a fund called and AEGF [the Advantage Early Growth Fund]. The process couldn't be further from that presented on *Dragons' Den*. The investors did not try to take a huge percentage. They analysed our business plan and in fact invested nearly £100k more than was proposed in the deal for only a few per cent more of the business. We have an extremely positive relationship with our investors – two of whom are active non-execs and AEGF attend board meetings each month. We have since gone through a second round where the majority of first round investors reinvested. We have learned a great deal from these guys – the knowledge, advice and referrals have been so valuable if not more than the money.'

So if it is really that different, let's look at it in more detail.

The pitch

Before a pitch

Unlike *Dragons' Den*, real investors take entrepreneurs very seriously and tend to treat them with respect. Whoever reviews your plan knows in the back of their minds that even if it is not very good, maybe one day you will come back with a better one; they would be fools to be rude to you or to try and unsettle you in the manner suggested by *Dragons' Den*.

And the people who help you raise money from investors will usually have personal interest and a financial incentive to help you raise the sums you need, so they are most likely to give you lots of training on how to present, rather than just throwing you to the wolves unarmed.

At a pitch

Investors watching your pitch will be as cross as the Dragons if you mess it up. After all they have given up their time for free to listen to you. The difference is they are much more likely to tell you how they feel by ignoring you than by making rude comments. Just like the Dragons, they will talk about you behind your back after you have pitched, but if you challenge them about what they think of you, they will probably try to make constructive comments about how you could improve your business or your pitch so that next time everything goes better.

Private investors like very simple things, like *'Numbers that make sense'*, according to Henry Pound, a very experienced investor. They also like entrepreneurs to focus on the returns they will get, according to Andrew Burton who has been closely involved with dozens of deals involving angels. Angels also look at how they will get their money back, known as the exit route. This is a crucial issue rarely discussed on *Dragons' Den*, though no doubt it affects the Dragon's decisions.

The other key issues that real investors look for are based on the entrepreneur satisfying them that the opportunity is real and that the entrepreneur really believes in it. Entrepreneurs *'need to have good ideas on why their product has market traction'*, Martin Rigby a well-known early-stage venture capitalist and investor told me. And as Chris Arnold, another private investor said, '[they should] have done their homework and still believe in their idea'.

Private investors take the presentation the entrepreneur makes very seriously indeed. In a survey I conducted of some of the investors I know, around 85% of them said the pitch itself was a fundamental aspect of the investment opportunity and key in helping them to decide whether to pursue the opportunity afterwards. So Peter Jones is right to make such a fuss about how people dress when they pitch; he is echoing what real investors think.

Funnily enough it was an entrepreneur who summed up the real point about a pitch for money. *'People buy people'* said James Davies, the founder of Upad. He is right, the investment game is all about people – entrepreneurs succeeding, investors getting a satisfactory investment and outcome and both working on common goals to achieve this. For any deal to work, the people have to get on and respect each other, a point which does come across on *Dragons' Den*. Private investors would not get far in building up a group of investments if they were known to be as rude and aggressive as the Dragons appear to be. They know that setting off on a bad foot by being rude or insulting will mean that post-investment the entrepreneurs may hate them, or will at best tolerate them. And they know it is not a good idea to hand over large sums of money to someone who feels like this.

> *'Trading on the spot is unrealistic.'*
> Paul Gardner (ADVISER)

One of the biggest complaints by private investors and their advisers is the implication on *Dragons' Den* that a deal can be struck in a few minutes. 'You can't judge an idea in a few minutes . . . what do they know outside their specialism?', investor Chris Arnold told me. Interestingly you often see one Dragon initially keen on an idea until another points out a major flaw, under time pressure it is all too easy to miss those flaws. Another investor said, 'it gives the investment market a bad name'.

About the money

On *Dragons' Den* entrepreneurs usually pitch for a sums of money from a few tens of thousands to £150,000. This reflects exactly what the real market is like in the UK, although it is rare to find an entrepreneur asking for £50,000 pitching at the same event as someone asking for £2m. One difference is that long before entrepreneurs get to pitch to investors they tend to have a clear idea why they need the money and what it is going to be spent on. As a rule, investors in the real world felt that the people who appeared on *Dragons' Den* had not really thought this through. They tended to agree with Robert Brown, a specialist insurance broker who works with small and medium businesses. He said, with some irony:

'The entrepreneurs [on Dragons' Den] rarely need investment. If something is that good, and could sell in the volumes that some of them describe, then you could get quite easily investors such as VC fund managers an old-fashioned loan.'

The real benefit of *Dragons' Den*?

There is no denying that the exposure the entrepreneurs get from being on the show can lead to them securing investment elsewhere or simply a huge boost to sales of their product, despite the Dragons laughing at the concept. James Finlayson, an entrepreneur, believes through *Dragons' Den* 'there is the added benefit of being able to say "as seen on TV", which is a great PR tool'. Many deals that are not successful on the show often find it easier to obtain investment following their exposure on TV. They can also find that the publicity does marvels for sales, sometimes meaning they no longer have to raise money at all.

There is a great example of this from the show. Ling Valentine pitched to secure £100,000 funding for 5% of her online car rental service. After two joint offers from Dragons Duncan Bannatyne and Richard Farleigh asking for a 30% share of the equity, Ling turned them down outright saying she would just get a loan from her bank without losing any of her business. Since the show, LINGsCARS.com has doubled turnover to £28 million, and her business is growing, without the financial backing of an investor. On being asked by Evan Davis about turning down the offer she said, 'Well, the Chinese eat dragons for breakfast.'

Are the Dragons like real private investors?

Several private investors have told us that they are not interested in becoming famous with the general public just because they are investors in early-stage businesses. Many have confided that they have been invited by the BBC to be a Dragon and have turned down the offer to keep their reputation as an investor intact. This may be the right call. A 2007 survey by Kashflow revealed that 65% of the owners of Small and Medium Enterprises (SME) said that they would turn their back on an offer from the Dragons as they didn't feel it represented good value for money, and would rather turn to banks or genuinely private investors for a more reasonable split of the business.

There are a few areas where private investors are very like the Dragons. The biggest is over what businesses are worth. There will always be a few businesses that really are worth a fortune from day one, but as a rule, most private investors agree that the Dragons are pretty smart about valuing businesses. All investors need to get a good deal because investing is so risky. Where private investors differ from the Dragons is the way they conduct the negotiations. Other ways in which the Dragons are just like the real world is they like entrepreneurs to dress properly and know their figures.

To be fair, this is not surprising because the Dragons are investors in the real world too, particularly Richard Farleigh who has made over 50 private investments in recent years. And all of them, except for Simon Woodroffe, have also made real investments via *Dragons' Den*.

The Dragons are all clearly successful and very intelligent. The ones I have met are charming too and I would be proud to have any of them as friends, just as I am very proud of having friends amongst the real private investment community. I would certainly take any of the Dragons seriously as an investor. It's just that on TV their personality and reactions are vastly exaggerated to make good TV and like anyone who finds long-lasting fame via the media, they use it as much for their own advantage as they permit it to use them.

Final thoughts

Like so many things that appear on TV, *Dragons' Den* is really an adaptation of what really happens. For those who know about the real world of private investment, just like devoted readers of books like *Pride and Prejudice* or even *Bridget Jones's Diary* that are filmed or televised, the TV version will never be quite the same or anything like as good as the original.

But something amazing happens when these are adapted to appeal to the mass market of TV. It means that a whole generation of people get to learn about and enjoy something very special. For the world of private investment, this means that many more people want to, and do become, private investors and even more other people decide to start their own business. And for those who have appeared on the show they have their five minutes of fame on TV which, for many of them, has given them amazing publicity which they could not possibly have afforded any other way. For some, the fame probably helped them to make their business a success in a more effective way than cash from the Dragons ever could or would have done.

Dragons' Den isn't a very accurate representation of what it is like to raise money from private investors. But most of the reasons the Dragons cite to invest or decline to invest are real. And it does what it sets out to do really well – it is excellent entertainment. Long may it stay on air.

CHAPTER 5

Nova-Flo: A case study on how *Dragons' Den* compares with the real world of business angel investment

In the rest of this book I will share my experiences of the real world of private or angel investment, but it seems fitting, before I start, to share this story with you. In early 2006 James Barnham, the inventor of Nova-Flo™ decided to pitch his business to the Dragons for investment to manufacture Nova-Flo™ and take it to market. Although he was offered investment from the Dragons, he rejected it and went on to raise the money he needed from real private investors. Here is his story in his own words.

'I think I was destined to become an entrepreneur. I failed all my A levels and so when I left school there was no chance of university. As I loved cycling, I went to work in one of London's top bike shops of the day. I was trained up as a cycle mechanic and progressed through the ranks till finally, nine years later, I was managing two highly regarded stores. But I wasn't using my head. The job had taught me three key things though. I had learned about sales, customer service and what people expect from a product; I had learned about hot new-technology materials and non-electronic mechanisms; and I wanted to do something more interesting than being a shopkeeper all my life!

'So I went off to study industrial design at South Bank University, but as I still needed money to live started managing a contemporary furniture store called Ocean on the weekends when I wasn't studying. There I learned what customers wanted in the home. It was another fantastic experience because I gained loads of experience in graphic design and furniture assembly. Another job I had while I was studying was working for the BBC special effects department. When I got to my third year at University I was told I had to design something innovative and create a working prototype, so all the skills I didn't know I had suddenly fell into place and I was away.

'I was scratching my head about what to design and then I realized that all over London (where I had lived in plenty of rental accommodation) there were signs of water damage in buildings. I decided to solve this problem and decided that the design I would make would be an anti-flooding device. That was the start of Nova-Flo! Crucially I knew that water and electricity do not mix and therefore if I could make the Nova-Flo mechanical rather than electric, I would have a winning design, and guess what, I did! The design I prototyped won a couple of awards at the University design show!

'It was then that I met Ian Sillett who worked at the University. In those days he was just my mentor, but now he is working with me running Nova-Flo and is a fellow shareholder. He persuaded me to take part in a scheme the University was running to help students turn into entrepreneurs. It was quite a risk; I was over 30 and had a mortgage, but he persuaded me to take the leap and spend a year (whilst being paid a meagre salary by the University) trying to commercialize Nova-Flo.'

Ian Sillett says of this moment:

> 'I thought James was looking a gift horse in the mouth. It's an entrepreneur's dream to get paid to kick the tyres!'

'So I started on the scheme and quickly realized that there was a lot of work to do. The design was too complicated and was unmarketable because I could see no profitable applications for it. So I scratched my head again and decided that the main reason there are floods in the home was because baths flood so I would need to make a product that would solve this problem. All the time I was thinking this I was getting more excited about Nova-Flo working and selling and it all happening very quickly! So we started work, won bits of grant money to show it off at the Ideal Home Show using a proper demonstration model and were up and running.

'By now Ian was really excited about the business opportunity. He was really a frustrated entrepreneur working for the University, but because of his job as head of IP there he knew an amazing amount about setting up businesses and patent protection, so his skills matched up perfectly with mine.

'We needed to raise some money, as we did not have any of our own to spare. The Emerald Fund gave us some in chunks so we knew that external people who knew what we were doing, liked us. Then I was asked to pitch at a Lions' Den event organized by the National Council for Graduate Entrepreneurs. We were one of the winning pitches and we asked for £150,000 for 20% and got it! We ended up turning the money down, because the terms weren't right, but it gave us the confidence to think that if we worked hard we could go on *Dragons' Den* and get a better price.

'Ian and I loved (and still love!) *Dragons' Den* as a TV show. We also realized that if we could get on the show it would probably be our only chance to get a 10 minute slot on prime time TV in front of our perfect audience at the perfect time (all those people sitting at home, just before they went off to have their night time bath). So we decided to apply to pitch. 'Even if we don't get the money, we will get the publicity' we thought.

'We took care about our application because we realized that so many people are presenting that we would need to work hard to stand out from the crowd. After we sent in our forms we did not hear for ages and so got on with running the business as we thought we had found a couple of profitable routes to market.

'After about two months we had heard nothing so Ian got on the phone and demanded to speak to the producer. He made a great case, talking about what a good product we had, how I was a photogenic guy and how it would make great TV. It worked. Two days later we were in the TV centre doing a test screening and the following Monday we were told we would actually be filmed that Friday.

'Those few days were really busy because we had to get pretty much everything together, from our financial plans to the justification for our valuation, and I had to practise making the pitch.

'Going on *Dragons' Den* was a unique experience of my life. Ian and I turned up in the morning and were shown into a room with eight entrepreneurs, many of whom were climbing the walls with nerves as they had been waiting since the day before to present. We were not allowed to exchange business cards and the BBC people did little to calm us all down. If anything, they egged us on by making us practise our pitches and then making "helpful" suggestions as to how we could change it at the last minute. One of the other entrepreneurs broke down in tears and could not go on.

'We waited all day. I wasn't called up until 5pm. We were in the old building then so I really had to walk up the stairs, having had a quick five minutes beforehand to set up the Nova-Flo demonstrator when the Dragons weren't in the room. Ian was left downstairs and could not see or hear anything. So I was alone and out of breath when I walked to my designated spot in the room. Really hot lights were blasting above the Dragons' heads – and it felt like I was walking into my own TV because I had seen the room so many times before. There was a bank of people sitting on the side taking notes, but it is deathly quiet and you can hear your footsteps as you cross the floor. The first thing I noticed was that the money on the tables was fake!

'I was even asked to change part of my pitch five minutes before we went on! Off we went and it all went pretty smoothly, but it wasn't like it appeared on TV months later. In fact all the Dragons were interested and when I defended myself on the valuation – explaining that the valuation I had offered the Dragons was actually lower than the valuation I had really put on the business, that I was reducing the price to take account of the extra risk they would be facing – there was an enormous cheer and laughter from them and they applauded me saying it was the best answer they had ever had. That was cut out of the TV clip.

'After I called Ian up to answer Theo's question on patents everything went a bit wild with the producers dashing around trying to get hold of the piece of paper Theo wanted to see. They did not know it, but both of us had been caught completely off the hoof about whether the University would sell the patent (they own the patent and I have licensed it for Nova-Flo – that was the deal). We just blagged it and thought we would answer to the University afterwards.

'And then suddenly we saw the Dragons looking at their watches. They wanted to wrap it up as they seemed to be going off in Peter Jones's private jet somewhere. They even forgot to film a clip of Deborah Meaden turning me down, so we had to quickly film it. In fact Deborah had not wanted to turn me down. When it was on TV they chopped the film around so it would look like only four Dragons were interested, so they didn't really show the true story to the public.

'Because we did not take the investment, they did not let us have a say in how it was cut. So we knew nothing about how it would look until the night the show was aired. I was at home with my family and some friends and Ian was crouching on the sofa with his wife and kids at his house.

'The response was amazing. For two weeks I struggled just to answer the non-stop phone calls and emails. Everyone must watch *Dragons' Den* – we had offers of funding from all sorts of people, including some pretty well-known business people! And we got loads of calls from prospective customers in all the areas we had listed in our marketing plan!

'Then it started to quieten down and we accepted that we should look for investment properly. One of the people who had called us was John White, from e-Synergy, the company that ran The Emerald Fund. He said that he had watched the show and as they already knew us, he thought his fellow angels could invest in us. We got into discussions which were very open and not at all predatory, and worked out a deal with them that also included some of our friends and family. More people wanted shares than we could offer, but we raised the £200,000 we needed on the back of the work e-Synergy did. They also found us our fantastic chairman Michael Stoddart.

'Now it's been a while since we did *Dragons' Den* I can tell you that we planned it like a battle and milked it for as much as it was worth. They played a game with us, so we played a game with them. We would have taken the Dragons' money if they had agreed our deal, but we knew that the publicity would be invaluable. From the show we flushed out our real investors and lots of potential customers. Our real investors invested at a considerably better price than the Dragons offered, so it is not right that all businesses have ridiculously low valuations.

'Our time on *Dragons' Den* is up on YouTube so we still get calls about it and people ask, "Didn't I see you on *Dragons' Den*?", but now it just seems like one step in the path the company has followed. We have now moved on a long way. In a way I feel sorry for the Dragons. Real investors don't have the cameras rolling and the lights on them when they try to strike a deal. And who wants to be most famous for appearing on a TV show rather than from their real achievements such as their business successes or their charity work?'

PART 2

How to raise money from investors

CHAPTER 6

Do I need a dragon?

Could your business attract an investor like the Dragons?

By the time you finish this book I want you to know what it takes to raise money to grow your business. Why? Because I know just how exciting, but also what hard work it is to build a business, especially if you have never done it before. Not only do I watch others as they build their businesses, but I am also running my own. I too have been where you are today. I've done the research, prepared the figures and thought up the plan, changed it, changed it again, got ready, got steady and then gone! I get the same tingly feeling of excitement when I think up something new and the incredible sense of excitement when one of my plans has paid off.

I was asked to write this book because for almost 10 years, I have worked in the world of putting businesses and investors together. I started long before *Dragons' Den* came along. I may not be a Dragon on TV, but I have been a dragon investor in real life. And because of what my business does, I spend my days with people who, like the Dragons, invest in exciting young businesses, but unlike them, do not seek fame on TV. I also know a lot of people who have refused an offer from the BBC to become a *Dragons' Den* dragon, but who are investing all the time in the types of businesses that you see on the TV programme. In the real world, these people are called angels or private investors, but I also like the term 'dragon investor'. So from now on when you see the terms 'angel', 'dragon investor' or 'private investor', you will know who I am talking about.

This book is my way of sharing with you what I know and what investors tell me, so that you can use it to build your own successful business.

One of the most important things to think about before setting off on your road to fundraising is whether you really need to raise money from private investors. Seeking dragon investment is time-consuming and very hard work. It is also nerve-wracking as you will have to tell influential strangers all about your business without any guarantee that they will invest any money. You may well end up feeling it would have been easier to appear on *Dragons' Den*! So before you put yourself through this trial, make sure that it is outside investment that your business really needs and wants. In the real world, most businesses do not really need to raise money from private investors. In fact, lots of real dragons think that many of the companies that pitched on *Dragons' Den* would have been better off not trying to raise money. Why? These were the typical reasons they gave:

- It would be more suitable for them to raise bank debt; or
- Their business would do better to grow itself organically, that is by increasing sales; or

- Their business would need so much money in order to succeed that the entrepreneurs would be better off going to venture capitalists who could invest the millions needed; or
- Their business could not be sold to anyone else easily and therefore they, the investors, would never get their money back.

Of course, many of the entrepreneurs who pitch on Dragons' Den understandably also do it to get a five minute advert for their business, but this is not a reason to pitch in the real world where you will probably only be pitching to an audience of 1–100 investors in real life not 3 million people on TV.

When I challenged the angels on what they think of people who pitch to them in real life, they confirmed that in the real world too most companies should not seek to raise money from them for exactly the same reasons listed above.

Remember selling shares in your business is the most expensive money you can raise

'It's no longer your baby.'
James Davies, founder of Upad

A wise investor once advised never to forget that selling shares in your company for money is the most expensive sort of money you can raise. By selling those shares, you will have a permanent co-owner, who unless you plan very carefully, you may never be able to get rid of. In contrast, if you grow organically, the business remains yours and if you raise bank debt, as long as you pay back your loan according to your agreement the bank will not interfere in how you run the business.

All shareholders have rights under the law and, if they are smart, investors will also negotiate additional rights which will be set out in a legally binding agreement which you will have to sign, called the **Shareholders Agreement**. Even the simplest deal will have terms that will affect your freedom to run the business, down to what targets you must meet and even when you must sell it. That can be a big cost and can lead to problems between you and the investor. If you talked in private to some of the entrepreneurs who have raised money from the Dragons they would tell you stories of board meetings where their investors question the decisions they have made or how the money has been spent. In fact it would be amazing if the Dragons did not have the right to refuse to let the management spend largish sums of money without their express permission. Of course, when hearing about the deals that have been struck on *Dragons' Den*, everything appears to be rosy, but there is at least one *Dragons' Den* deal which went terribly sour. The details are bound up in a confidentiality agreement which means no-one can talk about it, but insider sources report the deal had to be unwound and the entrepreneurs ended up having to borrow money to pay off their Dragon investors. So think carefully about whether an investor is right for you.

There are lots of ways to raise money to grow your business which do not involve anyone else having a say in what you do. As well as bank debt there are lots of grants available for young companies, as well as subsidized support from government, councils and even charities such as The Prince's Trust. The cheapest money of all is what you get from your customers, assuming you are selling things at a profit. Other cheap money can be had from your suppliers letting you delay payment for a while.

Let's assume though that these routes are not suitable for you. Perhaps you need more money than they can give you or that you have already exhausted these sources. Maybe you cannot get venture capital yet because you are not big enough or even you think that venture capitalists really are Vulture Capitalists and will suck the life out of your business.

The first angel investor in Facebook invested $500,000.

The ideal time for raising business finance is if you need between £100,000 and £2,000,000. However, there are always exceptions to prove the rule, and some investors put as little as £25,000 into a business and some as much as £3m or more.

Unlike on *Dragons' Den*, the typical business investment deal will not be a start-up like so many of the businesses you see on the show. Instead they are more likely to be already trading and have shown that there is real demand for their products and services (known as having shown 'proof of concept'). They will also be moving towards the point where they could be sold at a great profit to someone else.

Other characteristics of ideal companies for private investors are those that have a great product that no-one can copy such as Nova-Flo's mechanical bath anti-overflow system where their patent gives them exclusive rights to produce it, ones that have an excellent (and complete) management team and ones that have high profit margins.

Many businesses could become a world leading business. You too could shape your business to achieve this if you really want to. But if you want to raise money from other people to help you get there, there is one really important decision you will have to make. Are you prepared to try and build an explosively large business which you can sell quickly for millions of pounds or do you want to run a business for yourself that will give you a job for life and a great lifestyle?

Is your business really a lifestyle business?

If you want to build a business for yourself and your family that is great. You might also be able to build it very big. Companies like Mars, JCB and Yeo Valley are all enormous family-owned businesses. In fact the vast majority of businesses are privately owned by a family or some close friends/colleagues. Many investors would love to be able to buy a stake in them, but cannot because the family owners either do not need or want them.

However, private business investors do not want to invest in a business which you are going to run for yourself and your family. They describe this type of business as a lifestyle business and do not see enough potential for profit. So if this is what you want to do, don't bother to seek this type of investment.

And note that although you may have dreams of growing your business enormously, the investors may decide that because of the plan you are adopting, you will never be able to grow in such a way that it becomes big enough for it to be sold, which is an investor's way of making profit. The Dragons often make this point on TV.

Case study: Joanne Morrison and Emma McPherson

In the very first series of *Dragons' Den* Joanne Morrison and Emma McPherson pitched to the Dragons for £60,000 to open a shop for their fashion brand in Glasgow. They made a very good pitch, but Duncan Bannatyne explained that he thought their business was a lifestyle business and therefore not suitable for investment. It was not a potential Top Shop, because it would be very difficult for the designer to provide enough variety of clothes and to get the supply chains set up that would be able to provide enough clothes to fill every shop in the chain. Also, because it was high fashion, the clothes would have to be changing all the time to keep the customers happy and he believed that Joanne and Emma would not be able to do this month after month, year after year without becoming worn out.

If you want to build a lifestyle business for your lifetime or even an enormous family-owned business that will last for generations, you will be better off going to borrow some money from the bank, dip into your own savings or sell something you own. But assuming you are not, you then need to ask yourself some more questions.

How much money do you really need?

Some businesses simply do not need much investment to get going and be a success. Investors like these, but do you need them? It might be that you only need a small sum of money and it is not worth the time and trouble of getting private investment. Think hard about whether you really need money or whether you can beg and borrow your way through the early difficult days if you only need a few thousand pounds.

The Internet makes it much easier to build a big business without much investment. If you know how to build your website for yourself you will not need to pay other people to do it for you. And if you know about website optimization you can make your website come out top in the search engines so your customers will find you and you will not have to spend much on sales and marketing. You will not need premises because nobody will be visiting your 'office' or 'shop'. So as long as you can survive on as little money as possible when you start, you can build a business which does not actually need much money to get going. Don't be put off by entrepreneurs who say you need at least £500,000 to start a website business. It is simply not true and there are many examples of people starting their own website business with just £1,000.

Some businesses do need large amounts of capital to grow. For example, a manufacturing business or one that needs a lot of research and development before a product can be sold or a retail chain with lots of shops. Coffee Republic needed the investment it took from Nitin Shah, a famous angel investor, to go from being one or two restaurants to a national chain.

If this is the case, it is a good idea to consider private business investment, but remember that most private of investors normally do not have the deep pockets of venture capitalists. They either can or will only invest a certain amount of money in any one business. So if you have a really large need for cash, for example £2 million, you would be better off looking for venture capital.

Even if you don't need money, you may want to find yourself an investor because they can provide support and advice. These investors act as mentors for your business as well as giving you money. They may not invest much money in your business, but they will definitely add an enormous amount of value in other ways. So don't completely ignore angels just because you do not actually need much money from them. The Dragons have a point when they emphasize the value they can add to businesses on TV. I will talk more about this later in the book.

Is my business more suitable for bank debt?

In many cases this would be a resounding yes! If you have a business that is based on owning physical assets you should always look for bank debt. The banks like businesses with assets because they can value the assets and lend a proportion of the value to you.

If you want to build a business that invests in property, buys and sells second-hand cars or machinery or other items, go and talk to your bank manager first. You may have to start relatively small while you prove you can sell on at a profit, but once you have proven yourself it should be a straightforward process to borrow more and grow your business.

Many banks will also lend to other types of business so long as you are prepared to offer security for the loan, i.e. you agree that if the business cannot pay off the debt, you will instead. Typically they will ask you to offer your house as security, which is a very good test of your commitment – for if you won't risk your own assets on your business, why should the bank? If you do not have any assets you can offer, the government has set up a scheme with the banks called the Small Firms Loan Guarantee Scheme (check out www.businesslink.gov.uk to find out more) where it guarantees most of the money your business borrows and you only have to promise to repay 15% if everything goes wrong.

How Leaf Systems did it

Leaf Systems is a very successful company that sells educational software and IT services to prisons and colleges to help offenders gain education and qualifications whilst they are locked away. Its founder Matt originally went to his local business angel network to pitch for the money he needed. Though successful in raising interest he found, like many on *Dragons' Den*, that the offers did not reflect the opportunity the business had. He therefore looked to alternative funding methods for the business.

'We approached a number of high street lenders with the view to moving our account to the most accommodating,' said Matt 'and found a number of schemes were on offer. From the Small firms loan guarantee scheme to a straightforward loan with security. The problem was that many of the high street lenders were not willing to do the leg work involved in helping a business to obtain a government funded loan under any scheme. It simply wasn't worth their while.'

This left Matt with a dilemma. The bank would be willing to lend the required six figure sum, but only with the family home as security. As a father of three young children, this is a decision that he could not make on his own. Having consulted with his wife, they decided that if the business was to achieve its full potential that this was a risk worth taking.

'Ultimately it was a risk that we, as a family, were prepared to take. I appreciate that this is not always an option for many start up entrepreneurs and the support of my wife meant that we could borrow the money to give the business the boost it needed. Having the house at risk helped to crystallize our attention and achieve things that I now don't think we would have been able to do if we were simply "playing" with someone else's money – no matter what equity holding they had in the business.'

Matt also believes that a supportive business bank manager is critical to the success of any lending relationship.

'We are very lucky to have had the same bank manager for a number of years now. On occasion, when we have had late paying customers, or required additional support they have done what they can to support the business. The current climate has meant that support has not always been forthcoming from higher up within the institution – but without the support of our direct contact at the bank, I don't think we would have seen the year on year growth experienced by the business.'

Organic growth has meant Leaf has doubled turnover and staffing year on year since starting life behind a makeshift desk in Matt's cloakroom!

Should I sell something so I have the money for my business?

Did you know that Fitness First, started by Mike Balfour, originally started because Mike spotted an opportunity to take over a site and start his first fitness club? So he sold his house to raise the cash, put his family into a rented flat and moved himself into a bed and breakfast. George Gallagher, founder of Zi Medical plc, a bio-tec company worth millions did something even more amazing. He did not have any money or a house, only owned a beloved motorbike. Having had several false starts at raising venture capital investment he was about to give up when he heard that he might have some luck from business angels. But he needed some money to start the process of getting in front of those investors, so he sold his bike to pay the fees to his local adviser to help get in front these people. It worked; he raised the money and the rest, as they say, is history.

If you are really certain about your business idea, be prepared to sell other assets to raise the money you need if you cannot get it any other way.

Help! I need money really quickly

It is not easy to raise money quickly for a business from strangers, especially from private investors. It is no good looking for money if you are about to go bust or if you are so heavily in debt that the business will fail if you don't raise money quickly. Look at what happened to Grails. The Dragons who invested in it got caught out here because all the money they invested went on paying the company's existing debts. So there was no money left to build the business. Although this was bad news for the Dragons, they could afford to write it off to experience, but for the founder of the business it meant her chance to build the business was gone.

There are people who will invest in situations where it is all going wrong, called distressed investors. Theo Paphitis is known for investing in failing businesses that have gone wrong, but the difference is that he invests in businesses that have been established for a long time and which have a great brand name like La Senza or Rymans. Unless your business is very well established you are unlikely to attract investment from Theo Paphitis or people like him. However, if you are in this situation, your accountant should know where to find them.

I still need the money, so when is my business right for business angels?

Your business is right for private investment if the opportunity is enormous and you need a reasonable, but not ridiculous, amount of money. It may also be right if you need the advice and support that experienced business people (who are also business investors) can give to you. For example, Levi Roots would be the first person to acknowledge that without the experience and contacts of his Dragon investors, he would never have got Reggae Reggae Sauce onto the shelves at Sainsbury's.

What makes your business ideal for investment

1 Your business has real potential to become a mega-success and a leader in its field.

2 You have spent all your own money.

3 You have asked all the friends, family and anyone else you can think of.

4 The bank will not touch you because it says the business plan is too risky.

5 Your customers cannot fund your business by pre-ordering from you.

6 You have taken all the grants or other support on offer.

7 You need between £100,000 and £2 million.

8 As well as money, you need people to help you run the business or give you the right introductions.

CHAPTER 7

Why a dragon is good for you

What investors can do for you

Angel investors are saints rather than dragons, honestly! They are also people. They bring money, but they can also bring a whole lot more.

If you want angels to invest in your business and then to have a successful relationship with them afterwards so you both make a lot of money rather than lose the lot, you need to understand what you can do for them and what they can do for you. But don't be naïve, even saints can go to the dark side. People can change, especially if they are treated the wrong way. This applies to you, but it also applies to investors. You need to think about why you want to have an investor and what they can do for you and you can do for them BEFORE you start talking to them.

The way *Dragons' Den* portrays the Dragons might make you think that all dragon investors are rude, greedy people, but don't be misled, this is because showing the mean or tough side of people makes much better TV than filming people being nice and sympathetic.

In the real world, private investors tend to be very different from the Dragons for the simple reason that to be a successful angel investor you have to have better emotional intelligence, experience and judgement than normal. Most investors are more like Richard Farleigh or possibly Peter Jones in the way they approach deals. They understand that it is difficult to build a very successful business and that there will be lots of risks along the way. Not everyone will agree with me on this. Nick Boles who is also involved in the real world said to me,

> 'Real life investors are just as harsh – the problem is the Dragons are forced to reject propositions on air, while in real life they just don't return calls.'

What *Dragons' Den* portrays correctly is that both the Dragons and private investors are very experienced, successful people and they are very wealthy. Nearly every investor has made their money for themselves by building a business. From first-hand experience they know what it is like to be an entrepreneur and how difficult it is to succeed.

To get the most out of any investor in your business it is essential that you try to see things from their point of view and to make the best of what they can offer to you. By understanding this you will have a better idea of what to ask for when you eventually meet one.

One of the best reasons for seeking investment from any investor is not only the money they will give to your business, but also what they can do for you. In *Dragons' Den* you can see this when the Dragons start talking about the way they can offer their experience to help build the business or introduce the entrepreneur to key contacts who will become customers or suppliers. Just think of the times in the show when the Dragons try to outbid each other in terms of what extra they can offer when they are competing to invest in a business such as Reggae Reggae Sauce. The sort of things private investors might be able to do for you include helping with your business strategy; sharing their experience, contacts and knowledge; introducing you to other investors and generally acting as a trusted mentor to whom you can go with your problems.

> **Case study: Reggae Reggae Sauce**
>
> When you watch the pitch made by Levi Roots on *Dragons' Den* it is immediately clear how much value investors can add, whether it is someone like Richard Farleigh picking up the holes in the numbers or Theo Paphitis explaining that the contract from a potential customer was not quite so set in stone as it seemed. Since he won the investment from the Dragons, Levi Roots has seen the evidence of what having angels on board can do, not least helping him to win the contract with Sainsbury's to sell Reggae Reggae Sauce in its supermarkets.

These are the things any investor can offer you.

Money

An investor cannot call themselves an investor unless they invest real cash into your business. There are four key questions to ask about the cash an investor can offer you.

1. How much money do they really have available for you (and not just how much money do they have overall)?

2. Are they giving you all the money they have right now or might they be able to invest again if you decide to raise more money?

3. Will they want to approve exactly how you spend the money? And

4. If they are going to get involved in helping you to grow the business will they be charging for their time and expenses?

One of the biggest debates around investors is often how much money they really have to invest. The general answer is that we will never know. Most investors have a pot of money for investment and then form a view on how they are going to spend it. But for most of them, neither you nor I will ever know how much that is. Some of them invest large sums (over £100,000) in a few deals; others will spread the money around in £10,000 chunks. Some invest all their money quickly and others take years. In Part 3 I will give you some profiles of different investors to show you how different they all are.

Most investors get 'fully invested' every two to three years and then stop investing for a while. Therefore, one of the most important things to talk through with them when you are negotiating the deal is whether they will consider investing again if your business will need more money in the future. They are unlikely to make a firm commitment, but if you expect need more money, it is worth discussing whether they will agree to reserve some funds in a separate bank account, which can be used if needed.

Money is never the most important thing an investor can offer you and you should never judge an investor on the amount of money they are proposing to give you. Instead, look at the whole package on offer.: From my experience of watching hundreds of deals over the last 10 years you should consider the following things, as well as money, before you take investment from an investor.

- Are they a 'big name' who will add credibility if they are your shareholder, even if they invest a token amount?
- Can they offer you support in terms of mentoring, introductions or management support?
- Are they 'buying themselves a job' – in which case maybe they will do it for a cheaper wage than if you had to hire someone on a proper commercial rate?

Sometimes a private investor will offer you just money and it may be an awful lot of money. Well done if you can find one of these angels! But before you take the money make sure you really understand whether they will be buying you with the money and whether they may end up having more influence over your business than you might expect. They may get this influence by negotiating extra rights when you strike the deal, which will be clear, but remember that if they have a very large shareholding, it will be difficult to resist what they want in the future even if the rights are not set in stone in the legal agreements.

Mentoring

One of the very best examples of how effective an investor can be as a mentor as well as a provider of cash was in Series Six of *Dragons' Den*, when Peter Jones invested in Victoria McGrane's new catwalk line. Many of the Dragons declared themselves out of this deal because Victoria was not asking for enough money to fund the growth of the business. Peter Jones wisely spotted that Victoria had done everything else right. She knew had made sales, knew her numbers and had made an excellent presentation. Peter also felt that she needed more investment and told her so, but put his money where his mouth was an offered her the additional £21,000 she needed. This is what mentoring means. Offering good advice and then helping the entrepreneur to act on it.

Most private investors genuinely enjoy the idea of being able to 'give something back' or sharing their experience with younger entrepreneurs. In fact this can be an even more important reason than making money when an investor decides to invest in you. Some investors want to see businesses grow as a result of the money they invest and others like the idea of creating jobs. One of the most positive things about this world is that many investors admit they were helped by an angel investor themselves when they were starting out and that they see their investment activities as a way of repaying a debt to that long dead investor who supported them.

Some angels just like the idea of making other people rich like them. As one private investor I know put it, 'I like to be a millionaire maker!'

If you can find someone who is willing to mentor you, especially by giving you advice and support on the phone or in person, for free, grab them, even if they never give you a penny!

Becoming a director of the business

Some investors want to become directors of the companies in which they invest. Others do not, but may want to receive copies of board minutes, management accounts and/or to have the right to attend board meetings and listen but not speak. This is known as observer status. They will ask for these things so they can stay close to their investment and so they can step in to help if there are warning signs, but by not being a director they avoid any legal liability if things go wrong.

> **Case study: media business**
>
> I have known a media business since it was a start-up. This business puts screens in ante-natal clinics and sells advertising on the screens to businesses wanting to market products to pregnant women and their families. When their private investors made their first investment in the company they both became directors of the company. Since then they have provided enormous amounts of support to the management team, from helping with preparation of the financial forecasts and the business plan to working on the company's subsequent rounds of fundraising. In fact they are so important to the company that the current venture capitalist investors have demanded that they stay involved.

A good investor who becomes a director could be just what you need. This is especially true if they are very highly regarded in your industry or are very well known. It will give you credibility and a greater likelihood that they will really try to help your business succeed. A really good director will work next to you, coming to meetings with you (whether it is the bank manager or a customer) and help to advise you on how to develop your business strategy as you grow.

If anyone becomes a director of a company they have duties and obligations under the law. They also have powers, especially at board meetings which can be very significant.

If you want your investor to become a director, you should make sure that you sign a proper contract. It should set out their duties as director, the numbers of hours they will work each week or month and also put in place a mechanism so that they can be removed if necessary. You will probably need a lawyer to advise you on this as it is a complicated part of the law.

Watch out for investors who collect directorships like trophies. How useful will they be to you if they are always being a director elsewhere and do not have any time to advise you? Take up references from other companies where they also have a directorship. Remember also that it is a time-consuming process to get rid of a company director if they are not willing to leave voluntarily, so take care that you only give an investor a directorship if you are sure that they will do a good job in that role.

Becoming part of the management team

Most entrepreneurs who pitch for investment will not have complete management teams. Many of them would love to find the right sort of investor who is also prepared to come and work in the business on a regular basis.

Some, but not all, investors actively want to get involved in the management of the businesses they invest in. They do this for a variety of reasons – perhaps they can offer specific skills, perhaps they want to keep an eye on things or possibly they are bored and want something to do.

Occasionally they will look to invest and join the company drawing a proper 'management' salary which, coincidentally, is the same amount (or even more than) they have invested. You should be careful with these types of people as it could be that they are looking to get their investment 'for free'. Treat each person on a case-by-case basis and always ask them about their motives before you agree to anything.

If they are to become part of the team you will need to look at them both as an investor and as a colleague. It is very important that the fit is good, especially if you will be working alongside them all the time. It can be tempting to set things up on an informal basis at first with a plan to move to something more formal, but even if the investor wants it that way, you should insist that all the paperwork is done properly, with one set of documents for the investment and a separate set for the employment. If the company does not have much money, your new member of the management team should share the pain with you. They should not draw a salary while you starve. Therefore, set up arrangements from the beginning that give you the same opportunities and risks. For example, you may agree that all of you can claim your expenses, but that all salaries will only be paid when the company can afford it.

Parachuting in to help on special things

For many investors, the perfect relationship is one where they are called upon when their skills are needed, but they are not expected to become a director or an employee. For example, if your investor is also a lawyer, you can probably ask them to check over your employment or commercial contracts. And if they are an accountant they may come in to help you set up the accounting system or to help with preparation for the annual audit of your accounts.

One great private investor I know is a dab hand at writing employee handbooks and another is a lawyer who looks very closely and really thinks about every legal agreement she sees.

Usually these investors will not charge you for the work they do. They see rolling up their sleeves and helping you out when you have a particular problem as part of their role as your investor. Sometimes they even see it as a way of protecting their investment! Don't be surprised though if your personal dragon starts asking for fees if they end up doing a lot of work for you. Usually you will find that their request is reasonable and they will accept that actual payment can be deferred until the company has enough money to pay them.

Here is a great story of how private investors saved a company.

Case study: entrepreneur Nick Dyne

Our angels saved the company from a VC that had invested in the business but had no idea about how it worked. The VC threatened the ongoing existence to the point that our angel investors acted together to buy them out. They believe in our business in a way that VCs just don't.

Providing contacts

Angel investors are successful people, and because they are successful they generally have very good networks. This means they probably have an enviable ability to open the doors you need, just by making a phone call.

As Tim Duffy of MeetingZone says:

'We have a good mix of business angels as investors and I have found them all highly supportive and willing to open up their network of contacts for the benefit of the business. This has been very positive for the company. We always keep them well-informed with shareholder updates and requests for help if we need it. I think it's good to have them as passive supportive shareholders rather than directors or board members.'

Investors may introduce you to potential customers or to better suppliers. They may even introduce you to other dragons. Take advantage of any offers and do not be afraid to ask, even if they have not offered. However, be a bit sensitive and try to use investors well. Remember they may be using up a favour on your behalf and, after they have used it, they may not be able to do so again. They may also have other entrepreneurs who they may want to help, so do not try to grab all the contacts for yourself. Try also only to ask for contacts when you really need them. Sometimes it is better to go cold into a company and impress the day-to-day team, before you ask your investor to introduce you to the Chairman. For all you know the staff at your potential customer may hate him!

Case study: Everyclick

Everyclick is a search engine (like Google) with a difference. It gives half of its revenue to charities chosen by the users of the search engine. Everyclick has raised lots of money from business angels and the founder Polly Gowers regularly talks about how helpful her investors have been in giving her introductions to customers and suppliers, including some leads that have led to pretty amazing contracts.

The benefits and pitfalls of having a group of investors as your shareholders

Before you start fundraising think about what you want your group of shareholders to look like after the fundraising and also in the long term. Do you want to have lots of shareholders (a syndicate) or just a few?

> **Case study: Procession . . .**
>
> Procession . . . raised most of its money from business angels in the late 1990s. It has over 200 shareholders — with only two institutions. When asked at a Cambridge conference in 1999 'how do you manage over 100 individual investors' the reply from the then MD was 'a lot easier than managing the two institutions!' The company feels that this sums up a key difference. Angels, once investment has been made where there is no direct involvement, like to know how can they help. Angels react quickly and it is as much about the eye balling and a judgement call about the people. They generally are not driven by 'greed'. There is nothing wrong with greed but often where this dominates then control is a close relation!

The Procession story is a long one (a 10 year startup!) and whilst many shareholders may have written off their investment they remain interested and very supportive. It may be a personal thing, but such loyalty from these brave individuals is a big driver to the management to ensure they see their rewards. The company has rejected a number of 'spivy' deals to drop existing shareholders and 'restart' and such loyalty is a two-way flow. In Procession all shareholders are equal. In other deals shareholders will have different rights depending either on the degree of influence they have over the company and/or the size of shareholding they own.

Angel investment deals tend to fall into two categories, one where just one or two people invest in the business, or the other where you have lots of smaller shareholders. How the shareholder register looks after the deal will affect the future in lots of ways. These are the issues you should address when you are thinking about your shareholder group.

What sort of exit do you want?

If you want to sell your business or possibly buy back the shares yourself one day, it is probably better to aim for one or two large investors. If you are planning to float your business, it may be a good idea to try to get lots of dragons to invest so that when you float you are already used to dealing with a lot of shareholders and you will also have a lot of shareholders who will act as a base group of investors once the business is quoted.

Raising new rounds of funding

If you know you want to raise further rounds of finance, it may be worth having a lot of shareholders; this is provided, of course, that you know you can go back to them to ask for more money.

However, if you are going to need to get venture capital funding later on, be wary of having too many shareholders. Venture capitalists typically do not like investing in businesses where there are already lots of private investors as they think it makes the deal too complicated. Too many people will have rights at shareholder meetings and they may interfere in the business. They may also take up too much of the management team's time when they ask questions. Venture capitalists like deals where there are one or two 'good quality' experienced private investors (preferably who they know) because they will be able to help the management team and will also know when to interfere and when to leave things up to the venture capitalist.

Interfering in the business after the deal

Weigh up the benefits of only having to talk to one or two investors, who may get heavily involved in the business, versus having a lot of 'passive investors'. When you negotiate the legal agreements around the investment you can set some rules about the amount of influence new investors will have, but generally if you have a lot of small investors they will each have less power over you and what you do. The downside is that all shareholders have rights and some companies find they have one very annoying small shareholder who can cause a lot of headaches and end up spending as much time dealing with this as if they had only one big involved investor.

Communicating with your investors post the deal

Talking to your new shareholders regularly is going to be vital. If you have one or two shareholders you may be able to do this more informally by email and phone. If they become a director of the company you will also see them at board meetings. If they are not a director you can invite them to attend your board meetings as an observer, which means they can attend the meeting, but that they cannot speak or contribute to the meeting.

With a lot of shareholders it can be tricky keeping up a good relationship with them. Think how much time and effort quoted companies spend on investor relations! As a small company getting this right can make all the difference. Consider sending out a quarterly newsletter or having a special section on your website that is only for investors. Also think how much you want to tell them; consistency and no surprises are always what investors want. If you get your investor relations wrong, you will find yourself continually fire-fighting queries from your shareholders which will take up a lot of time.

> ### Case study: Cambridge Biostability
>
> Cambridge Biostability is a biotechnology company which has fascinating technology which can stabilize vaccines, meaning that they can be taken all over the world and be just as effective as when they were made in the factory. This has the potential to revolutionize the effectiveness of vaccinations in the Third World where there is a real problem with vaccines becoming ineffective long before they get injected into the person who needs them so badly. Cambridge Biostability has over 100 angel investors. Some have been investors since the early days and others have invested as the company has grown and developed. The company has always had a policy of proactively communicating with its angels. It sends out regular letters from the CEO explaining about the achievements the company has made and also about its plans for the future. It also tells its angels when there are changes to management and is delighted to have angels visit the head office to see what is going on and to talk to the senior management.

The main benefits and pitfalls of private investors

Benefits

1. Money

2. Mentoring

3. Giving value as a director of the business

4. Actually working in the business (often for free!)

5. Providing you with business introductions to customers and suppliers.

Pitfalls

1. Do not have enough money for further investment

2. Interfering with and distracting the management

3. Try to take over as management

4. Not giving you any help with the business

5. Wasting time by giving you the wrong contacts

CHAPTER 8

Will a dragon want me?

When you see the amazing variety of businesses pitching on *Dragons' Den* and which ones the Dragons choose to back it is really hard to get a handle on why some businesses win investment and some fail to. Do you remember iTeddy? Personally I would have agreed with Duncan Bannatyne about that opportunity, but it appears that Theo Paphitis was right as the business has been incredibly successful.

In the real world of private investing life is a bit different; angel or dragon investors tend to have similar reasons for liking and disliking businesses and similar objectives as to what they want to achieve from their investment. So while it is always worth remembering that every dragon investor is an individual and may do something atypical, most will have the same issues. To have the best chance of winning investment you will need to be exciting to *most* investors not just one or two, so here are some tips on how to position yourself and your business. When you are pitching you should not lie, but you need to try to bring out the points about your business that are most like the questions covered below.

Are you a business with potential for explosive growth?

I have already talked a bit about lifestyle businesses and why they are unsuitable for dragon investment. What you really need to do to win with dragons and angels is to show them that you have a business with 'Potential for Explosive Growth' or 'PEG' businesses as they are known.

PEG companies are those where the ambition of the people running the company is to *build* it as big as they possibly can and then *sell* it so that their investors receive at least 10 times their original investment and they personally receive an enormous amount of cash. PEG businesses are not defined by their size or sector, or anything else, just by their *potential* for enormous growth in the future. Think of Igloo Thermo Logistics, which is not in a sexy sector like the Internet, but is growing massively by offering added value and concentrating on excellent processes and service levels.

No company is definitely a PEG company or a lifestyle business, especially when it starts out. Some big businesses may have been lifestyle businesses for years, but a new management team may decide to turn it into a PEG company. Equally the team at a PEG business may discover that the opportunity for immense growth does not become a reality, but that they can build a very profitable business that gives them and their staff excellent pay and a great way of life with sensible working hours.

Dragons and private investors alike want to back PEG companies, not just for the money they might make but also because they have a good chance of being able to sell their shares in the future. For a private investor there is no point in holding shares in a business where they can never get their money out. They are very unlikely deliberately to invest in a lifestyle business, unless they have other reasons for doing so, e.g. they are helping out a friend.

So how do you know if you have a PEG business? The following questions may help you to decide.

Is your business in the right sector?

Dragons' Den shows entrepreneurs pitching an incredible number of business ideas. One programme alone may have businesses in everything from new foods to hi-tech products that will be used on mobile phones. Like the show, dragon investors also look at businesses in all sorts of sectors and, as a general rule, there is no 'sure-fire' sector to be in, if you want to get investment.

The Dragons are just like private investors in this respect. In the first couple of episodes they invested in businesses as unlikely as Hamfatter, a pop group and Victoria McGrane's fashion line, both of which are in sectors that would not typically be the "right" sectors to invest in. Of course, they were really backing the talent of the people in both these deals. These deals are not the norm, and if you look at the long line of investments made over every series you will see that most of the deals have been in businesses with unique products such as the Youdoodoll and Chocbox.

It is true that some sectors have a good history of creating businesses that have explosive growth and others that have a reputation for failing to make investors any money. These are the signs that investors look for when deciding if the business is in the right sector.

Good signs:

- A small amount of money is needed to grow the business quickly in that particular sector.
- It is easy to build a position which is protected and prevents other businesses from competing with you.
- The sector is ripe for 'disruption' i.e. a new technology or a new business model can enter it quickly and relatively easily.
- The sector has established businesses which have a history of acquiring their competitors.
- The sector has high profit margins.
- It is a sector that operates in the same way all over the world.
- Is it a sector that is recession proof.
- The sales cycle is short.
- There are regular repeat sales to customers and it is easy to increase the variety of products you sell to your customers.

Bad signs:

- The sector has dominant players who will squeeze out new companies if they can.
- The sector is fiercely competitive and price driven.
- The sector has established businesses with a history of squashing out their competitors.
- The sector has low profit margins.
- In each country the sector operates differently.
- It is a sector vulnerable in a recession.
- The sales cycle is long.
- Each sale, even though large, is a one-off.

The sectors that tend to make investors rich

These are the sectors that have a good reputation for making angels rich.

- Technologies around the Internet or telecommunications e.g. software or physical products used in phones or computers.
- Businesses that can build quickly on or via the web, think of Skype, myspace, YouTube etc.
- Sectors that sell products or services to governments or to big corporations.
- Medical instruments or technologies.
- Sectors with a product that will win acceptance from all types of customers, think of Dyson vacuum cleaners.
- Consumer products where the product will sell and sell.
- 'Fashionable sectors'. A good example at the moment is the Clean Tech sector as investors are very interested in environmental technologies.

In the last year or so, there is also one other area that has also evolved as a popular sector for investors, although traditionally it has been seen as very risky. This is the area of Creative Arts businesses. Creative Arts ranges from music, film and TV to jewellery and art. The Dragons have invested in a number of these businesses over the years. Private investors are now catching on to this sector as well, but it has quite different characteristics to other sectors as the businesses will remain very dependent on the continuing creativity of the entrepreneur for their success.

The sectors that find it hard to make investors rich

These are the sectors with a much poorer reputation for making angels rich.

- Biotechnology, because of the large amounts of money needed to commercialize the product.
- Retail and restaurants, unless the business is already well established and just looking for money to expand a proven business model (you need a specialist investor such as Theo Paphitis if you are in a sector like retail).

- Services businesses where the biggest asset is the staff, their contacts and their knowledge. If your biggest assets walk out of the office each night and may not come back, an investor will be worried.
- Sectors selling to a niche audience or sectors that will disappear after a time because of issues like technological advancements.
- Speculative sectors such as mining.

Is your business protectable?

You cannot protect an idea, but you can protect something real. The Dragons always ask about this on the TV show and with good reason. If a business does not have anything that it can use to protect its market share, the chances of it being beaten by the competition rise considerably. No wonder the Dragons and private investors all switch off if a business cannot protect itself, but get very excited if a business does have patent protection. Think back to the Nova-Flo case study in Part One, where they got the interest of all the Dragons when on TV and had angels fighting to invest in them once they started fundraising in the real world.

PEG businesses nearly always have something that is real, whether it is a patent over a technology, a great brand, an amazing trade secret or just the best processes and systems. All these things give PEG businesses an edge over their competition and therefore enable them to grow more quickly and make more money than others.

So to win dragon investment you must show that someone else cannot just come along tomorrow and copy exactly what you are doing and then take away your customers. There are various ways to protect your business and some are more important than others.

Legal ways to protect your business

There are three main ways to protect your business.

1. Have legally binding contracts with all your customers, suppliers and employees for long periods and preferably with the option to renew them at improved rates in the future.

2. Obtain a patent over your product or process which prevents other people from selling it without.

3. Get a trademark over your brand or business names so that other people cannot use them or use a copycat name.

Remember good businesses ALWAYS protect themselves using the first route, even if they cannot use the others

Soft ways to protect your business

Trade secrets

There are some businesses that don't worry the same way as others about things like patents or trademarks. They rely on what is known as a trade secret to ensure that nobody can copy them. One of the most famous examples is Coca-Cola. You may choose to rely on keeping the secrets of your business, well, secret – but if you are going to rely on this, make sure you know exactly who knows the secrets (and that there are only very few of them) and also have a back-up strategy if you cannot get hold of these people (e.g. keep a copy of your formula in the bank!). Make sure that anyone who knows the secret has signed a document to ensure that their life will not be worth living if they reveal it to anyone. Best of all do not let any one person have more than a part of the total secret!

Branding

One of the strongest ways to protect your business is to build a brand that reflects what you do and who you are. A strong brand is much more difficult to destroy than you might think and as most business sectors mature over time, it is usually only the top two or three brands that make any big money; everyone else ends up as a poor fourth or stuck in a small niche. Think of the UK chocolate industry which is dominated by Cadbury, Mars and Nestlé.

Thinking about chocolate – did you know that the business that owns Green & Black's chocolate had private investors? They are a great example who built a very strong brand that enabled them to dominate a niche in their industry. Not only did this help them to charge a premium price, but it also helped them to sell out to Cadbury's for a very good price. This makes it an excellent example of a good dragon deal.

Customer loyalty

How customers feel about a business can make or break it. The more that customers feel loyal and engaged with a business, the more likely they are to stay with it and not turn to a competitor for products or services. Therefore, using the right techniques to build customer loyalty are the key to explosive growth. Loyalty will only be built if both your product and the customer service behind it is excellent, so plan accordingly.

A reliable supply chain

When you are a very small business, getting reliable suppliers who are loyal is very difficult. Make sure that the correct legal agreements are in place to protect your business, but also try to build a relationship with your suppliers so that they are engaged with what you are doing. They will give you more for your money if you get this right.

Private investors will look to see if your suppliers can easily offer to others what they are doing for you, so talk to suppliers and if your business is doing something very special, get confidentiality and exclusivity agreements in place, so they do not take your idea to someone else.

You can also protect yourself by trying to use more than one supplier for a job or by using different suppliers for each part of the production process.

Is your business at the right stage?

One of the biggest complaints from Dragons and private investors alike is that entrepreneurs ask for money at the wrong time in the life of their business. Business angels like some risk but they really want to back entrepreneurs who have shown that they can build something for themselves.

It is quite rare nowadays to see investors backing businesses that are only ideas or have not yet started trading. If you are still at that stage, it is probably better to look for bank debt, grant funding or awards from local government and other agencies that specialize in supporting new ideas. There are always exceptions, however, as you can see from this story from Roger Wilmott of Airetrak.

> ### Case study: Airetrak
>
> As a startup company Airetrak was looking for seed funding to provide the investment to support initial product development and the first few initial customers. With a small staff, who were focused and knew what had to be done and how to do it, what we didn't need was to have to spend time with investors providing progress updates, justification, financial reports etc. We were extremely lucky in securing a bunch of angel investors who saw the value in the proposition and were willing to commit investment and leave us to it. At the stage of the company we were at, it was exactly what we needed. I can see the value in more active investment but for us that would come at a later stage when we require help with geographical expansion etc.

The Dragons are always asking entrepreneurs about what sales they have achieved already. Real dragons will ask the same question because they want to see signs of real customer demand. Clearly the more sales you have the better it will be.

One of the complaints I occasionally hear is that private investors only want to back young companies. This is not true. They do want to back young companies, but only when they are just about to have a period of massive growth. They do not want to back businesses that are already well established because it is so difficult for them to make great profits on their investment. One angel investor complains that many of the deals he is shown are now too late and therefore want to raise sums of money that are too large and at too high a valuation for him to make money. He is turning to places where he can find really young deals where the great returns can still be found.

Some investors do like older businesses – Theo Paphitis specializes in investing in companies that are tired and old and need restructuring, but this type of investor in the real world is rarer than you might think.

If you have an established business, especially if it has cash flow and assets, you should probably talk to the bank or the venture capital community. If you want to buy out an established business because you think you can revolutionize it, talk to the Private Equity Buy-Out houses. Some of these will invest in surprisingly small existing businesses if the future opportunity is big enough.

Do you have the right management team?

Private investors back people. The saying goes that an A list team can make a good business out of a B list product, but a B list team will not be able to make the best of an A list product.

To win dragon backing, the team should be right and if you have holes in your team, e.g. you do not have a finance guy, you should do two things. First, find someone who can do that job, even if you have to outsource it and second acknowledge that you have a hole and describe how you are going to solve the problem.

The best teams have a leader and up to four people playing a supporting role, each of whom specializes in one thing e.g. sales, but who is prepared to turn their hands to anything.

It's best to be honest with yourself from day one about your team – don't be tempted to fill your team with friends or acquaintances just because they are around. Instead, think about what the role will need, write a job description and then start talking to people.

Private investors also look for serial entrepreneurs. These are the people who have already built a successful business and sold it so that it made money for the investors. If you are one of these people, you will be taken very seriously by investors. If you are not one, you will have to show similar characteristics, so remember to point out that you were the kid in the playground who was trading sweets or whatever.

Do you have the right business model?

To win investment you must show that you can grow your business very quickly and get large profits from the sales you make. You also need to show how you can upgrade your products so you can resell more products to the same customers. When investors talk about a business being scaleable, this is what they mean.

The business also needs to be able to develop itself. It needs to show that it has the opportunity to launch its products or services into new markets or sectors. A great example from *Dragons' Den* is Laban Roome's 'Goldgenie' gold-plating business that started out with gold-plating the Emmy Awards. After winning investment from James Caan it won a contract from Harrods to supply gold-plated luxury items such as iPods.

The profit margins (net profits divided by sales) in your business must be high to be attractive. This is because all businesses need to be able to cope with pressure from customers to cut prices and pressure from suppliers to raise costs. If the margins in your business are low, then you will need to show that you can make very high volumes of sales and also that you will be able to cope with high volumes of sales, which means there have to have very efficient systems. A good example is Google (which was backed originally by angel investors) which can accept millions of payments from advertisers using Google Adwords in tiny and large amounts online every minute of every day all over the world.

If the business is in a very specialist niche, you will need to show also that you can find enough 'experts' or highly trained people whom you can employ in your growing business. So before you talk to potential investors find out where will you get these people from or have a solution to how you will train them yourself once they have joined you.

Another thing to think about is how you will deal with a sudden massive growth in customers. You need to be able to show that you can outsource parts of your business to someone else if you cannot deal with demand with your own team. Take a look at your current suppliers to see if they will be able to help you if necessary.

Is your business ready for investment?

One of the hot topics in the private investment world is how to get more businesses ready to take investment from people they do not know. In fact this is an issue that worries people as high up as the European Commission. As a result there are many course available that offer companies support in getting ready for investment, many of which are funded by governments and so cost nothing for you, the entrepreneur to attend. You can also get help from many firms of advisers, particularly accountants and your local BusinessLink.

I recommend that you look into going on one of these courses before you start looking for private investment. Some of the best are run by the CONNECT group (including www.connectyorkshire.org and www.connectmidlands.org), Finance South East www.financesoutheast.com and G2i www.g2i.org. One of the advantages of these courses is that they will usually have a crowd of private investors they know and they will allow you to pitch to these people.

Are you personally ready for investment?

If you have got this far in the book, you are probably wondering why we have asked this question, but have a think about whether you really want to share your business with other investors. The hard work with an investor starts – and not stops – with the successful closing of your fundraising round.

Are you ready to share the management and strategic development of the business with someone else? Think about how you will deal with this extra involvement and what ground rules to lay down from day one, especially the time you plan to spend with the investor. Remember that many investors believe that the time may come when someone else will be better than you at taking the business forward, so your role may change. You have to be prepared to have this conversation, and if you are determined to stay in charge, will have to show how you plan to grow and develop yourself so you are ready to meet the challenges of running a large business.

Can investors supply all the money you need?

In every episode of *Dragons' Den* there is a deal where the Dragons offer to invest some, but not all of the money the entrepreneur needs. When the entrepreneurs pitch they ask for all sorts of sums of money from the Dragons. Often the sums are less than £100,000. In real life they usually request much more, starting from at least £250,000. This is for the simple reason that they need to raise enough money to help their business catapult itself into becoming a global concern. Of course there is always an exception to the norm. Recently one investor told me how one dragon investor only invested £40,000 in a publishing business and sold his stake for millions only a few years later.

The same is true in the real world, but this does not mean the sum they are asking for is the right amount from the perspective of the dragon investors they are pitching to. The investors, however, tend to look at what sort of sum of money they think the company actually needs and make decisions accordingly. They will walk away from deals that need too much and equally reject deals that are 'too small'.

This is hard for most entrepreneurs to understand, but at the end of the day it is the customer who decides and, therefore, knowing your customer becomes very important.

Some private investors invest millions, but these are very rare. Most investors put between £10,000 and £100,000 in each company they back. Some will put in £500,000 or more, but it is very rare indeed for them to put in more than £1 million. Occasionally groups of investors will put in more. A fuel cell company called Bac2 recently raised £2 million from private investors in London, but this is very unusual and you should not assume you will be able to achieve this.

It is usually best to look for dragon investors if you need less than £1 million. If you need more than that you should probably start talking to the specialist early-stage venture capitalists. You can find details of these at the website of the British Venture Capital Association www.bvca.co.uk which has a page where you can search for investors by the amount you need to raise as well as by sector and location. It is also worth checking another website that I run called www.vcrdirectory.co.uk which has details of VCs that are not members of the BVCA.

If you need less than £100,000, it is arguable whether it is worth seeking dragon investment because of the time and costs in trying to raise the money. It usually costs between £5,000 and £15,000 minimum to raise any private investment, so either make a plan to raise more than £100,000 or try to raise the money from your friends and family or the bank.

How much will it cost to raise money from dragon investors?

Something that is often not talked about in the entrepreneurial world is how much it costs to raise money from private investors.

Typically you will have to pay fees for advisers who will help you negotiate the deal and you may also have to pay the fees the investors will face. You will probably also have to pay commissions (usually 5%–10% of the money you raise) to the people who introduce you to the investors. Make sure you factor this money into the funds you raise and into your financial projections.

What is your business worth at the time you seek investment?

When the Dragons like a business on *Dragons' Den* the conversation rapidly moves into a discussion about the valuation of the business. Valuation is an area that people spend hours and hours discussing. University professors have made and lost their reputations writing about theories of valuation. So this is not an easy area, but there are some clues which can help anyone to understand the basic valuation of a business.

The value of any business is based on a mixture of what it is worth today if you sold it on the open market (i.e. if you just put it up for sale and asked anyone to buy it) PLUS what extra value might be in the business in the future, which would mean if it was sold in the future it would sell for a much higher price.

Your business's value today is usually based on a multiple of the current profits after all costs have been taken out, including tax, most commonly described as the 'profit after tax' or the 'net profit'.

This figure is usually adjusted for 'funnies' e.g. if you are not taking a salary, but a buyer would have to employ you or someone else to do your job once they own it, then the net profit would be reduced further by the cost of this salary. When seeking investment, investors will immediately look for these funnies and adjust the profits and therefore the valuation downwards.

If the business is loss-making, most investors will take a view on its value based on other measures. Good examples are the Web 2.0 businesses like MySpace and YouTube. They were valued on a 'value per user'. This price will have been set by working out roughly what each user is really worth to the business. It could be £1 or maybe £100 depending on how much an average user is likely to spend with the business as a customer and how much profit the business will be able to take from that spending.

Investors then look at the future potential of the business. This will be based on your sales and profit projections and also the amount of cash the business will generate. The more they understand and trust your projections, the easier it will be for them to form a view on this.

However, they look at it this way because any cash left over in the business after all the bills have been paid can potentially be shared out amongst the shareholders. This money is the return they will get from having invested if you all decide to close the business down instead of selling it.

Most importantly of all, they will think about how much the business will eventually sell for one day, as this is the most likely way they will get their money back.

Clearly they want to get much more back than they have invested. In fact they usually invest with the expectation that they may get 10 times back or more. The reason they want to get this much back is to make up for the losses on all the other private investments they make and also to take into account the big risks they are taking by investing in you.

Coming to a valuation

Having thought about all these things, investors will chose a final 'profit' number or sales number they most believe in and multiply it by a number which is appropriate for the sector the business is in. They will come to this sector number by looking at two major things:

1. The number the stock market uses to value quoted business in the same sector.

2. The number that other people buying similar businesses have paid.

They will then adjust this number to take into account comparisons between the size of the business they are investing in and the size of the businesses they are comparing with it. In all likelihood your business will be much smaller than these businesses so the investor will apply a discount of perhaps 30%. So if quoted companies are selling for a multiple of 12 times their net profits, they will probably apply a value of 9 times the net profits of your business.

The next thing that investors do is think about what percentage they will need to own in order to get a good enough return on the money they are investing. They will also think about how long it will take them to get their money back.

Dragon investors will typically want to get ten times their investment when they sell their shares. So if they are investing £100,000, they will want to get back £1 million.

If they think it is going to be worth £10m when they sell their shares, they will ask for 10% of your business, but if they think the business is going to be worth £2 million they will want 50% of your business.

When the business is sold will also be important to the investors. If they think it will be sold quickly, in two or three years for example, they may ask for a smaller percentage because they will get their money back quicker, but if it is going to take five to seven years or more, they will ask for a larger number of shares.

Is the market ready to give you investment?

All investment markets go through times when they grow quickly and others when business is slow. Sometimes investors are attracted by one particular sector and are prepared to pay a premium to get a stake in a business in that sector. As an entrepreneur, you will have the best chance of successful fundraising when the investment market is very active and especially if you are operating in a popular sector. It is well worth taking some advice from people who know the private investment market well to find out when to time your fundraising.

What is going to happen to your dragon investors if you raise money from a venture capitalist in the future?

If your business is going to need lots of new investment in the future, make sure that you have thought about this and talked the issue through with your investors.

When a new investor puts money in a business, all the existing investors, including you, will have your stake in the business diluted accordingly, because there is only ever 100% of the business to be shared out.

The good news is that a new investor will probably want to make sure that you are still very motivated to build the business so they will try to make sure that you keep a big enough stake to remain keen.

New investors are much less interested in taking care of your old investors, especially if they are not actively contributing to the growth of the business. It is almost unheard of for new investors to buy the shares of current investors. They want to put their cash into growing the business itself, not to make other people rich.

Usually this means that private investors get their shareholdings more heavily diluted when new investment is made. As an example, suppose when they first invest in you they take a 25% stake and you keep 75%. A new investor then comes on board who wants 50% of the business. As a result after that investment, the new investor would have 50%, your private investor l would have 12.5% and you would have 37.5%.

Dragon investors know and understand this, but it will affect the stake they will want. They will think like this.

> 'I have £100,000 to invest in the business and want to get back £1m. If I take 10% now I should get that £1m, but if new investment comes in and I end up with only 5%, then I will only get £500,000. So I had better get 20% now, just in case! Then I will ensure I have 10% when the business sells and get the £1m back that I want.'

When you are doing your calculations remember that if you do not think you can make your investors any money, for whatever reason, they are going to be able to work this out too!

Ten questions to ask to decide if your business is suitable for private investment

1   Does the business have potential for explosive growth?

2   Is the business in the right sector?

3   Is the business protectable?

4   Is the business at the right stage to receive investment?

5   Do we have the right management team?

6   Do we have the right business model?

7   Are you personally ready for investment?

8   Can private investors supply all the money you need?

9   Is the business worth enough to attract investors?

10   What is going to happen to my investors if I seek more investment in the future from venture capitalists?

CHAPTER 9

How to find a dragon

Now that you are sure private investors are the source of money for the business and you think you will be able to make them some money, you will need to know where to look to find some.

Private investors tend to keep quiet about their dragon investments, for the simple reason that once everyone knows they are a wealthy investor who likes risky investments, the requests for funding from entrepreneurs start flooding in. And most of the opportunities they see will not be of interest so they end up wasting a lot of time and money, when they could be doing better things. Dragon investors, like all wealthy people, suffer from other people trying to sell them things. Not just fun things like luxury holidays and fast cars, but also rather boring things like people offering to help them manage all their money. No wonder they work hard to stay under the radar and don't go flaunting their wealth like a City trader!

So how do you catch yourself a dragon, assuming you do not want to spend days hanging around backstage at the studio hoping to meet a real Dragon from TV.

There are various routes.

Routes for finding a dragon

Asking around

The first thing you should do is ask your friends, family, current and former colleagues at work, mates in the City, customers, suppliers and anyone else you can think of. After all, a personal recommendation is worth a lot and if you can find an investor for yourself, it can also be cheaper because you may not have to pay fees on the funds you raise, which will be the case if you follow any of the other four routes.

> **Case study: media business**
>
> Do you remember that we mentioned a screen-based advertising business in Chapter 7? When I first met the founders, the company was really only an idea, with just one screen being trialled in an ante-natal unit in one of the London hospitals. They wanted to raise £1m to fund the business and came to me because I was then working for a business angel network. There was no way that the angel investors I knew would have backed the business at that stage, not least because they did not know the founders at all. But I loved the business concept which would clearly be very profitable once all the screens had been put into the hospitals and were full of advertising. So I asked the founders to go away and see if they could find someone they knew, probably from the media industry where they both had good track records. About 18 months later, they came back to me having found two excellent private investors. We struck the deal and the business was up and running.

Attend events where you will find investors

This is a route that is most suited to people based in urban areas. Every city will have several groups that encourage investors and entrepreneurs to attend. Some of these organizations are based in more than one city and some even span the globe. Some of these groups also hold specific investor fairs or other events where entrepreneurs can pitch to investors.

Talk to business people you know to find out the current popular networking events, but you can also try out the following:

Growing Business magazine (www.growingbusiness.co.uk) holds an annual Growth Strategies Conference at which you can often see real Dragons such as Rachel Elnaugh and Doug Richard.

It is worth getting in touch with local accountancy firms, lawyers and banks to find out about other smaller networking groups locally. Check out the website of your local Regional Development Agency because they may list good events as well.

Mashup* www.mashupevent.com

Second Chance Tuesday http://www.theglasshouse.net/content/sctlondon

Appoint an adviser to help you find private investors

There are numerous people who will help you to find private investment. They will usually charge a fee for this service and it may be that you have to pay the fee up front or pay a monthly fee, known as a retainer. These advisers will also want to charge you a percentage of the funds you raise via them, though sometimes they will take part or all of their fee as shares or an option to buy shares in the future in your business. However, most of them will give you an hour of free advice before they charge you anything.

If you are a first-time entrepreneur and if the business opportunity is very exciting, it is well worth finding yourself a good adviser. They can make sure that you are ready for private investment. Also, if they are known to and trusted by investors, they will 'fast track' you towards the right people.

Talk to plenty of advisers before choosing one and make sure that you have a good rapport with the people who will be helping you. Also, negotiate hard when it comes to fees. Remember that the more certain an adviser is that they can raise you money, the more likely they are to undertake work for you and accept that they will be paid once the funds have actually been raised.

You can find suitable advisers by talking to your local business angel network, BusinessLink, your Chamber of Commerce and also your local legal and accountancy firms. If you are really stuck try asking the Institute of Chartered Accountants Corporate Finance Faculty and the Law Society.

> ### Case study: Vibrant Media
>
> These days Vibrant Media is the leading business selling in-text advertising on websites. It has been a remarkable success story starting with Doug Stevenson and Craig Gooding using a couple of desks in an incubator in London in July 2000 and an initial $500,000 of investment. Doug and Craig developed Vibrant Media into a global online advertising business, with over 200 employees located in New York, San Francisco, London, Hamburg and Paris. Vibrant Media's in-text advertising reaches over 120m Unique Users on over 3,000 publisher websites in 13 different languages and its advertisers include Fortune 500 global brands such as Microsoft, Daimler-Chrysler and Sony. When Vibrant Media first started to look for business angel funding, they appointed a corporate finance adviser to help them and they managed the investment process together very cleverly. They followed a timetable so the deal went through smoothly and the adviser, Hugh Campbell, provided considerable help in negotiating the best deal, especially in terms of valuation.

Approach the business angel networks

The vast majority of serious investors will belong to one or more business angel networks, but not all business angel networks are the same! ALWAYS ask any network if you can get a reference on them from two or three other companies that have used them before so you can find out if they will suit you.

The first thing to understand about business angel networks is who they see as their client. Is it you, the investors or both? Make sure that if you are the client then they serve your interests first, but if the investor is the client, you will have to recognize that they will look after their interests first. Some networks will claim to have both of you as clients. If this is the case, just remember that you will probably only use them once in your life, but the investor will be back again next month. Therefore, whatever they say, they will be thinking this too and you will be of secondary importance.

The types of business angel networks vary. Here are some of the types.

Online matching services

These are a bit like dating websites, where you will typically pay a fee to post your business plan or summary of your plan on the website and virtually anyone can go and look at it. This is not the route to follow if you have a highly sensitive plan, but it may be suitable if you are hoping that as many people as possible will see you. The risk with using such sites is that you do not know whom you will be dealing with if someone does approach you, and you will not know who has seen your plan.

Business advisers masking themselves as business angel networks

There are some groups whose primary purpose is to give advice to small companies and to charge fees for this advice. That advice may include helping you to raise money from private investors, venture capitalists and from banks and may be very helpful if you are unsure about where to raise money.

Informal clubs of private investors

Sometimes groups of friends and colleagues, particularly in the technology sector, form themselves into a club so they can invest together. Sometimes groups also form with people who live or work nearby or who have known each other for a long time. They may be an organized group that meets regularly or just meet up when a good deal comes along. Sometimes they only look at deals when one of the club members brings it along and sometimes they will look at deals where they are approached by someone they do not know.

In these clubs, the members will typically ask the entrepreneur to pitch to the whole club and then if they want to take the deal forward, they will share out the due diligence work between themselves. They will probably appoint a lead investor who will look after all their shareholdings in the investment after the money has been handed over and liaise between the company and the club members when necessary. That lead investor may also wish to become a director of the company.

There are great advantages to these groups, especially if their members really understand your business and the sector it is operating in. The members are usually very well connected and not only the lead investor, but also the other club members will offer to help build the business with you. They also probably know venture capitalists who may be interested in investing in you one day.

One of the big advantages of informal clubs is that they will not charge you money to present to them, nor will they charge you fees if they invest in you because they are spending their own money, so the main cost will be paying the lawyers and the financial advisers such as accountants.

You are likely to find informal clubs of investors by asking around and by talking to your local BusinessLink or Chamber of Commerce and also the Regional Development Agency. You may also find them at places where wealthy people tend to congregate e.g. the local golf club, sports club or social club. Local venture capitalists may also be able to point you in the right direction.

Formal business angel networks

Every region of the UK has at least one and sometimes more formal business angel networks. Most are members of the British Business Angels Association www.bbaa. org.uk (BBAA). You will find a list of these networks at the end of this book.

As members of the BBAA they agree to abide by a code of conduct to ensure that both entrepreneurs and investors are treated properly and fairly. If you are not happy with how you are treated there is a complaints procedure, which is managed by the BBAA.

Some of these networks are also regulated by the Financial Services Authority (FSA), but some trade under special exemptions that have been set up by HM Government to help the business angel community. From your point of view there is probably no difference between those that are regulated by the FSA or those that trade under the exemptions, as long as they are full members of the BBAA.

Some only perform a matching role, where they let you present to their investor members, but do not help you with following up after you have presented. Others will have a full service approach where they will work with you to prepare you for your presentation, set up the presentation meeting or meetings and also stay involved afterwards until the investment is completed. The majority charge fees according to the amount of assistance they offer, but some do not charge any fees at all. Some may take an equity stake in the business they are helping instead of a cash fee.

Most business angel networks hold investor meetings about six to eight times a year, where they invite their members to come and see four to six presentations by entrepreneurs. The location is usually somewhere really nice, e.g. a hotel or perhaps in the office of a local law or accountancy firm. These venues are nothing like the set of *Dragons' Den* by the way!

Some of them will also help other companies to raise money in other ways, including putting your details on their website for the investors to have a look at.

Good business angel networks are very selective. It is in their interests to show deals to the investors that will raise money, so if you are selected it is a good sign.

Understanding the gatekeepers

Before you get to meet any of the investors in a business angel network you will typically have to get through the person who manages the network. These people are known as the 'gatekeepers'.

If you want to raise investment you will find that the gatekeepers are some of the most important people you will meet. They can make or break your chance to get in front of people who will invest.

Most gatekeepers work for business angel networks, but occasionally they work in firms of accountants, private banks and anywhere else that private investors go to for deals. Their job is to receive all the business plans they possibly can and then to choose which businesses they think are most likely to win investment from their investors.

Dragon investors like good gatekeepers because they save them from having to look through and reject bad plans themselves. They really dislike gatekeepers who they think are showing them the wrong deals. If a gatekeeper shows too many of the wrong deals (too big, too small, not exciting enough, wrong sector, bad team etc), the investors start to worry that they are missing the good ones. They then leave the gatekeeper's network and look elsewhere for deals. If too many investors leave, the gatekeeper will lose his or her job, so they work very hard to get the selection process right.

Gatekeepers will always focus on the investors first and foremost and entrepreneurs will come second because investors will hopefully invest again, but it is much less likely that the entrepreneur will return to raise more money, especially if they are not successful the first time. There are always hundreds of entrepreneurs looking to raise money, but people who actively invest are much rarer. Investors tend to know other investors and gossip spreads quickly among them. If the gossip is that a gatekeeper is no good, this will mean the investors will turn to other places for deals, taking their fellow investors with them. Entrepreneurs, especially when they first start out in business, do not tend to know each other so well, so gossip between them spreads more slowly. This means that if they are unhappy with a gatekeeper it is unlikely to get out amongst other entrepreneurs and the gatekeeper will still get more entrepreneurs approaching them to help with funding.

So, for a gatekeeper, it is a bad thing to lose an investor, but not such a bad thing to lose an entrepreneur, unless of course that entrepreneur is a future Bill Gates!

Gatekeepers receive deals all the time from all over the place. Some of the deals will already be pretty good, with established teams and trading businesses and others will be way off the other end of the scale – perhaps just one entrepreneur with what seems like a crazy idea. The gatekeeper will typically see between 600 and 1,000 plans a year and will only select around 40 or 50.

The job of a gatekeeper is interesting. They need to find enough variety to keep their investors happy, but they also need to find those that have a real chance of getting invested in. Sometimes the two are not quite the same. Dragon investors like to feel they are seeing the best deals that are available even if they do not actually decide to invest in them!

To understand gatekeepers, you must understand what motivates them. As they are usually employees of someone else, they need to justify their salary by making money for the business. So they have to get fees from someone. That someone is normally the entrepreneur or his company who have to 'pay to play' i.e. they pay for the opportunity to pitch to the investors. Sometimes they charge membership fees to their investors, too.

It is normal for networks to receive and review a business plan for free, but if they select you to present, you pay a presentation fee (around £1,000+VAT) and then if you raise cash from their investors you pay a success fee (usually 3%–5% of the cash raised). So remember that they are directly motivated to raise you as much money as possible. Some networks also ask for share options in your company as part of their fee. Make sure you factor this into your costs when raising money and also think about how you will react if the gatekeeper asks for share options for themselves in your business. Will you be happy to have them as a shareholder in your business one day? Remember also that if they have share options that will shrink the amount of the company you will own.

Some business angel networks do not charge any fees, like xénos, the Wales Business Angel Network, www.xenos.co.uk, as their costs are met by their regional development agency. The gatekeepers at this type of network are not motivated by fees, but will be motivated by targets set by the organization funding the network. These targets are based on all sorts of things such as getting a certain number of women or ethnic minorities to present to just raising funding for as many companies as possible.

Try to find out if you can help them meet their target by being one of the companies they select.

Remember good business angel networks will be very honest with you about their procedures and charges and will be very helpful. More unscrupulous people will be more reluctant to explain how they make money from helping to raise money for companies.

Gatekeepers make their selections based on the following:

1 Do you fulfil their selection criteria?
   Broadly speaking you will fulfil the criteria which I have discussed in previous chapters, plus any specific criteria such as being in the right sector.
   Are you raising the sum of money that they think their investors can invest?
   One of the biggest problems for gatekeepers these days is companies that are not raising enough money!

2 Will you perform well on the night?
   Many networks will train you to present in the best way possible for their investors.
   And last but not least.

3 Do they have a slot for you?
   Most networks need to have a certain number of companies pitch at each event. So you may find that you get the chance to present on the grounds that they need someone to fill up a slot!

Actually meeting real investors

Unlike *Dragons' Den* it is quite rare to have your first meeting with investors in a 5:1 ratio. It is much more likely that a network will arrange one-on-one meetings with investors, or, more likely create a contact point at one of their investment events where 50–150 investors will be in the room. The investors who come to these meetings and events will probably have already been told something about you. They are not left completely in the dark as the Dragons on TV are. So it will be up to you and your colleagues to network like mad with them to take advantage of the opportunity. On the day, try to bring a couple of extra people along with you so you can say hello to as many investors as possible.

You may have to try more than one network

However good the business angel network, it may be that it does not have enough private investors interested in your business. Therefore, you may have to try several networks to raise all the money you want. Most networks will understand this and will be supportive of your efforts, but remember that the private investment world is still pretty small and both the gatekeepers and the investors talk to each other, so if you do try several networks you may find that your reputation precedes you.

Ten top tips for finding potential investors

1 Dragon investors are not easy to find, but there are clusters all over the place. Most investors know other investors, even if they do not invest with them and many investors belong to more than one club, network or cluster.

2 Talk to friends, family and other people you know to see if they know someone who might invest.

3 Find out about and attend networking events.

4 Consider appointing an adviser to help you find good-quality investors, quickly.

5 Get in touch with private business angel clubs, which specialize in your sector.

6 Think carefully before you post your opportunity on a website where anyone can see it.

7 Understand what motivates the people helping you to find investors and try to align their interests with yours.

8 Beware of any 'independent business adviser' asking for money to help you raise private investor finance. Ask them to justify their charges and get references.

9 You may have to try several networks before you find all the money you need.

10 Look for networks that are BBAA members, who have to adhere to a Code of Conduct or groups regulated by the Financial Services Authority (the FSA). Both these accreditations should ensure that you are dealt with fairly and you have a way to complain if you are unhappy.

CHAPTER 10

Befriending your dragon

Dragon investors meet dozens of entrepreneurs every year, so they get pretty good at judging those they want to back. They have so much choice that they don't have to bother anyone who does not meet their exacting criteria, so it is vital that you plan your strategy like a military campaign.

You may meet an investor anywhere and you need to make an excellent first impression. Take a lesson from Gavin Drake of Art Out There in series one of *Dragons' Den* in how not to offend a private investor. Never say to any investor 'just a minute' in a rude way, which he said to Rachel Elnaugh, just because you are already talking to someone else.

If a dragon asks you questions you think are dumb, still answer them politely. Don't whatever you do call them 'stupid', which is what Gayle Blanchflower unwisely said to Duncan Bannatyne, when pitching her cardboard beach furniture idea.

Momentum is vital in any fundraising. In an ideal world you will contact as many people as possible at the same time and then start negotiating with interested private investors in parallel with each other. This tactic is the equivalent of when people on *Dragons' Den* play the Dragons off each other, something that Igloo Thermo Logistics did brilliantly.

Fundraising takes time, but it is much worse if you approach one person, wait for rejection, then approach another and get rejected again.

Try following these steps to help make your approaches successful.

Making a successful approach

Step 1: Be prepared

It is very important to find out who might be your ideal investor and where you will find them. Do lots of research on the business angel networks and other places where you might find groups of investors. Set yourself a budget for the costs you will incur, especially for the presentation fees charged by different networks.

Make sure that both you and your business are ready from day one for investment. This means preparing the business, including the business plan so that there are no nasty surprises for the investors to discover. It also means being prepared yourself; try to make sure when people ask about you, they hear good things. If there is something funny in your background, have an explanation ready.

Practise making your five minute introductory pitch, known as an elevator pitch, and your full presentation, until you are word perfect. If you have a PowerPoint presentation, make sure it is really good, with not too many words or figures and that it will support what you are speaking about rather than being your speech. Decide now what aids you need e.g. product samples, customer references or contracts etc.

Step 2: Research the market

From now on you should keep a specific notebook (either a paper book or on your PC or personal digital assistant [PDA]) to hold all the information about your fundraising. Use it to keep a record of who you have spoken to and when, what they are interested in and what the follow-up steps are.

Then do lots of research about how you are going to find investors. Investors dislike deals which they think have been touted around everywhere, so have an A list of targets and a back-up plan if you have no luck from this list.

Step 3: Non-disclosure agreement (NDA)

A NDA is a legally binding document where the recipient of a business plan promises not to use it other than to consider the investment proposition. They also must not use it to copy the idea for themselves or use it to the detriment of your business (e.g. they cannot tell your competitors about what is in the plan or even that you are fundraising). Some investors are happy to sign NDAs. Others will refuse, so consider what you will do if an investor does refuse to sign one.

Step 4: Start to contact your targets

Depending who you approach or how you come across them, you will need different strategies. However, try to contact all your A list within a few days of one another. If you get lots of rejections turn to your B list and approach them as soon as possible.

In general it is normal to send an executive summary first (see Chapter 11), followed by the business plan if it is requested. This means that you do not reveal too much about the business before you are sure there is real interest. If you want to use an NDA send this with the executive summary.

If you are approaching individuals – especially very busy people – send a polite letter attaching the executive summary of the business plan and mentioning why you have decided to approach them and how you found them.

With others you could try using email, but ALWAYS ring first to check this is a good idea and make a polite follow-up call to confirm that the email has arrived.

Some business angel networks may ask you to submit a summary via their online form. If this is the case, DO NOT send the plan in by email or post until asked. The only exception to this is if you have an adviser that already knows the network who may be able to shortcut the online route and send the plan for you.

If you meet an investor at an event, be ready with your elevator pitch. Ask them if they want to hear it and if they do, off you go! Even if they do not want to hear it ask politely if you may take down their details in your notebook and contact them by email or post. Many investors deliberately do not carry business cards and they can be hard to find on a Google search afterwards! Ask their permission if you may contact them and, if they agree, how you should contact them and when. Whatever you do, don't let Julie White's experience happen to you. Do you remember that despite having interest from Peter Jones, she did not manage to take down his contact details on the day and then could not make contact with him afterwards, so the investment never happened.

Step 5: Follow up your initial approach

Usually a polite phone call or email will do the trick. Aim for a positive tone and suggest various dates for a meeting. When you arrange the meeting ask how long you will have and if there are any particular things the investor would like to cover or if they have a preferred approach to conducting the meeting. Find out if you should bring your adviser, your colleagues or come alone. Suggest that you send an agenda before the meeting, and then remember to send it! You may like to offer to have the meeting at your office so they can see the business in action or they may want you to come to their office because they are very busy.

Step 6: Accept rejection politely

Even if the investor does not respond positively always end the conversation politely as you never know when you might need them in the future. Remember also that investors talk to each other and if you annoy them, other investors will find out.

Do you remember Peter Jones apologizing to Rachel Elnaugh on behalf of all men after Gavin Drake was so rude to her? Well, just like the Dragons, private investors will also normally stick together in the real world.

Step 7: Stick to the agreed time and date of the follow-up meeting

Remember that gatekeepers and investors are busy people, so do not get annoyed if they rearrange the meeting, but try to fit around them. Only rearrange the meeting from your side if absolutely necessary and for a reason that shows you are 100% committed to your business; for example it is acceptable to change it if you get a chance to make a big sales pitch to a new customer.

Step 8: Attend the follow-up meeting

Make sure that you have all the necessary documents/samples with you. If you are presenting using PowerPoint, bring your laptop and a cable, just in case they do not have a computer for you to use. Print off a copy of your presentation, as well, just in case your laptop does not work and also so you can leave it with the investor to review.

Try to arrive in the rough location of the meeting 30 minutes early so you have time to relax before the meeting starts. Turn off your mobile phone so that it does not go off at the wrong moment. Go to the toilet or get a drink of water if you need to, because you are likely to be in the meeting for over an hour if it goes well.

If the meeting has gone well and the investor wants to take it forward, establish how you should go about following up. Maybe they will want a site visit if they have not already had one, or maybe they will want to follow-up via email for a while.

If, following this meeting, you are told by the investor that he or she does not want to follow up, this gives you another opportunity to ask politely for the reasons why you have been rejected and ask them if there is anyone else you could talk to.

Step 9: After the meeting

Write up some notes of the meeting, even if it has gone badly. Think about what went down well and what went down badly. If the meeting has gone well and the investor wants to follow up, send them a copy of your meeting notes, so that they have a record of the conversation they had with you.

Step 10: The next step...

If it has gone well, you may be asked to meet the investor's advisers or even to pitch to some other investors he or she knows. In due course you will then move into a phase called 'due diligence' when the investor really starts looking into your business to see if it is suitable for investment.

If it has gone badly, take out your notebook and start following up your other leads!

Ten top tips for making the first contact

1 Do your research on who you would like to invest in you and why.

2 Prepare all the paperwork you will need before you start contacting investors, including your business plan and executive summary.

3 Prepare and practise your elevator pitch and your presentation.

4 Decide how you will target your ideal investors.

5 Keep records of everyone you talk to and what outcomes arise.

6 Decide whether you are going to insist that investors sign a non-disclosure agreement before you give them full details of your business plan.

7 Approach every potential investor on your A list first; then approach people on your B list.

8 Agree a follow-up process with every investor you talk to and stick to it.

9 When it comes to arranging meetings, try to be flexible and fit in with the investor's timetable if you can; good investors are usually busy people.

10 If you have been asked questions that need to be answered at a follow-up meeting, make sure you have got the answers ready.

CHAPTER 11

Opening up to a dragon

The thought of sharing the innermost secrets of your business with potential investors is pretty scary. After all, they will ask for information and it may take hours and hours while they check and recheck it. The trick to managing this is to collect all the information you will need before you start and then to give it out in an organized way.

It is really easy to get into a muddle if you have a lot of different investors looking into your business. The best entrepreneurs I know who have raised money from private investors tell me that they usually give one person in their team the dedicated job of looking after the information, the investors and their advisers. One of the main jobs of this person is to keep a record of who has been sent what details. It is vital that you get this right, because if you start sending the information to the wrong people your chances of getting a successful deal done will probably collapse.

The types of documents you will share with potential investors while you are fundraising are:

The executive summary – the first document you will normally send out

The executive summary is a two to four page document, which has a paragraph or two describing each of the key parts of a business. You should write it after you have written the rest of the business plan (see below), not before, but it is a very important document as it is probably the first thing the investors will see on your business.

The executive summary is different from the form used to apply to pitch on *Dragons' Den*, although it will use some of the same information, such as basic facts and figures, e.g. your business's and your own name and contact details." Some information that the BBC asks for, should not be included in an Executive Summary as it is not relevant to private investors. This includes details of your ethnic background and whether or not you have been on TV before. In fact, it would definitely not be in your interests to tell new investors that you have already approached other people. Investors like to feel special and do not want to feel that they are just one in a long line of people you have talked to.

These are the sections that should be included in your executive summary:

Introduction

- What the company does, e.g. *We are a social networking website focused on students.*
- What stage it is at, *e.g. start-up, expanding etc.*
- Where it and its customers are based, *e.g. the head office is in Leeds, UK and our customers are based in UK and US.*
- How it delivers its products or services, *e.g. The company operates via an online shop and we also have a mail-order catalogue that is sent out four times a year to everyone on our database.*
- What the competition is like, *e.g. the company has two major competitors both of which are smaller in terms of sales and number of customers.*
- Describe the opportunity, *e.g. following market research, the company has identified that it should start selling 25 new ranges online and open its first shop in central London.*
- How much money is being raised, *e.g. the company is seeking to raise £500,000 to fund the costs of expanding the range and to lease and fit out the premises for the new shop.*

Company background

- Number of staff and offices.
- The management team.
- Recent trading history *e.g. the company has grown revenue and profits each year for the last three years.*
- The business model *e.g. we are a virtual business. The company generates sales from thousands of consumers who pay online for their orders via their debit and credit cards. Goods are delivered via post within two to five working days, although customers can pay extra for delivery within 24 hours. We have a full refunds policy provided the goods are delivered unharmed. Our fulfilment is managed by XYZ plc who also look after ABC plc, DEF plc and GHI plc etc.*
- A description of the market in which the company operates, *e.g. we are part of the multi £billion online retail market which is currently growing at 10% a year.*
- What is different about the company compared with the competition *e.g. we are the only business which has a website in 24 different languages.*
- Major achievements so far, *e.g. with only £5,000 of investment the company has generated £250,000 in sales and has customers in 24 countries around the world. No customer has ever claimed a refund! The company has won two major retailing awards in the last 12 months.*
- The immediate potential for the business *e.g. we expect demand from customers to grow at 30% a year for the next two years.*

Future growth

This should describe the medium and long-term growth prospects for the business and explain why you have come to this view *e.g. 75% of our customers have pre-ordered products from our 2008/9 catalogue even though the goods will not be available until summer 2008.*

Forecast

This section should have a table summarizing the key financial numbers including sales, profit before tax and a net cash flow projection for the last two years (if you have been in business that long), the current year and three years into the future.

Funding requirement

- How much money that will be raised.
- What it will be spent on.
- Your ideas of the value of the business.
- Any special terms to the deal e.g. *The company wants to raise 50% of the money as a loan and 50% for shares. The company also qualifies for the Enterprise Investment Scheme for private investors.*
- Whether you intend to raise more money after this round.

Typically, the executive summary is made available to investors on request, or you may just send it out to your target list.

The Non-disclosure Agreement (NDA)

Unlike on *Dragons' Den* where you agree to waive your rights and have to hand over lots of information to strangers, in the world of private investment you can ask potential investors to sign a document where they promise not to share the information you give them with anyone else. This is known as a non-disclosure agreement or NDA.

The NDA is a document that is one to two pages long. It is a legally binding document that obliges all the people who sign it to stick to what they have agreed. It is well worth asking your lawyer to help you with this as a poorly drafted NDA will not be worth much if there is a problem in the future.

Some investors will sign NDAs and others will not. Most venture capitalists will not sign one. If you want to raise money from people who will not sign the NDA, you will have to judge for yourself whether you want to deal with them. As a rule, you can trust angels and venture capitalists even if they will not sign the NDA, but it is worth having a NDA agreement ready just in case.

The business plan

The business plan is one of the most important documents a company ever prepares. It is not a day to day plan of how you run your business, but is a document to attract investment. So it is really a detailed advert for the company and it is the accepted route that entrepreneurs use to tell potential investors all about their business and why they need to raise money.

I have seen dozens and dozens of business plans in my life. Many of them are atrocious and may well have hidden a perfectly good business idea. It's a bit like the paper equivalent of a terrible pitch on *Dragons' Den*. The trouble is that a bad business plan will usually stop your fundraising in its tracks, whereas a well written plan will get you a long way into negotiations with investors.

The business plan is important for another reason. Don't be surprised when it comes to closing the investment if your investors ask you to sign a document confirming that everything in the plan is completely accurate as far as you are aware! So it is a good idea to get it right from the beginning.

Numerous books can be found on writing business plans. You can also hire people to help write business plans. One of the best is Business Plan Services www.bizplans.co.uk.

I will not go into lots of detail here because it will be more helpful for you to read the books I have mentioned, but in case you just need a quick checklist, here are the main things that you need to think about.

1. The main part of the plan should be 20–30 pages.

2. There should be attachments/appendices to the plan which include management team CVs, printed copies of the spreadsheets with your financial projection spreadsheets, customer references/orders, any intellectual property the company owns e.g. patent details.

3. Pay particular attention to the following sections of the plan: the business growth plans; competitor analysis; and use of the cash being raised.

4. Watch out for using jargon that everyone in your industry uses, but that investors may not understand.

'Due diligence' meetings with investors

The hard work really starts when you have follow-up meetings with a potential investor. These are called 'due diligence' meetings. But before we go into these in detail, here is a word of warning. Some investors will give you money without doing proper due diligence. If this happens you may think that it is brilliant that you have got off so lightly, but remember that if you do not properly understand the basis for the investor giving you the money, you may find yourself in trouble afterwards. I suspect that the SnowBone team were delighted when Rachel Elnaugh gave them her first cheque, before they realized that there was no legal agreement in place to ensure that she handed over the rest of the money they were hoping for.

These meetings are the start of a detailed fact-finding mission by the investor and a chance for them to work out if they like, trust and respect you. It is also a chance for you to find out more about them. All the companies that have raised investment from the Dragons will have got very used to having due diligence meetings with the Dragons or their advisers.

Case study: Umbrolly

Charles Ejogo from Umbrolly described the period after he pitched in the Den to us:

Due diligence meetings find out interesting and important facts such as the time Dragons Peter Jones and Duncan Bannatyne did their research on Umbrolly. They discovered the company's contract with the London Underground to provide umbrella vending machines stated that the company would have to pay £2,000 rent per year per machine, something Charles Ejogo had not fully explained when he pitched.

They also discovered another hidden problem that, when the company had more than 50 machines, it would have to pay a huge one off fee of £1 million to Cadbury's who had a preferential vending contract with London Underground. Further research by the Dragons unearthed more information that ended up causing the deal to collapse. The contract stated that the only products that could be advertised on the outside of the machine were the products for sale in the machine, which meant that it would be impossible to make money from advertising other products such as mobile phones on them, which would have been the most lucrative part of the business.

Typically it will take between three and four months for the various due diligence meetings to take place. Some will be just with the investors and some will be with their advisers. You may also have meetings with syndicates of investors. It is quite likely that if lots of people are interested, you will find yourself having similar meetings with different investors at different times. So prepare to be very busy!

Try to be as well prepared as you can for these meetings. Set aside a couple of hours or an afternoon for each meeting. Gather as much information about your business as you can and have it ready to pull out to show the investors. The sort of things you should always have ready are:

- The business plan and financial projections.
- Official company documents e.g. Companies House documents, VAT registration details, patents etc.
- Customer contracts, sales prospects lists and customer references.
- Supplier contacts and quotes.
- Product samples.
- Employment contacts.
- Minutes of board meetings and other key meetings such as staff meetings.
- Details of any legal disputes you have had or are involved in.
- Bank statements and loan documentation.
- The sales ledger and the purchases ledger.

Try to ensure that the investors can meet some of the team while they are with you and arrange for some time when you can chat informally before or after the meeting, but don't feel obliged to pay for expensive lunches.

Quite often you will find that the investors will ask you to redo things like the financial projections to test what happens if things go better or worse for the company. You may even be asked to change your business model to make it more profitable and to rewrite your business plan. It pays to listen to the investors, they will usually have more experience than you do, but do not feel you have to say yes to everything they suggest. If you disagree with them, prepare your arguments about why you are right and then talk the issue through with them.

Once these meetings are over, the investor will make you an offer either informally in person or on the phone. Some may even send you a document called a term sheet. This sets out the detailed terms of how much they are offering you and what they want for the money in terms of shareholding and influence over how the business will be run.

Once the term sheet has been issued, the investor will probably put you in touch with their lawyers and probably their accountants so you can all start hammering out the details of the deal. Both the lawyers and the accountants may send reports to the investor about what they have found out. The trick to managing all this is to agree a timetable and then stick to it.

Keeping investors up-to-date while due diligence is taking place

Once all the advisers start getting involved, it is worth making sure that you also keep up direct contact with the investor, just in case. Copy them in on emails and give them a ring sometimes to catch up. One of the things they will be most interested in is how current trading is going, so you could send out a short weekly update to each investor. (*Remember not to copy all of them in on the same email if they do not know each other!*) Try to relate this update to how things have changed compared with the original business plan.

An overriding thing to remember is that transparency is of paramount importance to investors and it is important that you assume this when you are dealing with lots of investors, even if you think they do not know each other. Most angel investors know each other and talk regularly. They will get very worried if you tell them a different story to the one they heard that you had told to another investor. If they think you are telling different stories they will get nervous and/or angry and will probably use this as an excuse to back out of the deal.

Lastly, take particular care when you are communicating with investors by email, as these can be forwarded without your knowledge very easily. Be careful about using the 'cc' function on email. Always double check to whom you are sending an email before you press the send button. If you do need to copy emails to people, but you do not want the recipients to know who else it is being sent to, use the "bcc" field for all the names.

Ten top tips about sharing information with investors

1 Write the business plan first and the executive summary afterwards, but send the summary FIRST and the business plan SECOND.

2 Organize the other information you will need before you start fundraising. Keep it all in one place.

3 Allocate responsibility to one person to manage the information and the requests that come in from investors.

4 Decide whether to have an NDA and when you might insist on using it.

5 Try to be as organized as possible about arranging the different meetings, so you do not waste your own time.

6 Don't be surprised (or offended) when investors ask you to change your financial projections and to rewrite your business plan.

7 A successful deal will depend on mutual respect, so do not be afraid to put across your own point of view – just make sure you have the back-up arguments ready!

8 Most investors will also ask their advisers to look you over, so be prepared to deal with them politely even if they initially seem unnecessary.

9 The hard negotiations about valuation will only really start when the due diligence is complete.

10 From your first proper meeting with an investor it is likely to take three to six months to close the investment; the more efficient you are the more quickly you will be able to close the investment.

CHAPTER 12

How to impress a dragon

'[I want to see] passion and energy, plus a good understanding of the market they are planning to fill.'
Rowena Ironside (ANGEL INVESTOR)

In his autobiography, *Enter the Dragon*, Theo Paphitis gives some tips for impressing him. He says that he has to like the person and the business proposal best and says that, 'if they can make a fantastic pitch under the pressure of the television cameras, that's an added bonus'. Most of the investors I know would agree with him in part, but be less forgiving about a bad pitch; they see being able to present well as one of the key skills you need when you are building a business.

The best pitch I have ever seen was given by Scott Pielsticker the founder of Blueback Cabs, a business that has now been sold to Addison Lee, the London cab company. Scott was amazing. He spoke without notes and was totally relaxed. In fact he was so confident that when he spotted me in the audience (we had not seen each other for a couple of years) he broke off, said hello, and then went straight back to his pitch!

Why was he so good? Well, he was very used to presenting and knew how to do it. He was very well-rehearsed and had all the facts at his fingertips so he did not have to refer to notes. He also had the confidence of having raised investment previously in Canada so he knew how to talk to investors and even more importantly, how to make them money.

Scott presented alone so he did not have to worry about how his co-presenters might look. Often entrepreneurs will make a pitch with two or more people. When this happens, warn all the people on the stage to look permanently fascinated (or at least engaged) with the person who is doing the speaking at any one time. There is nothing more fatal to a pitch than the audience seeing the co-presenters looking bored, picking their nails or even surreptitiously checking their Blackberries.

On *Dragons' Den* the entrepreneurs frequently go horribly wrong with their pitches. Rumour has it that some of this is due to the producers of the show wrong-footing them by suddenly taking away their props just before they walk up that flight of steps – I am not sure if this is strictly correct, but it is worth pointing out that if something can go wrong it always will, so always be prepared.

Whether you are an experienced presenter or not, do not worry. Investors will be in the room because they want to invest in something. All you have to do is impress them so much that they decide they really must back you. In fact, many investors tell me that they have often backed a business (despite everything I am telling you in this book!) based on the fantastic first presentation they saw.

So your pitch must be spot on perfect and when you realize that 15 minutes could make all the difference between getting anything between £0 and £2 million, it makes sense to do all you can to get the £2 million and not walk away with nothing.

'[I want to see] passion, balance, good market research, [they have] done homework and still believe in [the] idea.'
Chris Arnold (INVESTOR)

Deciding who should present

As a general rule, the most important person in the company on a day-to-day basis should present. This is usually the founder or the CEO/Managing Director.

However, chat to the team about this issue. Sometimes this person is not the person who will make the best presentation, perhaps it should be the head of sales or marketing, or even the head of finance. It may be worth getting the presentation ready and then two or three of you each having a go at making the presentation and then deciding who should make it on the day.

Before the presentation day

Find out from the gatekeeper how the format will work, what you will be expected to talk about and how long you will be presenting for. Find out if you can use props and if there is audio or visual available to you. Accept any offers to help you with presentation training.

Agree the deal you will have with the people organizing the presentation, especially around costs. It is also worth checking how much assistance they will give you in terms of presentation training, what the audience likes and dislikes, how long you should present for (the usual rule is one slide per minute of presentation) and also how you are expected to follow up at the event and afterwards.

One particularly important thing to understand is who will guide you on the day if you are speaking to a strict time slot. Some networks ring a bell and will actually stop you in your tracks if you go over time, and there is nothing worse than having your pitch cut off before you are finished. If you have someone sitting nearby who can give you a warning signal when your time is about to run out, it will be a great help, because even if you have practised your pitch to perfection, on the day it is easy to get off track and take longer than your rehearsal.

Regardless of who might be watching out for you on the day, you must practise your presentation several times in front of anyone who will listen beforehand. It can take hours of practise to get a pitch perfect, but it will, I promise you, be worth it.

The day before you present

Double check that your presentation is as perfect as you can make it. Practise one more time.

Collect all the copies of NDAs, executive summaries, business plans, business cards, samples, props you may need and put them in one place so you do not forget anything on the day.

Prepare a list of questions you think you might be asked and first write down the answer and then practise it, so that if you are asked it you can answer it off pat.

On the day

Dress code

Like Peter Jones, most investors like to be treated with a modicum of respect. One of the worst presentations I have ever seen was by some entrepreneurs who turned up late off a plane in crumpled clothes. They sloped onto the stage and made their presentation whilst swigging on cans of Coca Cola. A good ad for Coke maybe, but the investors were not impressed and the gatekeeper was FURIOUS.

The reason that the investors were unhappy was that they felt that they could not be sure that the men pitching would not turn up at a sales meeting and behave the same way!

Talk to the gatekeepers about how formally you should be dressed. Some people are more relaxed than others and on some occasions are also more informal. Especially if you are a tech entrepreneur or are in the film/TV/radio world, dress codes are often more relaxed, so it may be that jeans and a T-shirt are the right dress code on the day.

What to do with your name badge

At nearly every big event you will be given a name badge. Make sure it is prominently displayed high up on your suit/dress. For female entrepreneurs the very best place is actually high up, almost on your shoulder. There are two reasons for this:

1. Most investors are men and will be taller than you, so it is easier for them to read it if you put it here.

2. If it is well away from your cleavage, there is no reason for men to have to look too hard at your bust, which is embarrassing for you and for them!

3. Put your name badge on the right hand side of your breast because when you shake hands it is where people's eyes natural turn.

Remember not to have your badge hidden by your jacket, coat or scarf. Some people replace their badge with their business card. This will depend largely on how clear your business card is. If by any chance the badge has spelled your name or your company's name wrongly, either ask for it to be changed or replace it with your business card. After all, there is no point in starting off a conversation with people calling you by the wrong name!

Feeling good with how you look

'No-one is going to criticise you for wearing a suit, but they might criticise you if you took too casual
anonymous investor

Wear an outfit that you feel comfortable in and that reflects two things – your company image and also your own personality. As a rule men should wear suits in a sober
colour, dark blue, black or grey with a jacket, smart clean shirt and possibly a tie.
Women should wear a business suit or dress, but can usually be more relaxed about
its colour.

One of the best tips I have ever been given about a presentation is to go and get a
haircut the day before you present. It is one of the quickest ways to make yourself
look smart and well put together! Another trick is to clean your teeth just before the
presentation starts – it will force you to look at yourself in the mirror and check you
look just right!

Make sure your shoes are polished and there are no holes in your socks or tights.
Have a clean handkerchief in your pocket, just in case you need to blow your nose or
mop your sweating brow!

Case study: Umbrolly

Charles Ejogo, who was the very first person in series one to be offered money from
the Dragons described his experience on the Den as follows: . . . 'then when your
moment comes you are thrust into the 'Den' where the five Dragons grill you under
intense spotlights, which can cause a few drops of sweat to appear, which the BBC
used to death in their ad run-up to the opening episode, at my expense!' And if you
are not sweating when you start a pitch, you may well be at the end of it. Do you
remember Glasgow vet Iain McGill and his About Time family board game which
aired in 2007? As he said in the *Daily Record* 'The *Dragons' Den* is terrifying and I was
sweating by the end of it.'

Be prepared!

Whatever else you may do or not do, you should have a pen and a small notebook and
plenty of business cards in your pockets, so you do not have to scrabble around when
an investor starts talking to you after the pitch.

'[I want to see them:] well prepared, good knowledge, convincing [and] numbers that make sense.'
Dave Auger (BUSINESS ANGEL)

Before the pitch starts

The chances are that you will be one of several people who are pitching to the investors that day. So the environment is likely to be fairly tense and maybe even quite
competitive. Try to relax with the other presenters and have a bit of a laugh about
the whole thing. You never know you might find yourself wanting to do business

with them and unlike *Dragons' Den* most gatekeepers will be delighted if you use the opportunity to network with each other.

Sometimes you will be asked to sit in the audience until just before your presentation and sometimes you will have to wait in a room outside and come in when asked. Check all this out with the gatekeeper, so that you are not surprised on the day. In particular, check how much time you will have and whether you will be expected to take questions immediately after your presentation.

If you are using PowerPoint, check whether you should use your own laptop or whether the presentation will already be uploaded on a PC in the room. Either way, before the presentation starts, have a quick practice so that you know how to use the equipment and that your presentation does actually work. In particular, double check any audio or video within the presentation.

Setting up your stand

Many business angel investment meetings will allow you to have a stand, table and chairs outside the presentation room. Don't underestimate the power of your stand. Treat it like you would a stand at a trade show. After all you are here to sell and you can be sure that everyone else will be doing so. You do not want to be the one sitting at an empty table in a corner, whilst everyone else has a flashy display that is much more interesting for the investors to go over to. Use props wherever possible, including the obvious ones like a small bowl of sweets or free samples of your products. It may seem crude, but it works.

Get to the event early and if you can, grab the best table, ideally in the middle of the room, where most people will see you or pass you. Make sure you have a couple of colleagues who can stay by the stand all the time. If you do have to leave it unattended leave some business cards out.

'[I want to see] an edge.'
William Jones (BUSINESS ANGEL)

Making the pitch

You will notice that the entrepreneurs on *Dragons' Den* never use a PowerPoint presentation when they pitch. Occasionally they use a board to help them or some props, but the BBC does not give them a flashy screen and a laptop to present with. In the real world it could not be more different. I have not seen anyone use a board instead of a PowerPoint presentation for years. In fact, many investors feel they have almost seen too many PowerPoint presentations and become rather sick of seeing yet another groovy PowerPoint presentation when they would much rather just listen to the entrepreneur speak passionately about his or her business.

So think hard about what props you are going to use in your presentation and consider a PowerPoint slide show as just one of the many props you could use.

Not everyone will agree with me, and PowerPoint, used well, can be enormously helpful in supporting your pitch. It can be used to get crucial facts and figures across to an audience which illustrate what you are saying, for example. Ask yourself the following questions so you can make an informed decision about whether to use it or not.

1 Is it appropriate to use PowerPoint in the pitch you will be making?
   You can always check with the gatekeeper on this point.

2 If I am going to use it, how many slides should I have?
   1 slide per minute is the absolute maximum you should use.

3 What should appear on each slide?
   The general rules are: pictures speak a thousand words; text should be large enough for the audience to read it; do not go overboard on whizzy graphics – they slow things down and often don't work; everything should enhance the points you are making in your pitch and not repeat what you say or worse still go into even more detail!

When you set up your PowerPoint presentation, make sure your slides reflect your corporate branding. This is professional and will subliminally impress the audience. Make sure that you have a sensible order for your slides. Do not waste a slide on having an agenda, but do have a slide at the front and at the end with your company name on it, your logo and your contact details.

Have a paper copy or two to hand out to investors, or have a copy on a USB stick so that you can copy it onto an investor's laptop if asked.

What should be on your slides?

There are some things which must be on your slides. These are:

1 The name of your company and/or your logo.

2 On the first and last slides should be your name and contact details.

3 The other slides should contain the following information:

   • the names and job titles of the management team and directors including a picture of each one
   • a description of your business model
   • details of the product
   • details of the market you operate in including competitors and how you are unique or special
   • details of current customers and your sales pipeline
   • a summary of sales, profits and cash flows
   • how much money you need and what you intend to spend it on.

Speaking without PowerPoint

Sometimes investors (me included!) will demand that you do NOT bring a PowerPoint with you to a presentation, or perhaps you yourself would prefer not to use one.

That is fine, but it probably means you should bring notes with you in a notebook or on some small cards, which can act as an aid when you are presenting. Even if you are quite an experienced speaker, it is still worth bringing these along, because you may find that investors interrupt you or you may lose your place for some other reason.

> '[I want to see] evidence that there is a market today, drive, competence,
> willingness to obtain market characteristics.'
> John Caines, (INVESTOR)

Immediately after the presentation
Taking questions from investors

Typically you will be expected to take questions in one or both of the following formats.

Sometimes you will have a compere who will manage this session selecting people from the audience to ask the questions, but on other occasions you will have to do this yourself.

There are important things to understand about this question and answer session.

- Never be afraid to pause before you answer a question, while you gather your thoughts on how best to answer it, but don't take too long!
- NEVER get angry or insult the questioner when you respond, however tempting. It may that they are deliberately testing you to see how you respond under pressure.

Case study: The Phoney Box Company

One example of this is Andrew Peters from The Phoney Box Company, who appeared on *Dragons' Den* in 2007. He had a particularly difficult time because he was called to appear before the Dragons at only a day's notice. He had to work on his pitch while driving to London from North Wales and was first up in front of the Dragons at 7.30 the next morning. Here is how he describes it on his website.

'As I walked into the Den I saw Peter Jones, Deborah Meaden, Theo Paphitis, Duncan Bannatyne and Richard Farleigh sitting in front of me. Panic was threatening to take over as I worried about my lack of preparation. "How many people fit in a red telephone box?" said one of the Dragons. It was a simple *Guinness Book of Records* question and I couldn't remember the answer. I thought my pitch was over before it had begun. "Can five Dragons fit in the telephone box?" – Before my eyes all the Dragons got up from their seats and one by one entered my Phoney Box. A first for the programme and I'd done it!!!!

'The fun was over and the real grilling started. Questions were coming at me from all angles. My lack of preparation was beginning to show and I realized that humour was the only way to get me through. Theo Paphitis asked why he should give me £100,000 and my inspired reply "it's a phoney product but not a phoney business" had the Dragons in fits of laughter. At this point I knew investment from *Dragons' Den* was not going to happen and just as easily as they entered the Phoney Box they one by one declared themselves "out".'

- The best investors do not always ask questions in a public arena.
- There are likely to be some investors in the audience that all the other investors particularly respect or like, though you may not know who they are
  yourself. So you need to treat all people who ask you questions equally so
  that you do not inadvertently insult someone all the others are looking at
  to see if they are interested.
- Most people will ask open questions e.g. how do you expect to grow your
  sales, but some may ask for points of information e.g. how many customers
  will you have in two years' time? In the appendix there is a list of the most
  common questions investors ask. Try to be informative when you reply but
  do not get caught up in too much detail but be aware that many investors
  will not like it if you duck a question.
- Sometimes you will be asked a question that you are not prepared to answer
  in such an open format. Before you present, ask the gatekeeper how you
  are expected to deal with such questions. If you do not want to answer a
  question in front of everyone, politely say so and invite the investor to talk
  to you at your stand afterwards.
- Some questions may be too technical to be easily understood by the whole
  audience. If this is the case, say that you will answer the question after the
  presentation.
- Most questions will not be designed to make you look a fool, but you never
  know. Don't be afraid to politely challenge the angel and ask for clarifica-
  tion on why they are asking the question.
- If you do not understand a question, don't be afraid to ask the angel to
  explain it again.

One-to-one or many-to-one questioning after the presentation

Many investors do not ask questions in an open arena, but will approach you before
or after your presentation. This is your big chance to impress and arrange a follow-up
meeting.

Always answer questions as best you can. If there is a small group of investors
around you, try to include them all in your answer by scanning their faces whilst giving the answers. Try to include the investors who hang around at the back of a group
as they may be the ones who are most interested in you.

Crowd control can be an issue if the investors particularly like your deal. You
may find that after this pitch it's like bees at a honey pot at your stand. The trick
here is to try to get the details of as many people as possible, without looking
too aggressive and pushy. If at all possible, have someone else standing nearby
who can note the names of the people who came to talk to you. Then you can ask
the gatekeeper the next day for their details, if you did not manage to get their
business card.

If someone is taking a serious interest in you, ask if you may take down their details and offer them an executive summary or business plan to take away with them. IF they take one of these away, MAKE SURE you have their name and contact details so you have a record.

One of the bits I like best about *Dragons' Den* is when the entrepreneurs are confident enough to ask the Dragons what they can offer as well as money. It is fascinating watching the Dragons explain themselves. Remember in the real world investing is a two way street as well, and you need to want the investor as much as they want you, so don't be afraid to ask them about themselves.

Jokes, irony and cynicism

Whether it is in your character to be jokey, ironic or cynical, or even if nerves tend make you behave like this when you are speaking in public, it is vital that you avoid this when you are presenting to investors. Remember that you will not know much about the investors to whom you are presenting. They may even be from another ethnic background and may simply not fully understand a joke you make. At worst they will be insulted. So even in the more informal session after the presentation do not joke or make ironic or cynical comments either about yourself, your business, your team or investors – however tempting it may be.

Networking a room successfully

The investment event is probably the time you will have the most investors in one place at one time and so you should maximize the opportunity.

Although you should make sure that someone stays near your stand at all times, do not be afraid to walk into the room during the networking session and say hello to people. Have your elevator pitch and business cards ready and introduce yourself to some likely-looking investors. If necessary, ask the gatekeeper or their assistants to introduce you to one or two.

After the presentation event

Without fail, follow up on all leads in the agreed way the minute you are back in the office. Aim to arrange a follow-up telephone call or meeting at this point. Suggest three or four dates and times that will suit you and send them to the investor.

You are likely to find that there is quite a high fall-out rate from the investors in the few days after the event. This may be because they were only vaguely interested at the time or because they looked at the plan and the opportunity was not what they thought it might be. You may also find that you get calls from accountants and lawyers offering to help you fundraise but who do not have any money to invest!

Talk to the gatekeeper about what they have heard from the investors and ask if there is anyone you might have missed and how to get in touch with them. Ask how they think your presentation went, so that you can improve on it next time.

Write up some notes on the experience, both the good bits and bad bits! If necessary take a look at your presentation again and change it to make it better. The business plan may also need a bit of adjustment or the financial projections.

This will ensure that you are even better prepared next time, if there needs to be a next time!

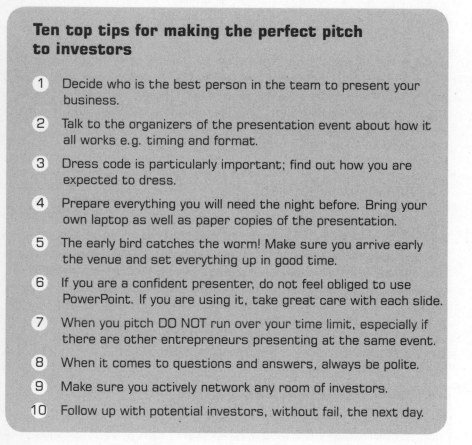

Ten top tips for making the perfect pitch to investors

1. Decide who is the best person in the team to present your business.

2. Talk to the organizers of the presentation event about how it all works e.g. timing and format.

3. Dress code is particularly important; find out how you are expected to dress.

4. Prepare everything you will need the night before. Bring your own laptop as well as paper copies of the presentation.

5. The early bird catches the worm! Make sure you arrive early the venue and set everything up in good time.

6. If you are a confident presenter, do not feel obliged to use PowerPoint. If you are using it, take great care with each slide.

7. When you pitch DO NOT run over your time limit, especially if there are other entrepreneurs presenting at the same event.

8. When it comes to questions and answers, always be polite.

9. Make sure you actively network any room of investors.

10. Follow up with potential investors, without fail, the next day.

CHAPTER 13

Striking a deal with a dragon

If you have got investors wanting to talk seriously to you about making an investment, well done. You probably had a 1 in 20 chance of getting this far. The trick
now is to pass the hurdle of striking a deal which suits both you and the investors.

But beware! If you thought the last step was challenging, this one will take twice as
much ingenuity and effort. Get it right and the rewards will be big; get it wrong and
you will have no money and will have wasted time, effort and money.

Timing is everything

At the end of the day timing is everything. Here is a great story of the ups and downs
of one deal.

> **Case study: CD Direct**
>
> In mid-1997 an entrepreneur I know purchased a turnaround dotcom called CD
> Direct (which later became Netcommerce Ltd) for £9,000. The company had a
> customer list of 17,500 on the day it was purchased. The previous owners had
> bought it for £250k in 1995 and then invested £750k in it over the next three years.
> The company needed £250k for working capital and the new entrepreneurial man-
> agement team raised unsecured overdrafts from two high street banks and mon-
> etized the stock to provide £17.5k additional working capital through an innovative
> Internet auction attracting registration from 55 countries around the world. With
> this they were through the working capital 'gap' and into a cash positive position in
> the space of five months.
>
> The key challenge was to revitalize the company's product set which was selling
> through the company's small call centre and online (one of the principal reasons
> why this purchase was so attractive). Over two years the company built a profitable
> £1m turnover company which attracted its first offer for purchase by a very large
> games publisher of £2.4 million. Just before this sale was finalized an angel investor
> became involved by putting in £400k. If the sale went through there would be an
> immediate return; if not, the market was positive so the prospects of a good longer
> term return were there.
>
> With the Internet market raging and the successful floatation stories building, the
> £2.4 million deal was pulled on the hunch that greater things for the company did
> in fact lie around the corner. This hunch was proven right as four months later the
> company achieved a valuation of £12.5 million and an investment of an additional
> £1.4 million.

Over two and a half years the management achieved a turnaround and transitioned the business twice from the original business model. This also involved finalizing negations for a sale twice as well as taking in two rounds of funding. This culminated with the agreement of a sale to a company in Seattle for $10 million, but the timing was out by about eight weeks as the share crash of 2000 meant that a mostly 'paper' sale did not complete.

Striking your first deal for investment is just a step on the path to success, but it is probably one of the most important you will ever take. It is vital that you get it right.

Keeping up the good work

Many investors tell me they were sold on an opportunity because of the first great pitch, but that does not mean they did not take the investment negotiations pretty seriously.

It is quite likely that you will have never raised money before but the investors you negotiate with will have done it time and again, so putting it quite simply, they will have the upper hand. Don't take fright, but bear in mind you will probably start negotiating things which you did not know existed when you started fundraising. This is the time, therefore, to pull in an adviser such as a lawyer or a corporate finance adviser to help you.

The negotiation timetable

Deals do get done in a week, but it is much more usual for deal negotiations to stretch out for three to six months. And you will not get your money until the day the deal is struck, so factor that into your plans. On page 108 is a list of the sort of things that slow down the negotiations and a list of things you can do to speed them up.

Case study: Umbrolly

This is how Charles Ejogo from Umbrolly described the period after he pitched in the Den.

'At the time of shaking hands on the deal (40% for £150,000) I was literally over the moon, as up until then it was massively difficult to find investors for the business as I had no track record, was relatively young (27), and was a one-man band . . . About 2 weeks after shaking hands on the deal, I went to meet with Jones and Bannatyne at Jones' office out of London . . . At the meeting the Dragons said that there were things in the contract that I had not mentioned during the filming. As the contract was over 100 pages long, there was no way that I could go over all of the clauses, though I did my best to make clear what the overall terms were. The meeting ended abruptly, and Peter said he would be in touch. Over the following weeks, Peter sent me a few emails asking for further documentation, but interest from Bannatyne dried up completely. At this point I knew things were not on the right track. Another month passed and with no news from either Peter or Duncan I felt lost and unsure about what to do. About a month before the programme aired, Peter rang to say that he had some ideas about how to move forward and wanted to know if I wanted to work with him alone, or both Duncan and him. As Duncan had never once called or emailed me, I said Peter and he said he would be back in touch, but that I shouldn't talk to the papers until he had spoken to me first. The programme aired, and despite not getting a deal done with Peter I was confident that he was working on something and would not forget about me. In the month following the programme, things were manic, hundreds of enquiries, invitations to events, and possible deals to be done, but still no news from Peter. Finally Peter called, and said he would have to pull out because he could not see any way forward... .

'I spent about 2 days feeling sorry for myself, but then was filled with some sort of energy telling me to get back up and try again...which I did. I went back to the drawing board.... After about a year working with a product design company, and funding the business through day and night jobs, etc, we had a new machine... . With a new company and my old partner out of the way, I finalized a new business plan and got to work looking for investors...At the same time as looking for investors I managed to raise £3,000 to visit a trade show in the US, which I had decided would be the make or break of the business. With a month to go before the show, I worked hard meeting potential investors, and partners, discussing the business plan and model, and getting closer to getting a deal done. About a week before I was due to fly to the US, one of the investors agreed to make an investment, so I focused my time with him. The night before I was due to fly to the US, we finally agreed the terms of the agreement, and the final version [of the deal documents] was due to go in a cab to his house, when he decided that he wanted to change the percentage I would sell or the deal was off.

'I could not believe it, the day before I was due to leave and the deal was about to collapse. Had I agreed to the changes the investor would effectively have taken control of the business, which I couldn't do, so I said "thanks, but no thanks" and got on the plane. While in Las Vegas, interest in the machine was great, but no firm orders. The day the show finished I received a call from one of the other interested investors, asking if I had secured the funds. I told him that I was still open to offers, and he suggested a meeting when we got back to London. Despite my earlier promise to call it a day, I decided to meet with David. Meeting David at his offices I knew he was serious, interested, but, most important, a genuine person. We discussed the business and the ups and downs, and he told me about his group. I left the meeting feeling very confident that we could work together but also wary that I had promised myself that I would move on, for myself and also my partner who by now was not very happy with my obsession. Over the course of about a month, I exchanged emails and spoke to David almost every day, discussing every aspect of the business, forwarding contracts, expressions of interest, emails, and other information, as well as going over the financial model, and business plan in great detail. By this point I was clear that if David did invest he would be a great partner, as he clearly wanted to understand the business he might be investing in. Finally about 3 weeks after coming back from Las Vegas, David wanted to make me an offer! Once we had settled on the valuation, within about a week we had subscriber agreements, and I had my first service contract for the Company. The day to sign the agreements came. I was now a father, and took my wife with me as she had been through so much that I wanted her to be there to share in the moment. Standing in the lawyers' offices looking out over London we signed what seemed like a mountain of paper. The day after, the investment hit the account!

'Since taking the investment on, the business has grown to having over 300 of our vending machines across the UK, with plans to grow to over 3,000 by the end of next year. Such has been our success that we are currently raising further funds to assist growth, and of the £1 million we are trying to raise, half has already been committed.'

Issue	What slows it down	How to speed it up
Due diligence on your own company.	Not having all the paperwork to hand or not being available to answer questions.	Have all the paperwork ready before you start; always be available or have a deputy available at all times. Keep your mobile switched on.
Market research on the industry you are operating in.	The investors not being able easily to understand the market and not having ready access to information on the size of the market, what the issues driving the market are, and what the big and little players are doing in the market.	Have as much market research available as possible; gear up customers and suppliers to be ready to take calls; consider getting hold of research from stock market analysts on your sector and on the quoted companies in your market; speak to trade bodies and get hold of as much research from them as you can as well as statistics on the size of your market; talk to consultants and government agencies who may have information. Once you have all this gather it together and have it ready for the angels.
Competitor analysis.	Not understanding the international competitive landscape and not understanding what makes you different and why others cannot copy you.	Identify ALL your competitors, both small and big and those overseas who may be planning to enter your home market. Try to understand their strategies properly not just in a light-hearted way.
Issues with the management team.	The management team is incomplete or not quite as 'together' as investors might like.	Be honest about issues with the management team and be in touch with someone e.g. a headhunter or interim manager who can get hold of people to join your team quickly.
Financials.	The financials are all over the place or the financial model is inflexible so it is difficult to test the assumptions behind the	Work really hard at your financial model before you even start looking for money. Get a friendly accountant to look it over and play with it yourself to see if

Issue	What slows it down	How to speed it up
	numbers; the assumptions behind the financials are not the right ones!	you can create a mega-success scenario and a disaster scenario.
Valuation.	Your valuation is wildly different from that of the investors.	Talk to everyone you can about how private investors might value your company and have your arguments ready to justify your own valuation. Remember to look at the prices that have been achieved for companies that are similar to your own.
How the business will be run after the investment is made.	There is disagreement about who will be responsible for delivering against the targets after the investment. There may also be disagreement about the role the investors will play post-investment.	Think hard about what your role will be after the investment and what the investor's role will be. Think about everything from the hours everyone will work each month to the roles they will play and the targets they will be expected to meet.
Good leaver/bad leaver issues.	Entrepreneurs not recognizing that once they accept investment in their business it is no longer their private empire. The time may come when you may actually make more money if you are not running or even working in the business anymore.	Examine your own conscience about your long-term objectives for the business. Be honest with yourself about the skills you have, the skills you will be able to learn and exploit and those things you never ever want to do again!
Negotiating the exact terms of the deal.	Dragon investors want to protect their investment as much as they can and have as much influence as possible; entrepreneurs want to hold onto as much of the company as possible and to limit the powers of the investors.	Before you start the negotiations think about how you might like the company share and loan structure to look after the deal has been struck; understand about different deal structures and the advantages and disadvantages for everyone; find out at the very beginning what type of deals the investors you are talking to typically negotiate and why.

(Continued)

Issue	What slows it down	How to speed it up
Investor demands for their investment to be protected.	The investors want large investment protections known as warranties and indemnities from the entrepreneurs, but the entrepreneurs feel they cannot agree to the demands.	Have the company as clean as possible before you start negotiations so investors have less reason to ask for protection from you for their investment. Ask your lawyer to get a draft list of warranties and indemnities prepared as soon as possible so you have plenty of time to negotiate with the investors about them.
Holidays.	Investors disappear for long Christmas, Easter or summer holidays.	Plan the timing of your fundraising to ensure the deal will not be finalized around these times or allow for the holidays in your timetable.

Case study: IT Ambulance

In early 2008, a company called IT Ambulance, which provides IT support to businesses, pitched to investors at the South West Angel and Investor Network (SWAIN). I attended the pitch which was excellent and it was clear that the dragon investors who also saw it were taking it very seriously. Thanks to the support of their advisers who ensured a smooth negotiation process, they invested in the company only six weeks later. This probably made it one of the fastest investment rounds made in recent years.

Valuation

If you watch *Dragons' Den* the real excitement comes when the Dragons start making offers to buy a stake in the company. Almost without fail the terms they offer are less attractive than the entrepreneur asked for. Of course they are going to ask for more for their money. It would not be good TV if they just rolled over and took the offer. But this is one area where the Dragons are usually right.

As an entrepreneur it would be crazy not to start the negotiations with as high a valuation as you can, but it must still be fairly sensible or you will not get anywhere. We have already talked about the ways dragon investors value businesses, so familiarize yourself with all of this.

Before you start your own negotiations, think about the valuation you would like and ask yourself, what would I really pay for a stake in my own business if I had the money? Ask around your friends and, of course, talk to advisers, gatekeepers and many others before valuing yourself as the next Facebook.

'The knotty issue of pre and post money valuation'

As you get more familiar with the language investors use, you will come across the phrases 'pre-money valuation' and 'post-money valuation.' Essentially the 'pre-money valuation' is the valuation placed on the equity of the business BEFORE the investment had been made. The 'post-money valuation' is the value of the equity of the business AFTER the investment had been made and is simply the pre-money valuation added to the value of the cash being invested.

It is important to understand these terms as you need to know upon which basis you are discussing what size of equity stake you will have compared with the new investors. 50% of a business based on a pre-money valuation can be worth lots less than 50% of a business based on a post-money valuation.

The terms of the deal

The terms of the deal are not just about valuation and selling shares in return for money.

For a start in the private investment world very few deals are just straight deals of cash for ordinary shares. More often than not the deal will end up being a mixture of ordinary shares, preferred shares (which have extra rights above and beyond ordinary shares), loans (often called loan stock), convertible loans and/or convertible shares. There may also be options involved and some investors love to use something called a ratchet, whereby they allow you, one day in the future, if you have met certain targets, to buy back shares you have sold them at a cheap price.

Therefore, as well as thinking about the valuation, sort out what sort of deal you want. Do you just want shares or shares and debt? Are you prepared to work for less salary if this means you can hold onto more shares? Think about your long-term fundraising plans and try to plan for a deal that will take these into account.

Long before you start agreeing the final valuation, talk to your investors about what the structure of the deal will be. Is it just shares, or shares and loans, or something else? The other thing to discuss are the issues around who will control the company both on a day-to-day basis, but also at a more strategic level. If you can get these right, you will find that the valuation will be agreed much more easily.

These are the typical terms of private investor deals

Ordinary share deals

Doing a deal for ordinary shares is the sort of deal the Dragons usually strike on TV. The benefit of these deals is that they are fairly straightforward and that after the deal all the shareholders are on equal terms. If you are planning to raise venture capitalist money in the future, this is the type of deal to go for, if possible, as VCs hate investing in businesses where there is a 'messy' (their word, not mine) share structure.

Some private investors, especially those that are taking advantage of the Enterprise Investment Scheme and those who are just passively investing, may be happy with simple deal terms based on ordinary shares, but many more will not accept a deal structure like this because they will want to protect their investment by getting better terms.

Mixture of ordinary shares and preferred shares

Preferred shares come in various forms. Typically they are shares that have one or more of the following rights:

- To have the capital value of the shares to be repaid before any other shareholders receive any money. Some have the right to have more than the capital value, perhaps two or three times the capital value to be repaid before the other shareholders receive any money.
- Special voting rights at shareholder meetings and also rights to appoint one or more directors to the company or to have observer rights at board meetings.
- Receiving a dividend payment before the ordinary shares are paid a dividend. Sometimes the amount of the dividend they will be paid is fixed from the start. Sometimes the dividend is not paid each year but is 'rolled up' until the business is sold, and the dividend has to be paid first before anyone else receives any money in the sale.
- To force or prevent the management to do or from doing things such as appointing people to certain management positions, making capital expenditure decisions, buying or selling parts of the business and much more.

A very common type of Preferred share used by private investors and by venture capitalists is known as the Preferred ordinary share which combines the advantages of ordinary shares with preferred shares.

Private investors may make some of their investment in ordinary shares upon which they can claim Enterprise Investment Scheme (EIS) relief and the rest in preferred ordinary shares.

Terms including share options

An option is a right to buy a share at a fixed price, set today, at some point in the future. It is usual to pay nothing or a tiny price for the option.

You can have an option to buy a share that has already been issued to someone else or to buy a new share that the company, will issue when the time comes.

It is more usual for private investors to take options over new shares, not over shares that have been already issued to other people. When the option is exercised, the investor pays the money to the company, which issues new shares. The company can use the money to grow the business.

Options are famously complicated so you should take specialist advice from both your accountant and your lawyer for any deals involving options.

The share option pool

Most private investment deals will also include some share options that are reserved for the employees and management of the company. This is usually called the share option pool. The terms of the share option pool will probably be different from the options that the private investor may want. Start thinking about how you would like the share option pool to work before you start talking to investors. One thing to think about is whether all staff are going to be entitled to share options once they have worked for the company for a certain period e.g. two years, or will the options only be granted to senior staff? You will also need to think about what happens to the share options if your employees leave the company.

Mixture of shares and debt

No private investor just wants to lend money to a company. That is the job for a bank. If they just lent money they would only get the interest, plus the original sum paid back, but they want to make 5x or 10x profit on their original investment.

However, some investors like to lend the company some money for the following reasons:

- The loan may carry an interest payment which means the investor starts to get repaid sooner than if they waited for the company to be sold.
- Loans usually have to be repaid before any shareholders receive money in a sale, which gives them a slightly greater degree of certainty in getting some of their investment back.
- If some of the money they are planning to invest is made via a loan, the investment is 'geared'. Essentially this means they get the same shareholding that they originally wanted, but will pay a lower price per share. Therefore, when the business is sold they will receive a proportionately higher return on their investment.

Mixture of shares and convertible loans

Convertible loans are loans which will convert into shares if the loan is not repaid within the agreed timeframe.

Convertible loans have all the benefits of being debt whilst they are still loans, but have the upside of becoming shares, if the loan is not repaid. They are also a way of establishing, at the start of the deal, a valuation for the shares at some point in the future. This can be very advantageous if the investors know that there will be another fundraising round in the future and will help them to protect their position when this round happens.

This simple illustration helps to explain why it is so important to get the deal terms right.

Great valuation, complex deal vs. Rubbish valuation, simple deal.

- Looking at the issue of valuation from the entrepreneur's perspective, deals will probably fall into one of these two categories.
- As an entrepreneur you will have to decide what you want the most and then try to find a way to get it, without destroying the whole opportunity.
- Suppose you want £150,000, but your business is only worth £100,000. If you took all that money as equity investment in ordinary shares, you would end up with 40% of the shares and the angels would end up with 60%.
- However, if you took £50,000 as investment in ordinary shares and £100,000 as a loan from the investors, you would end up with 66.6% of the shares and they would end up with 33.3% plus the right to receive interest on the loan and get the £100,000 repaid when the loan expires.

This may seem like a very good deal, but before you agree to deals like this remember that your company is going to have to make enough profit to pay the interest and the repayments on the loan.

Control – the other major issue to think about when negotiating the deal

When you are fundraising the first thing you will think about is getting the money you need, but you also need to think about how life is going to be after the investment has been made. In particular, you need to think about who will control the company on a day-to-day basis and also in the event that all the shareholders fall out with each other.

Formal control takes place at two levels. The first is control of the board and therefore the key strategic decisions the company will make on a month-by-month basis. Usually at board level each director has one vote and in the event of a tie, the Chairman has the casting vote. (So beware choosing a figurehead chairman who may not be on your side when the crunch comes!). Lots of investors want to have a say in control at board level by becoming a director.

The second area is control at shareholder level, which is the ultimate level where power games will be played. Quite simply, whoever controls 50.01% or more of the shares at shareholder level, ultimately controls the company and can make life very difficult for everyone else if things get nasty.

There are only ever 100% of the shares and 100% of control to be shared out between you, your fellow entrepreneurs, your staff and your investors and whenever you accept new investment these relationships will shift. The key thing to recognize is that the bigger the amount of money being invested and the smaller the valuation of the company, the bigger the swings in control and valuation will be.

Exit terms

When you are negotiating your first investment, you are probably not thinking too hard about what will happen when you sell the business. Meanwhile your investors will be thinking about this very hard.

Everyone wants to make money out of the deal and you will be amazed, when big money is at stake, how greedy everyone will get. So it is vital to sort out now what will happen when exit day (often known as the 'liquidity event') happens.

The most important thing to put in place to ensure a smooth exit are 'drag-along' and 'tag-along' rights. The purpose of these rights is to ensure that no shareholder can achieve a sale without the other shareholders also benefiting. Equally they ensure that no shareholder can prevent the others from selling their shares just because he or she does not want to sell.

It is also vital that you agree what will happen if any of you want to leave the business before it is sold. These are known as good and bad leaver terms and include, amongst other things, what will happen to your shareholding if you stop working for the business.

Ten top tips for striking the deal

1 Have your paperwork ready.

2 Have a timetable that fits around holidays; try to stick to it.

3 Make sure you or your deputy are always available to answer questions from potential investors.

4 Be open and realistic about the deal; don't be a martyr just to get the deal done but don't lose the deal because you are too greedy.

5 Try to understand the investors' point of view. They probably have your interests at heart as well as their own, even if it does not seem that way.

6 A deal is not just about exchanging money for shares.

7 Consider all the terms carefully.

8 Consider issues around control of the business post-investment before you start negotiating.

9 You will have to sign warranties and indemnities to satisfy the investors that what you have told them about yourself and your business is accurate and truthful. So be prepared; the financial penalties if you lie are very steep.

10 Plan for the exit as part of the investment negotiation.

CHAPTER 14

Closing a deal with a dragon

Watching *Dragons' Den*, anyone would think that a final deal can be struck in 10 minutes after the pitch. However, even in *Dragons' Den*, the deal that is struck on the TV is not the final one agreed. All investors go through a lengthy process of finding out more about a business they are going to invest in and then negotiating the terms of the deal. It is not unusual for this phase to take between three and six months.

Dragon investors like to have a good dig around a business before they decide to invest, then they agree the terms of the deal and set out what has been agreed in a solid set of legal agreements which will be signed by everyone. Once these legal agreements are ready they will transfer the money to their solicitor, ready to be handed over to the company (not you!) once everything has been signed.

Steps between an offer and your company receiving the money

Step 1 Initial due diligence

Do you remember my account earlier in the book about Charles Ejogo's experiences, first with the Dragons, and then with angel investors, as he tried to find funding for his business? He spoke about weeks of exchanging information with both of them. This exchange of information is known as 'due diligence'. Due diligence is the term used to explain the research that investors undertake to learn everything they can about the business they are going to invest in. While they are doing their due diligence, investors will also sound out entrepreneurs about the sort of offer they would like to receive. The sort of questions they will ask will include:

How much money do you need and when?

The reason they ask this question is to see if it would make more sense to drip feed the money into the company as and when the company actually needs it. If they do not need to give all the money up front, not only does it save them the cash, but it also protects them from the management team rushing off and spending it all at once!

Do you need to have all the money as equity investment or can we lend some of it to you?

This is explained in detail in the previous chapter.

I am interested in what I can offer you to help you with the business, but how am I going to get rewarded for my efforts?

Dragon investors will do a lot for free, but they are not charities. It is vital to sort out up front what you expect them to do for the company; not only specific tasks but also how much time they will give you. Another important point to be agreed will be if they are going to be paid or not for the work they do.

It is reasonable to pay any expenses investors incur when working for the company e.g. train and taxi fares. If they are happy to delay actually receiving payment for the work they do, you should set up a loan account for them. They will then charge their costs to the loan account but not claim any money until the company can afford to pay them.

What advisers shall we use?

Many experienced investors will have tame lawyers and accountants who they use to help them vet and close the deal. They may also use other experts to help them, for example patent attorneys and environmental impact specialists.

The lawyer

Whatever you may think about lawyers, this is the time you definitely need them. Sometimes the investors will have their own set of lawyers and you will have others. Sometimes you can agree to use one set of lawyers, though you should remember that contractually they will always be working either for you, for the company or for the investors and therefore their advice will only be addressed to their client. Usually, however many lawyers you have, the company will have to pay all the bills, although sometimes their fees can be paid out of the new investment being made in the company.

Agree up front who you will use and what you will use them for. In private investment deals the lawyer is usually very valuable. Always try to use a lawyer who has experience of private investment deals.

The accountant

Some investors will employ an accountant to help them consider the financial potential of the investment opportunity. Therefore you may well find them crawling all over your finances during due diligence. They prepare a report to the investor confirming that the company is in a financially fit state for the investment and help with valuation. They may also advise the investors about their own tax status in respect of the investment they are making.

The patent attorney

Patent attorneys are also known as Intellectual Property (IP) lawyers. They assess the strength of the intellectual property owned by the company. They will check out who actually owns the patents and trademarks and may advise on how many other similar or competing patents there are in the market. They may also make suggestions about what the company needs to do to improve the strength of its patents and trademarks.

The specialists

Investors may ask other people who are expert in your business sector for advice and help. Sometimes this is informal and may involve a couple of meetings or maybe a specialist will be formally appointed to do some work. If it is a formal appointment, you will need to agree before they are appointed who will pay for the work and to whom any reports or bits of advice are addressed. You should also make sure you have the right to respond to any report made by such specialists, even if you are not paying for them.

The private eye

Some investors will want to look into the backgrounds of the management team and the existing shareholders and directors of the company. They may appoint someone to do this or do it themselves. Sometimes the lawyer will help them out. Expect to give permission for credit checks to be made and personal references given.

Setting up a timetable

Take this opportunity to set up a timetable which you will work towards for closing the deal. A typical timetable will start with the day you plan to close the deal and then

D = the day you sign the deal	Date	Task	Responsibility (initials of person responsible)
D-60	*/*/****	Send draft timetable to all parties	AB
D-59	*/*/****	Set up meeting with investor X	BC
D-56	*/*/****	Due diligence meeting between Co accountants and investor X	CD
D-45	*/*/****	Meeting to agree terms	EF
D-43	*/*/****	Term sheet sent to entrepreneur	GH
D-24	*/*/****	Draft legal agreements circulated to all parties	IJ
Etc etc until			
D0	*/*/****	Final board meeting prior to investment Signing ceremony	KL All parties

work backwards. Each task should have a person (usually identified by their initials) allocated to execute it. A sample timetable might be as on page 119.

Step 2 The Term Sheet

The next step to closing the deal will be an offer made by the private investors. This might be verbal and emerge out of your discussions. Or it may be a formal term sheet which is a document sent to you from the investors listing the terms on which the money will be offered. A standard term sheet can be obtained from the BBAA.

Beware of the term sheet and take proper advice on it as often the terms seem good, but have a sting in their tail. Take a few days to think through the terms and work out some 'if and when' scenarios based on those you are offered.

One clause to watch out for in the term sheet is a request for an exclusive period for final due diligence and negotiations. The degree of interest there is from investors will affect how you react to this, but remember that other investors might walk away from the deal if you give exclusivity to someone else.

Feel free to go back to the investors to discuss the term sheet, especially if there is anything that is unacceptable. Good investors will consider issuing revised term sheets that meet reasonable requests.

Companies do reject term sheets, so if the one you receive is not right for you, reject it now rather than waiting and trying to move the goal posts later on in the deal.

Step 3 Formal due diligence

Once the term sheet has been signed expect the investor and his advisers to be all over the business. Expect enormous numbers of requests for information – anything from the documents such as the VAT registration document, to employee contracts, bank statements and product literature.

It will take some weeks for all the due diligence to be completed. Be prepared to have to send the same sets of documents to more than one person helping the investor. Investors are very likely to ring up your current and potential customers to take up references on you and whether they will continue working with you in the future. Make sure you have some customers who will be happy to take these calls.

Step 4 Heads of Agreement

Once these and all the other due diligence issues have been sorted out, it is usual to prepare a Heads of Agreement. This is a document which is half way to the full legal agreement and sets out everything that has been agreed so far.

The Heads of Agreement may be quite short, but usually ends up being longer than everyone expected! It is a vital document to get right as it will save a lot of legal fees if it is. Heads of Agreement will usually be prepared as subject to contract and if so, are not, in themselves, legally binding, but it is not good practice to move away from what has been agreed in the Heads of Agreement in the final documentation, so work hard to get them as right as you can.

The sort of things that the Heads of Agreement will cover will include:

1. The parties to the contract – this will be the company, the investors and probably individual members of the management team.

2. General principles of the deal, e.g. all the investors and the management will co-operate in the management of the business.

3. The pre-money valuation.

4. The terms of the deal e.g. the sale of x shares for £x. This may be in a table or may be written into paragraphs.

5. Anti-dilution clauses and pre-emption rights.

6. Protective provisions.

7. Proposed completion date.

8. Rights attaching to the shares that will be issued.

9. Information and contact rights for the investors.

10. Operational management of the company post-investment.

11. Board responsibilities and rights to appoint directors.

12. Warranties.

13. Removal of third party rights.

14. Proposed changes or otherwise to the Articles of Association of the Company.

15. Change of control provisions.

16. Proposed terms of an exit.

17. Restrictions or otherwise on one or more of the signatories regarding assigning the Shareholders Agreement and/or shares themselves.

18. Fees and expenses and who will pay for them, including cancellation fees.

19. Offer period and Exclusivity.

20. Closing conditions.

21. Confidentiality and Publicity.

22. Timetable.

23. Notices – this includes details of how everyone signing the contract should be contacted in respect of anything to do with the agreement.

Governing law. This section is very short and contains a simple statement which explains how and where any future disputes about the agreement will be dealt with. For example it will typically say something along the lines that any disputes will be dealt with in the Courts of England. It means that one of the signatories to the agreement who wants to have a row cannot go to court in some far-away place that is difficult for the other people to get to.

Warranties and indemnities

Any investor giving a company money will want to be sure that they know what they are buying into. Therefore they will ask the founders of the company (and sometimes other investors or management) to confirm that everything they have been told is true and correct and that nobody has failed to tell them something important. This is known as the warranties and indemnities. In order to ensure that the founders take this seriously they usually demand that they will receive financial compensation directly from the founders (and not the company) if they later discover that they were lied to. Normally the compensation they demand will be a large amount of money – sometimes the same amount as they will be investing! This ensures that the founders tell them the truth!

Step 5 The Shareholders Agreement and other legal documents

At this point the lawyers will take over. They turn the Heads of Agreement into a draft Shareholders Agreement and also prepare or amend lots of other documents in preparation for the final signing of the deal. At the first deal-closing that I attended there were 36 separate documents that had to be read and signed, so be prepared to deal with a lot of paper.

These are some of the documents that will be prepared by the lawyers.

Shareholders Agreement

The Shareholders Agreement is the BIG one. It is a document that is signed by the new shareholders, the existing shareholders and sometimes the directors of the company and even senior management. It is a lengthy document based on the Heads of Agreement that sets out all the terms of the deal from how many shares will be issued, to what will happen if the business is sold. It will also include things like the rules governing what will happen if the founders leave the business. It is also a document that remains confidential to the people who sign it.

It is vital that you use a lawyer to help you get the Shareholders Agreement right or you may find that you have signed up to something quite different to that which you thought you had agreed verbally.

Warranty Disclosure letter

This is also a confidential document. The warranties are usually laid out in the Shareholders Agreement, but the Warranty Disclosure letter is a separate document which contains all the detail about where the warranties do not apply. This letter is the second most important document after the Shareholders Agreement. It is the last chance the founders of the company and the existing management have to declare any oddities in their business or comments etc that they cannot warrant as totally true and correct.

The negotiations around the warranties can be the trickiest and most technical part of the deal as they may require the founders and management to reveal all the problems and difficulties the company is facing. Honesty is key in these negotiations as the investors normally demand severe financial penalties if they discover that the founders or management breach the warranties.

Memorandum and Articles of Association of the company

The memorandum and articles of association of a company are documents that are public and copies are held at Companies House. They contain certain rules about what the company and its shareholders can and cannot do.

Usually when there is a new investment, a company memorandum and articles of association have to be changed to reflect the company as it will stand after the investment. For example, the articles may have to be amended to allow the company to issue share options.

The best lawyers will aim to keep the Memorandum and Articles of Association as general as possible as these are public documents that anyone can get hold of from Companies House. All the juicy terms of the deal tend to be put into the Shareholders Agreement (see above).

Board minutes

The board minutes are actually prepared in advance of the final board meeting before the deal is signed. Then the board meeting is usually held very quickly just before the Shareholders Agreement is signed. The board meeting will approve the decision to go ahead with the investment and approve all the documents that need to be signed. There may be things like the resignation of some directors to be approved as well.

Relevant Companies House forms including directors' appointments and resignations forms and share issue and cancellation forms

There are usually lots of these forms to be filled in and signed, but the most important ones will be those relating to resignation and appointment of directors and the forms which will show to whom and in what amount the shares have been issued. All these forms are signed by the company's directors and copies are filed at Companies House.

Shareholders' certificate and cap table

Some, but not all, companies issue physical share certificates to the new shareholders either at the point of signing the deal or by sending them out sometime afterwards. Other companies keep a record of their shareholders in a document called a 'cap table', which is usually a spreadsheet.

EIS forms

Any forms that the Inland Revenue require in respect of the Enterprise Investment Scheme (see Appendix) will be prepared and then sent to the Inland Revenue for approval.

Share option and loan agreements

Separate agreements will normally be prepared for issues of share options and loan agreements. This ensures that each one is dealt with on a standalone basis and is not connected to other parts of the deal. It also means that in the future only the relevant agreement needs to be brought out if people like more new investors want to see them!

Directors' and key employees' contracts

Ideally all directors' and key employees' contracts will have been reviewed and updated to reflect the changes to the company, though sometimes these contracts are dealt with after the deal has been signed.

Step 6 Signing the deal

On *Dragons' Den* it always appears that the deal is signed on a handshake in the Den. In the real world, the last step to closing the deal is the actual signing of the documents. Depending on your investors and where they are based this may take place via email, fax, post (usually supported by frantic phone calls!) or it may take place with everyone present, followed by a celebratory party. The lawyers may offer to host the signing meeting or it may be at the company's office or even at the home of the founders or the investor.

However, once the deal is signed, this is a moment for celebration and so let your hair down a bit and party.

Ten top tips for closing the deal

1 Set a timetable for the closing process.

2 Help the investor and his or her advisers to find out as much about you and your business as quickly and efficiently as possible.

3 Find out about the investor as well as letting them find out about you.

4 Proactively manage the due diligence process in its various parts so that the timetable does not go off course.

5 Consider the term sheet carefully before agreeing to anything.

6 Consider the benefits and pitfalls of having an exclusive negotiating period with any one investor.

7 When it comes to the Heads of Agreement, make sure you set out the principles of the deal, as well as the finer print, so that when the lawyers start sorting out the Shareholders Agreement they can understand the intentions of the investors and yourself.

8 Expect to see a lot of paper flying around when it comes to the final documentation.

9 Watch out for the warranties and the disclosure letter – these should take almost as much time to negotiate as the Shareholders Agreement.

10 Negotiate, but don't leave things to the last minute – investors can and will walk away from a deal and the chances are that you, and not they, will have to pick up any costs!

CHAPTER 15

How to live happily ever after with a dragon

Taking an investor into your company is a bit like getting married. The only thing is that getting a divorce is a lot more difficult!

You might have thought that the hard work was in getting the deal done and that once the money is safely in the bank you can sit back and return to running the business in the way you have done in the past, only with more money around so you can get on with growing it really big.

But life will have now changed forever and you will need to adjust both your own attitude and the way the company is run to take this into account.

Changing your own approach

The investors will have backed you personally, as much as they have backed your business. Therefore, it is vital that you do not lose your own sense of ownership and passion in the business. Everyone will continue to look to you to provide the vision and guidance. They will want to support you as much as possible but they need you to achieve what you promise, and if you can't, to explain why. You are no longer alone in any sense and this can be hard to deal with, because of both the advantages and the disadvantages.

Depending on the deal you struck, you may find that you are left to your own devices more than you might have imagined, but it is much more likely that your investors will want to become much more involved with you and the business and it will be up to you to work with them to build a relationship where you both respect each other's skills and work together to take advantage of the extra resources you now have.

To build a really strong relationship will take some time and you should invest time and thought on this. You will have to learn to lead from the front but not take all the decisions on your own. You will also have to be able to argue your case if there is an issue where you find that your investor does not agree with you.

Try to establish good ground rules from the start and to get a happy balance between formal reporting and informal communications via phone, email or in person. It's quite likely that your investor will have been where you are now, but this may have been a long time ago, so bear with him if it seems he is always telling you what to do. Whatever you do, don't lapse into a cold formal relationship or upset your investor unnecessarily, or you may find that when you do need them, they are not there. Never forget that it is in the interests of investors to help you to make the company grow quickly, so use this to help yourself.

Confidentiality

One of the things to sort out with your investor is what he or she should talk about when discussing your company with others and what must remain confidential. Dragon investors can be great champions, so don't gag them too much, but make sure they do understand if there is something which is particularly sensitive.

Reporting

Formal reporting of company developments

The single biggest complaint amongst investors is the inability of entrepreneurs to recognize that they want and need to know what is happening at the company. In particular, they get very wound up if the formal reporting before and at board meetings is weak. Set up a system as soon as possible to ensure that you have formal board papers that are issued well in advance of each board meeting. Ensure also that these papers are circulated even if the investor cannot make the meeting. Always prepare minutes of each board meeting and send them out within a couple of days of the meeting, rather than waiting to send them out until just before the next one! Most people will be more than happy to receive copies by email, so you do not have to spend a fortune on photocopying and postage – it is more important to get the timing right. Try to win the reputation with your investor that you are the most efficient manager in his investment portfolio and you will not go far wrong.

If you are finding that the formal reporting starts to take up so much time that you cannot run the business, this is probably due to one of two things. Either the formal reporting is too much, in which case have a chat with the investor, or you are not managing your time properly, which is your problem. Before you rush off and complain to the investor, have a think about whether it is the former or the latter.

At board meetings, have an agenda and ask board members and observers to let you know beforehand if there is anything they would like to see discussed. Make sure your board meeting does not last for more than two hours. Any longer than this and everyone will be wasting their time. If there is a particularly big issue that needs discussing, set up a separate meeting.

Immediately after the meeting prepare the minutes and send them to the Chairman for approval; then send them out.

In between board meetings, it may be worth sending out interim information.

Dragon investors will always be extremely interested in how actual sales and the sales pipeline are growing. Research by Trinamo Consulting has shown that when sales targets are kept very tight, e.g. quarterly or more often, then companies tend to perform better than those that have a policy of longer lead times, so your investor is right to care. From day one, set up a system so that you can monitor sales and the sales pipeline – there should not be a problem with getting the sales team to create appropriate reports. This will be useful for you and will make it easy for you to forward them to your investor.

Some companies set up a password-protected part of their website for their investors. They can use this part of the website to store relevant information and papers and then the investors can keep up-to-date without bothering the entrepreneur all the time.

Informal reporting

Over time you should find that you settle into a healthy pattern of reporting back to your investor, but if you find that the phone calls or emails are getting too long-winded, try to find a good time of day which suits both of you to talk. This may be early in the morning, so that you can make a reasonable excuse to end the call as the working day starts, or it may be at the end of the day when you can politely end the conversation as it is time to go home.

Be careful about saying different things to different investors. They chat amongst themselves too!

Whatever you do, always copy your investor in on things like press releases. For the sake of adding them to an email circulation list you will save yourself time and keep them informed! Invite investors to events where you will have a starring role such as product launches and ask them to make themselves useful by acting as your informal sales team. It may also be a good idea to invite them to the office Christmas party.

Encourage them to meet with your staff from time to time. This will help your employees to understand that there are great people willing them to succeed and it will give the investors an opportunity to assess how things are at ground level and let you know if there is something that needs addressing.

Opening your investor's address book

It is a well known fact that one of the major reasons for accepting dragon investment is to get access to their business contacts. Investors know this and it will be one of the value-added things they can offer in addition to money. They will have different types of contacts. Some will be purely business and others may be through friendships. Therefore they will consider how they can use each contact to help you and may have different ways of setting up the contact and different timescales.

Case Study: Reggae Reggae Sauce

Have you noticed that Reggae Reggae sauce is now being sold as a dressing on sandwiches in Subway stores? I would lay bets that the deal with Subway has come about because of the help that Peter Jones and Richard Farleigh have given Levi Roots, just as they will have helped with the Sainsbury deal. As Levi Roots said in The Telegraph in May 2008:

'[Before the Show] I had already sent it to Sainsbury's who also liked it, but they were dragging their feet. So I had orders, but nothing was happening fast enough.

'Then, after I succeeded on Dragons' Den, Peter Jones got involved and made a call to Justin King, chief executive of Sainsbury's. The TV programme went out in February and they decided to move fast, so we had a factory produce 50,000 litres and got it on the shelves inside three weeks. Sainsbury's had the exclusive for six months and every time I launch a new flavour they get it first.'

The main thing to remember is that if an investor uses up a favour with a contact on your behalf, there is a cost to them. The biggest cost may be that they cannot use that contact again as a favour to someone else. They bear the risk that in making the contact you may do something to offend or annoy the contact who will go back to them and complain. For this reason, some investors may be cautious about giving you contacts.

To avoid this, find a good time to talk to your investor about who would be a good business contact for you and then agree sensible timescales for the introductions and also how it will be made e.g. phone or email or via a joint meeting over lunch or coffee. It will be very important to have a good follow-up process for these introductions, so set up a system to monitor this. This can also act as a record of who introduced you to whom.

Provide good feedback on how the contacts are shaping up and discuss how to make the leads more effective, if necessary. Agree a plan to deal with contacts going cold; find out whether the investor will try to get them warm again for you, or whether you are on your own.

One of the complaints by entrepreneurs is that investors give them bad leads that waste their time. If this happens it will be down to you to work out a solution, but don't be shy of explaining politely why you think that it will not be a good use of your time to chase any particular lead. Keep a bit of an eye out for investors who may give you a lead to help someone else they know. To take an example, they may have a pet website developer they want you to use. Particularly when you are given a lead for a supplier, always be friendly but don't get trapped into using someone who is too expensive, not right or whom you simply don't get on with, just because the lead was given to you by your investor.

Working in the business

Some investors love getting their hands dirty and coming into your office to help you run the business. It may be helping with setting up the systems in the company e.g. writing your employment handbook or grievance procedure; preparing the cash flow and profit projections; training the sales force or much more. If they are a really famous person it may just be coming in to give the team a motivational talk. Try to understand what operational skills they have and might be prepared to offer. Identify where they can help the most and agree the tasks they will perform as specific projects.

Always arrange a charging regime for the work done. If there is not enough money to actually pay for the work, arrange for the costs to be recorded and/or charged to a special loan account, which can be repaid in the future. By setting a value on the work it will ensure that the investor does it and also that you understand what it was worth to you both.

Helping with further rounds of fundraising

These days it is very common to see companies who are trying to raise more money from additional investors to make active use of their existing investors in the process.

Your investor probably has more experience of fundraising than you so he or she may be the ideal person to put in charge of the next round of fundraising, not least because they have a vested interest in getting a good deal for themselves as well as for you.

You will still have to attend fundraising meetings, on your own or with them, but they can still remove a lot of the leg work for you and can act as your champion with the new investors. I have known investors to stand up at a meeting of investors and personally endorse a business. If you can get them to do this for you, well done!

Help with tactical issues facing the business

Your investor may be a good person to help you judge new employees, so ask them to attend interviews, especially for senior appointments.

The day you have to sack or dismiss your first employee will be a big one for you and it will happen. This is just the sort of occasion which may benefit from having your investor present so they can support you and act as a semi-independent person in the room.

Other times to pull in your investor are meetings with bank managers and key sales targets or supplier negotiations.

Ten top tips for dealing with investors after the investment

1 Understand that your relationship (usually) is a partnership. If you feed into it, the experience will be richer.

2 Establish the ground rules for the investor's involvement in the business on day one – don't wait until things go wrong. If necessary, prepare a written contract setting out the arrangement.

3 Agree which things are confidential and/or need your approval before your investor talks/acts.

4 Get the formal reporting procedures set up immediately and stick to them.

5 Be flexible about informal reporting systems. Don't spend hours of your time chatting to investors when it could all be said at a board or shareholders meeting.

6 Agree the ground rules around business introductions.

7 Don't use a contact which will be no use to you, just because your investor says so.

8 If your investor is going to work in the business, agree the tasks, timescales and the charging regime.

9 Your investor may be just the person to organize your next round of fundraising.

10 Use your investor as a heavy hitter, e.g. when you have to sack staff or win a major sales contract.

CHAPTER 16

Making your dragons some money

None of the Dragons have yet seen an exit from their investments from the TV show, although it will not be surprising if one is announced in the next 12 months or so because some of the investments were made back in 2005/6. This is probably the reason why the *Dragons' Den* episodes do not tend to focus on how investors actually get their money back. Many of the Dragons have successfully exited businesses in the past, particularly James Caan and Deborah Meaden. Both of them have sold businesses via trade sales and have made themselves and their investors large fortunes.

In the private investment world people invest for lots of reasons and some investors will tell you that a sense of satisfaction and giving something back are two of the most important. But don't be fooled. If investors wanted to do charitable work they would go and work for a charity! Dragons invest to get big returns on their investment, so it is important to try to achieve this for them.

Getting an investor their money back is known as a liquidity event. It is not quite the same as getting an exit. For example, if a business is floated but the investors cannot or do not sell their shares, they may have an exit, but it will not be a liquidity event until those shares are sold for cash. Equally if the business is sold to another business in exchange for shares in the acquiring company, it is an exit, but it will not be a liquidity event until those shares are sold for cash.

Timescales for achieving a liquidity event

It's likely that when you originally made your investment pitch you promised an exit in three to five years via a flotation (IPO) or a trade sale. In practice, it is unusual to give shareholders their money back in this time frame. It is much more normal for it to take five to seven years although sometimes it will be less than three years. Experienced investors know this and will probably be pretty relaxed, but others may start getting frustrated if you do not return their money in the timeframe you originally hoped for. So be prepared to manage expectations in this area!

In the meantime, these are some of the ways to return money to your investors.

Fees

Some investors like to receive a fee to be a director of the company. Sometimes they may also charge a monitoring fee, if they are acting on behalf of a group of other investors.

Expenses

Investors should always be reimbursed the expenses they incur whilst working for the business.

Loan repayments

Director/employee loan repayments

In Chapter 15 we talked about investors working in the business. If they do take a job with your company, but do not draw a salary, they will expect to charge their costs to a loan account and to have them repaid when the company can afford it. If the loans cannot be repaid, it is normal for them to be converted into new shares either just before or as part of a new fundraising round.

Shareholder loan repayments

If the angel is not a director but is a shareholder, they may also make loans to the company. Normally these loans would be repaid in the same way as directors' loan repayments.

Dividends

'Dividend' is a magic word in the investor dictionary! If the business can perform so well that it can afford to pay dividends (after it has put aside all the money it needs to grow more), the angels will be delighted.

> **Case study: Cobra beer**
>
> Cobra Beer has made its investors very happy as it has paid 2.5 x their original investment back in dividends already and the shareholders still own their shares.

Whilst a company may have lots of cash knocking around with which to pay a dividend in theory, in fact a dividend cannot be paid unless the company has sufficient reserves on its balance sheet. Essentially until you have booked enough profits, you cannot pay a dividend. However, if you can get to this stage, you will find that your investors will be thrilled to receive a dividend.

Sale of the shares

Normally, a private investor will not be able to sell his or her shares until the business is sold. They understand this. Some enlightened venture capitalists, especially US-based ones, are beginning to buy shares off private investors when they make a big investment in a business, either to reward them for taking the first and most risky stage or (often) to try to get them to stop being a shareholder in the company, so they will not have to deal with them after the venture capitalist has invested.

Occasionally, if a company is very cash generative i.e. it makes lots of extra cash profit on each sale after direct costs have been taken into account; and this cash does not need to be spent on overheads, salaries, interest or capital expenditure it may offer to buy back shares from its investors. The effect of this will be to reduce the cash balances the company has and to reduce the number of shares issued by the company and therefore possibly the number of shareholders who own those shares. This can be a route to get rid of a particularly unhappy shareholder, if the company has sufficient cash, but it will probably require the approval of all the shareholders before it can take place.

If your company is EIS qualifying, remember that the investors who hold EIS shares may positively not want you to sell within three years because they will lose the tax breaks they are entitled to under the scheme. Bear it in mind that if you sell within the three years you will have to get an even bigger price to compensate them (as they will see it) for losing their tax breaks under the scheme.

One shareholder selling to another shareholder

Funnily enough, I recently received a letter from a fellow shareholder in one of my investee companies wanting to sell their shareholding to me. They offered the shares to me at quite a good price, but this was still a much higher price than I paid for mine. I was not tempted because although the company has grown a lot since I invested I did not think it was worth as much as the price of those shares suggested.

Sometimes there will be shareholders who are willing to buy shares off each other. Their main motives will either be because they believe there is really great potential in the business which the selling shareholder has not recognized or possibly it will be because they want to get hold of extra shares so they have more power as a shareholder. For example, it may be that they want to reach a 25% shareholding so they can block shareholder resolutions, or they may even want 50% or more so they get control of the company. Keep a record of any shareholders who are interested in buying or selling their stake so you know what might happen in the future.

Selling the whole business via a trade sale

Selling the business to another company is the real proof that you have achieved what you promised when you first raised money from your investors. Some businesses are so attractive to potential purchasers that they receive phone calls from people offering to buy them, but many others have to actively market their business to prospective purchasers before they can sell it.

Selling a successful business is in some ways like selling a house, but in others it is very different. Crucially a business is normally sold very quietly with only a small number of potential purchasers being invited to make an offer for it. However, just like selling a house, there is a lot you have to do to get a business ready for sale so that it is attractive to the buyers. So it is essential that you use advisers who are very familiar with the process, so that they can help you to get the best deal for your shareholders and for yourself personally.

Case study: Pout

Pout was a successful, private-investor-backed, cosmetics business that grew very rapidly in the early 2000s. From early on the management and the investors identified that it would be most likely to sell to a trade buyer and they identified the one who would be most likely to buy the business early on. When it became obvious to the investors that the company would need to raise a lot more money to continue with its international growth and that this would mean their own stakes would be very diluted, they agreed with the management that whilst looking for new investors they would also look to strike a deal with someone who would buy the whole business.

After a careful period of planning a negotiation, the business was sold to a trade buyer at a good profit for the investors and the management team. The team stayed in place at Pout after the sale to take it through its next phase of growth under the new owner. A year later the investors learnt that the new owner had closed down Pout so they were delighted that they had been smart enough to get out when they did. It was unfortunate for the founders, but they had already made money from the sale and because of the closure were freed to do other things.

Despite selling a business not all shareholders will get cash. Sometimes a buyer will offer you shares in their business in return for shares in yours rather than just cash. You and your investors will then have to sell those shares to get any cash back and this may be difficult unless the company is quoted on a stock market.

Ideally the buyer will pay cash, which will usually be great news for your investors, but it may not be such good news for you. Normally a buyer will want to keep you in the business for a while to ensure that everything is handed over smoothly. In fact, you may well find that while the investors walk away with the cash, you are left with a new fairly restrictive job contract reporting to the new owners and a stake in the business for which you are now working and a promise to give you your cash in a year or two's time.

So for you a trade sale may end up being a period of your life which is quite stressful. Lots of entrepreneurs tell me the time following a trade sale was the worst period of their lives. Suddenly they find they have to ask if they can buy office stationery when before they just told someone else to go out and buy it. But if you can deal with this period you will walk away with an enormous fortune, which more than makes up for it.

Floating the business

Another way to get investors their liquidity event is to float the business on a stock exchange. The two most popular stock exchanges in the UK for businesses backed by business angels are AIM, run by the London Stock Exchange and PLUS Markets which is a quoted company in its own right. There is also a new stock exchange called InvestBX, which has recently launched in the West Midlands. PLUS Markets specializes in having quoted companies which have been backed by private investors.

You must appoint advisers to assist you with a flotation and it will take at least 18 months to prepare one. You may find that when you float, neither you nor your bigger shareholders can actually sell any shares for up to six months after the flotation, to give the new investors confidence that you still have faith in the business yourselves. Therefore, do not assume that just because you have floated the business, you and they can rush off and spend all the money you have made.

Management buy-out

These days management buy-outs are a popular route to get investors their money back. Famous management buy-outs include Tom Singh's buy-out of New Look, Mark Dyne's buy-out of Virgin Interactive from Viacom and lastly, the buy-out from Virgin of Virgin Megastores which have recently been renamed Zavvi. This is when you, with the rest of your management team, buy the business back from your investors, usually with the financial backing of a venture capitalist or a bank. It can be a good way to give your investors their returns, but still leave you in a position of control in the business. You will usually find that the percentage of the business you will own after the management buy-out will change and it may give you the opportunity to enable other members of the management team to become shareholders.

Management buy-outs are complicated and you should appoint a proper financial adviser, usually a corporate finance professional, to help you structure the deal.

Selling a business at the right time

You might think that your investors would like you to sell the business at a profit as soon as possible, but this is not always the case.

In particular, if your investors buy shares in your business under the Enterprise Investment Scheme, they will lose the tax breaks attached to the Scheme if you sell the business in less than three years.

You may also find that they do not want you to sell because they believe that they can get a better price for their shares once the business is bigger and stronger. This is why it is so important to have a strategy in place for enabling shares in your company to be sold or bought in your original Shareholders Agreement. In particular, you need to ensure that one or two small shareholders cannot prevent you from selling the business if everyone else agrees. Likewise you should have arrangements in place that mean that if you do want to sell the business, the small shareholders are forced to sell their shares alongside you so that you can sell 100% of the business to the new owners. These arrangements are known as tag-along and drag-along rights.

Getting a return by closing down the business

Sometimes the time comes when a business that has done very well in the past does not have a profitable future. This is a time when it may be more profitable for the shareholders to close down the business, sell off any assets such as equipment and property and then share the cash left over amongst the investors, including the founder.

What happens if the business fails

Sometimes investors can get some of their money back, especially if the advisers sorting out the business can get a good deal for the shareholders. If a company goes into administration, the administrator who comes in and takes over the management of the company will try to keep it trading whilst they sell it or get it back on track. If the business is sold, the debts are paid and any remaining cash is shared amongst the investors. This is usually only a small amount compared with the original amount they invested. Often a business will only get properly back on track if it accepts more investment from new investors like Theo Paphitis who specialise in bringing failing companies back to life. If this happens the original investors will usually find that their investment shrinks to a tiny percentage, but at least they get the hope of a return one day when the business has recovered.

If the business collapses completely a receiver will be called in and the business will be dismantled with everything being sold to pay the company's debts. In this situation it is very unlikely that the investors will receive much money back at all.

It is worth noting that investors who have invested under the Enterprise Investment Scheme will be able to get some tax breaks if the business fails.

Ten top tips for getting the angels their money back

1. Acknowledge that dragons invest to make money.

2. If you can make them money, you will probably also make yourself a lot of money, so go for it!

3. Investors have really got their money back when they receive cash. They do not have a proper exit if they end up with shares in another business. A true exit is called a liquidity event.

4. It may take 5–7 years to get investors their exit, so learn to manage expectations early on.

5. It is reasonable to pay investors fees if they work for the company, especially if it is in a job that would normally be done by a paid employee.

6. It is acceptable to pay fees to an investor who is monitoring the investment on behalf of other investors.

7. Pay investors their expenses when they do work for the company.

8. Pay back investor loans as soon as you can.

9. Most private investors love being paid a dividend.

10. When investors look at the timing of an exit they will not only look for what is right for the business, but also what is right for themselves.

CHAPTER 17

What to do if your dragon turns bad

'[Angels are] wonderful people who need to get out more.'
Nick Boles

In the private investment world people all tend to talk about all the positive aspects of investors. But there can always be a downside to taking investment from private investors. There are even rumours that the Dragons themselves have a dark side and have not behaved as the entrepreneurs expected after the deal was struck.

However, in the time I have been in the market, I have heard plenty of complaints from entrepreneurs about what can go wrong as a result of having an investor.

Here are a few examples and some simple ways to sort them out.

Investors who do not deliver on their promises

Although the majority of private investors do far more than entrepreneurs acknowledge or are even aware of, there are always some who let the rest down. The typical things that entrepreneurs complain about are:

- investors failing to open their address books or not having such good contacts as had been suggested at the time of the investment
- not spending the time they promised with the business
- failing to come up with more money, even though they had promised that they would.

The best way to avoid these issues from arising is to check out your investor before you accept the investment. Talk to as many people as you can who have worked with or been invested in by them before you take any money or sign any legal agreements.

Investors who are too mean or greedy

As a rule, people get rich by knowing how not to spend money. They are also the type of people who are always after a bargain. Dragon investors are no exception even if it appears that these days they are wallowing in the joys of having lots of money themselves. It can seem that they are just being miserly by not investing some more money in you or are being greedy by asking for a larger stake. In some cases these views will be right, especially if they are a serious investor with many investments who knows what he or she is doing. But it may be for other reasons too – perhaps they have lost faith in you and your business or quite simply they have allocated all their investment money to other places for now.

If you think your dragon investor is being too mean, it could be because of these reasons:

- They have reached their own personal limit for how much they will invest in your business. Some have very strict rules for themselves about their investment strategy and no amount of arguing will shift them. The only solution is to respect this and look elsewhere.
- They have run out of money, in which case they will not want to tell you.
- They do not have faith that giving you any more money will enable them to make a better return. If this is the case, it will be up to you to provide them with the evidence to make them change their mind!
- They believe that it would be wrong to hand over any more money because the company would spend it wrongly.

If an angel is being too greedy, for example if they are demanding a larger number of shares in the business than you thought had been agreed, it is probable that either:

- they are just plain greedy or are being a chancer, or
- they genuinely believe that they will not get the returns they need unless they take a larger stake.

The best way to avoid these pitfalls is to make sure that you assess the investor before you take any investment from them. Post-investment, work hard to understand their point of view and investment strategy so you are forewarned about how they will act.

Investors who resist the company raising more money

Some dragon investors get very nervous about what will happen to their investment if the company takes on new investors, especially venture capitalists. Historically, investors have done very badly when bigger investors come in, having their stake significantly diluted and therefore making it much harder for them to make good returns on their investment. A few venture capitalists, though by no means all, simply do not respect their fellow private investors.

Case study: technology company

Back in the early 2000s a Midlands-based technology company raised investment from private investors and a venture capitalist in a big investment round. Six months later the venture capitalist who was meant to invest a further sum pulled out of their commitment, claiming that the company was following the wrong strategy. No-one talked to the private investors and in time the business collapsed to a shadow of its former self and none of the investors have got their money back. Many of the private investors still do not know the full story of why the venture capitalist behaved in this way and did not talk to them about how to deal with the problems the company was facing.

It is worth discussing well in advance about future fundraising plans and what issues this will raise with your investors. Typical solutions to the dilution issue are:

- Allowing the private investor to convert their directors and/or shareholder loans so that they take a greater stake in the business just before the venture capitalist dilutes you all.
- Giving the investor a management or other key role in the business so they effectively become part of the core management team, which the new investor has to incentivize with salary and/or share options.

It is also worth getting your strongest investors involved in the fundraising so that they can engage with the new investors before the investment is made.

Investors who interfere in the running of the business or just take over

Some investors may take their interest in your business more seriously than you either want or need them to. This may result in you wasting a lot of time trying to keep them happy, but which has no practical benefit to the future growth of the company. If this happens, either have a quiet word with them yourself or seek the help of your chairman or a trusted other shareholder.

Here is a good story of an angel investor who took advantage of an entrepreneur.

Case study: chocolate company

An entrepreneur told me an interesting story about an angel who turned bad. The entrepreneur ran a chocolate producing company and was introduced to the investor by his advisers. The investor offered his time and a loan in return for a minority equity stake in the company. All went well between the two people, but then it all went wrong. It came to a head when the investor wrote a letter to the entrepreneur saying he was not happy with how he was managing the business and that based on the size of his investment in the business (even though much of it was in the form of a loan), in his opinion, he was therefore entitled to take over the management of the business. He then threatened to start a lawsuit if the entrepreneur did not accept this.

It is possible that your investor might start interfering after a period of being very quiet. This might mean they think something is going wrong with how you are running the business. If this is the case, try to address it as quickly as possible or you may find the next thing on your desk is a letter requesting your resignation from your post and either your departure from the company or a sideways move into a role that they think is more suited to your skills.

Investors who cause trouble amongst the management team

Anybody can be a troublemaker, but some are definitely more mischievous than others! This is true for private investors as much as anyone else, although as a rule most are pretty calm people and recognize that their chances of making money out of an investment will only decrease if they start causing trouble.

If you think an investor is stirring up trouble, take the time to find out the facts before making any accusations. You could find that the investor is trying to sort out your troubling colleague rather than the other way around.

Investors who invest in competing businesses

Ideally you will put a clause in the Shareholders Agreement stating that your investors may not invest in a competing business, but your investors may not accept this on principle or they may already be invested in one of your competitors so cannot accept it. If this is the situation, there is nothing you can do about this. In practice, the best way to stop an investor doing this is to perform really strongly which will give the investors the evidence they need to believe you will be the winner in your market. There is nothing like seeing sales growing to make an investor believe that you are the best bet and give their money to you rather than to another company.

Investors who have rows with each other and then involve the company

Usually rows will only start when things are going wrong at the company they have all invested in. Often a row will start because the management team is divided and each member has a group of investors who line up on their side against other members of the team. One of your jobs as the key management person at the company is to ensure things do not go wrong and that your team stays united, so that there is no reason to start a conflict.

When rows do break out, you will have to behave tactically and try to keep both sides on your side. If all else fails, one of the best arguments to use to resolve rows is that continuing the row will decrease the chance of anyone or everyone making any money.

Investors who try to 'kill' the business or demand an exit at all cost

In an ideal world the legal agreements that were set up when you first raised money will prevent this, but even with legal agreements investors can still put you under pressure to act in a way you do not agree with. Keeping your investors fully informed of how the business is performing will help to prevent it from getting to a stage where they stop supporting you.

There will inevitably be some investors, some of the time, who will decide that being involved with you is damaging them in some other way and they may decide that the only solution is to try and 'kill' you off. A typical reason might be that your business is unlikely to give them great returns and it will be less effort to close you down than carry on supporting you while you struggle on.

There are three solutions to this.

You can agree with them that they will simply drop you, but retain a passive shareholding, accepting as part of this strategy that they may find the shareholding significantly diluted if you take on new investment.

You can make an arrangement whereby they exit from the investment, either by selling the shares back to you or perhaps selling out to another investor. This may mean you have to find the money to pay them off, but it could be worth it in the long-term.

Lastly, it may be a good idea for you to then buy out the business from them and then close down the company.

Whichever route you agree, always take legal advice and make sure that you get everything put down in writing so that there is no comeback in the future when you have made the business an outstanding success!

Ten top tips to help you avoid any pitfalls caused by investors

1   Remember that private investors are people too; they can make mistakes and they can also be mischievous.

2   Some of them, for good reasons and bad, will want to take control of your business or at the least stop you from being the boss.

3   Investors can fail to deliver on their promises. Mitigate this by checking them out before you take their money and keeping open communications with them post-investment.

4   Dragon investors can appear mean or greedy, especially when you are poor and short of money and they are on holiday in the Caribbean. Try to look at how your business appears as if you were sitting in their shoes and then work out how to align your interests.

5   Keep your investors fully informed about your fundraising plans so that they are supportive and not obstructive when the time comes.

6   Agree from day one the levels of involvement your investors will have in the business.

7   If you think an investor is making trouble, make sure you check and double check your facts and prepare a plan before making any accusations.

(Continued)

8   There is not much you can do to prevent people investing in a competing business unless you can show them that you are the only one worth backing.

9   If your investors are rowing with each other, do not take sides. If it is affecting the company, use the argument that the situation is decimating the value of the business.

10 Remember that sometimes investors want to exit their investment even if they are going to make a loss. If this happens you will need to form a strategy to try to give them what they want without it hurting you too badly.

Final thoughts

Private investors are currently a vital source of funding for high growth potential businesses and from the way the investment industry is moving they are likely to become even more important in the future. The vast majority of individuals are very generous people who give money, time and contacts to help growing businesses. They are also human, only answerable for their investment decisions to their families, so they may think and act based on a very personal agenda rather than have a long-term standard or professional investment strategy.

Without private investors we would not have companies like Google, Amazon, Dyson and many more. There is clear evidence that they do enormous amounts of good for early stage businesses. Very few do something bad. If you can find yourself a investor, I suggest you try to capture him or her as soon as possible!

PART 3

How to become an investor

CHAPTER 18

Meeting the real dragons

All sorts of people invest in private businesses. But mostly, it's people who have sold their own businesses. They can invest anything from £5,000 to over £1 million. And they can make huge profit.

As a rule, private investors work very hard to keep themselves out of the limelight. Of course there are some famous business angels – did you know Peter Gabriel, the rock star, is a business angel? But put the phrase 'private investor' or 'business angel' into a search engine and you will have to search for pages and pages before you find a reference to an individual. If you try to talk to the business angel networks, private investor groups or the other places that investors hang out, you will find you get the cold shoulder if you ask for a list of names. Just as an aside, though, they do say that investors love football and that one of the first things they do when they make a lot of money is buy the local football club. So it may be that you should pop down the road to your local club to spot your first dragon as he is probably sitting in the directors' box watching a game!

So who are these people and how many of them are there? I am going to devote a whole chapter to telling you about the ones I know. Many of them agreed to let me tell you all about them, from what motivates them to what sort of investments they have made and even how much money they have made. The only thing they asked me was not to reveal their names or to include anything that might let you identify exactly who they are.

Their stories will hopefully inspire you towards becoming an investor too. But before I talk about them in detail I would like to dispel some myths about real-world dragon investors.

Assumption 1: Private investors are just like the Dragons on *Dragons' Den*

'Real life investors [are] not as harsh once they understand the project.'
James Davis (ENTREPRENEUR)

Yes and no. When I talk to my investor friends about *Dragons' Den* they almost universally hate the show because they think it gives them a bad name. No private investor worth his salt would ever be rude or aggressive when talking to an entrepreneur about his or her business. And most of them spend hours and hours doing research before even offering to invest in a business. They will not try to strike a deal within only one or two hours (which is what really happens) or 10 minutes (as it appears on the TV show) of meeting an entrepreneur however good he or she is. Most importantly of all they are quiet, private people who avoid telling as many people as possible that they are investors, let alone on TV!

However, there are some key ways in which private investors are like the Dragons. They will ask similar questions and like the Dragons, will have a good handle on the issues young businesses typically face. They are also only human. They make personal investment decisions and therefore each one will make investments for different reasons. Just think how different the Dragons are on TV and how much they scoff at each other's investments. The other point is that they are only answerable to themselves (and their families!) for the decisions they make, so they will not react in the same way as venture capitalists who have to report back to their own investors who are enormous organizations like pension funds.

Although private investors do not boast about being investors, they do know that it is a badge of honour to be one and that making a dragon investment brings you into a select club of special people. So they are quietly proud about what they do. When I meet old friends and colleagues who have made a lot of money and been successful, they nearly always let slip to me about private investment activities and we share our tales of triumph and disaster in the investments we have made.

I have not yet met a real dragon investor who is disappointed that they have not been asked to be on *Dragons' Den*. In fact many of them have turned down offers from the BBC to appear, but they tell me that if you are keen you can talk to the BBC about it!

Assumption 2: You have to be incredibly rich to be a private investor

Private investors are rich compared with the average person in the street, but they are not necessarily in the league of the people who appear in the *Sunday Times* Rich List.

What they do have is money they can afford to lose. Think about the Dragons. They are all worth tens of millions of pounds, but only invest tens of thousands of pounds in the dragon investments. Therefore, normally, they have made their own money and choose to spend some of it investing in exciting new businesses. I know another gang of private investors who have come out of the City and venture capital. They enjoy working with much smaller businesses and supporting them privately because they would never be able to do so in their main jobs. There are even a few private investors who have inherited wealth, but I have found that they are usually pretty entrepreneurial in spirit and are almost certainly the children or grandchildren of great entrepreneurs.

They will normally own their own house (and usually more than one) outright and have enough wealth that they will never have to get a 'normal' job again unless they want to. But some angels are worth £1m whilst others are worth £10m or £100m or more.

Maybe you have the sort of wealth that means you too can become a private investor, but remember some people with much less money than this have been successful investors in the past. I know of one story where an investor put only £25,000 into a company and this made him an incredible amount of wealth – in the millions in fact. After that it was not relevant how much money he had when he made that original investment.

Assumption 3: You have to invest loads of money to be a investor

'Angel investment offered me the right balance of engagement and lifestyle.'

I have made a couple of business angel investments myself, but I have not invested loads of money. The trick is to work out how much money you can genuinely afford to lose without it affecting you in any way and then invest that and only that. Here are some other tips which may help you to decide if you have enough money to be a dragon yourself.

Exactly how much money overall do I have spare for investment?

This is quite straightforward to work out as private investment is known as an alternative asset class, like property. This means it is a much riskier way to invest than putting your money in the bank or investing in large quoted companies on the stock market.

Lots of research has been done over the years and the general rule to follow is that you should not invest more than 5%–10% of your spare capital (i.e. after your house and your pension and any other money you may need for living) in alternative assets such as private investment.

But as a general rule, it is probably best to start investing when you have at least £100,000 or perhaps £200,000 of cash available. You really need this sort of amount so that you have enough money to make a few investments and still have some money left over in case the entrepreneurs you back need some more money.

If you have less than £100,000 to spend but still want to have a go, talk to some of the groups that specialize in arranging investments for people with less to invest, for example, Hotbed www.hotbed.eu.com and Endeavour Ventures www.endven.com.

When you are thinking about how much money you have to spare, remember that most businesses you will back will return to you at least once, but possibly 2, 3, or even more times for further investment. They will either need more money because they are not performing as well as expected and need more money to keep going or because they are doing really well and need extra money to expand further. Most investors follow a simple rule of thumb to cope with this issue. They work out how much money in total that they want to put into any particular business. They then divide that amount in half or even in three. It is this smaller amount that they invest in the first round.

How much money will I have to invest in each company I back?

Depending on the type of company you invest in, their needs will be different. How much money they will need long-term will depend on how long it takes for the business to generate enough profits to support itself or until the bank or someone else is also prepared to invest in them to help with their growth. This may be a matter of months or it may be years. As a private investor you will not need to give them all the money they ask for. You can choose to give them a little or a lot. Although it is usual that the minimum amount private investors give is £10,000, the sky's the limit and I also know of investors who prefer to invest £5,000 a time. If the company needs more money it is up to them and their advisers to go and find more investors.

Some companies may not want you as an investor if you only have a small sum to invest because they may prefer to find a few very large investors, but I can promise you that they will not ever worry about whether you can afford to give them any money or not!

From a private investor's point of view it is more important to understand how you want to spread the money you have between the companies you would like to invest in. Do you want to back one or two with a large amount or dozens with a little bit each?

Assumption 4: Private investors only invest in businesses like Google or Facebook, not in normal businesses

This is not true. I know investors who have invested in everything from Internet businesses to biotechnology and from retail to fast moving consumer goods. And the Dragons have invested in everything from a logistics business to a dancing school and a dog's treadmill! I even heard a story of an investor in Wales who invested in a second-hand car dealership (that one did not go well!). Some private investors like business to business (B2B) investments, some like business to consumer (B2C) businesses. But the common theme running through all their investments is that there is a hope that the ones they back will give them a much better return on their investment than if they put the money in the stock market, the bank and, these days, especially property.

It is said that the smartest private investors only invest in businesses they understand. Sometimes they will back a business in a sector they know about because they can understand it quickly, but in other cases I have seen people spend ages working out a business in a sector they knew nothing about, just so they could invest in it. And of course there are always investors who will back the crazy outsiders because they know they have found a great entrepreneur or a great new technology! A few years ago a bunch of city traders found themselves millionaires because they had backed a former colleague who built one of the first really successful dating websites.

The only advice I can really give you is that when you make your first investment you should probably have a good reason to invest in that particular deal. Maybe it will be a friend, like the way Ian McGlinn backed Anita Roddick, or maybe it will be because it is the business you know will dominate your own industry in years to come.

Assumption 5: Private investors only invest in tiny start-ups

'I like to have a balanced portfolio between real technology stuff and some easier business cases.'

Private investors invest in businesses of all types. This is because companies at all stages and of all types seek investment, and much of the time there is someone who will be impressed by the pitch that is made to them. However, as a rule, the best private investors avoid businesses that have not yet proved that there is a real business opportunity. You can see this on *Dragons' Den* where the Dragons reserve their most insulting comments for the people who pitch businesses where there is nothing but a crazy idea. The best example of this was Denise or Jaq D Hawkins and her pitch for funding for a film based on her book *Dance of the Goblins*. Denise made a pitch based on a book that had sold virtually no copies, published by a publisher who had only ever published two books (his own and hers), with a producer who had never done a feature film. As Theo said,

> 'I think you should go home, turn off the lights, get under your quilt and go to sleep. When you wake up in the morning, if you think you still have a good idea you should turn the lights off, get under your quilt and go back to sleep! It's a no goer.'

If the team is good, private investors will always listen to a pitch, but good teams know they have to come to the table with some proof that they and the opportunity they are presenting are also good. They also know that the best proof is that they have already sold something and this therefore stops them from being a start-up.

A good example of this is former Dragon, Doug Richard, who recently received serious venture capital backing for his start-up TruTap. This shows that people who have a good track record and/or who are experienced entrepreneurs will have a better chance of getting backing.

Assumption 6: Private investors only invest close to home

> '. . . I stick to areas I know, preferably geographically close (as an active investor) and ones that I feel passionate enough about to commit time to them.'

As a rule investors do tend to back businesses that are close to home because they can then add real value contributing their advice and skills without having to spend hours of each day travelling to and from the company. There are signs that some private investors are getting more adventurous in their investments. The European Commission is currently funding a project called the EASY Project which I am involved in, that encourages investors to invest internationally. And groups such as Hotbed, which serve investors who are happy not to get involved in helping the businesses they back, offer deals to investors who are based all over the UK.

Assumption 7: Private investors like to invest alone

> 'When deals come along, I prefer investing as part of a syndicate.'

Most private investors recognize that they are involved in a risky game and that if possible they are much better off sharing that risk with other people, especially if the other investors think and act like they do, so they will agree on what is to be done if problems arise in the future. Once you start meeting investors you will find that some like to invest in twos or threes, others invest alone, but most are very happy to invest as part of a group, where they join up with perhaps five or ten other investors to provide the company with the money it needs.

Some even invest happily alongside venture capitalists, especially the venture capitalists who have a reputation for treating private investors well.

If you are new to this world one of the best ways to learn about investing is to join up with other people who have already done it. The best way to do this is to join a business angel network. There is a list of networks at the end of this book. The great advantage in joining a network is that you can watch what other investors are doing before you start investing yourself. I know a lovely story about a private investor who spent a year attending as many business angel network events as possible. He spotted the clever angels in the pack and then followed them around for a whole year before he made any investments at all. Clever him – he is now one of the best investors in the country! However, I do sometimes wonder if the investors he was following around might have been concerned that they had a stalker in their midst!

Assumption 8: Private investors are hobby investors who do not take their investments seriously

'[We like] the intellectual challenge of supporting and building early stage businesses.'

Clearly some people will always invest in punt and just wait to see how it turns out, but most private investors take their investments seriously and respect the entrepreneurs they are backing. Their level of involvement will depend on what the entrepreneur wants and needs from them and on their view on their own ability to add value to the business.

The fatal mistake many people make is to muddle up hobby investing with investing where the people investing want to have fun whilst making money. As one friendly investor I know put it:

'I decided to become a business angel to make a difference, learn about new sectors and to see if I could identify winners.'

This is hardly the comment of a hobby investor.

I would not recommend that anyone becomes a hobby private investor. Honestly, you will have more fun if you spend your money at the races.

Assumption 9: Private investors are not open to new things

No investor can be successful if they are fixated on only investing in a few things. If anything the investors I know are particularly receptive to new things, especially if they are interesting or clearly offering a solution to a big unsolved problem. They also like to learn about new things. As a couple of them said to me:

> '. . . we never thought we would invest in this sector. However, through our
> active involvement we learnt a great deal . . . '

A useful tip I have had from several private investors is that you should invest in new things, but only when the entrepreneur has convinced you about the opportunity and you properly understand it.

Assumption 10: All private investors are men

No they are not, but 98 or 99 out of 100 are! Over in France there is a business angel network called Femmes Angels which only has women business angels in its group and there are no doubt some similar groups in the United States. The interesting thing about women and men investors is that even if their backgrounds are similar, the way they invest is quite different. Do you remember Rachel Elnaugh backing Le Beanock when all the male Dragons had rejected it?

As a rule, women tend to spend much more time researching which investments to make, whereas men rely much more on gut instinct. However, it is going to be a few more years before we have enough women business angels to see if being a different sex makes you a better or worse investor!

Did you know that there are now more women millionaires aged between 45 and 54 than there are men millionaires in this age group in the UK? So if you are a woman who wants to be a private investor, please come forward. And the first person you should talk to is Sally Goodsell, CEO of Finance South East www.financesoutheast. co.uk, who is spearheading the drive to encourage more women to become business angels. And if you are a man, go and visit your local business angel network, where you will find plenty of male bonding opportunities as well as some great deals. You will find details of your local network in the Appendix.

Assumption 11: All investors are old

Well if you are 18 years old, you probably would think that most private investors are old, but the youngest business angels I have met are in their late 20s or early 30s. It is true that most investors are over 45 and many will be over 60, but this is largely a function of the fact that many of them are self-made and it has taken them time to build up their own businesses and then sell out to get the wealth they need to become investors.

Many in the private investor world would love to see more young investors. Particularly today, when there is so much cool technology around, they would welcome having the expertise of a younger generation that not only understands it, but uses it!

Assumption 12: All investors are the same

If only all my angel friends would let me publish photos of them in this book. They are even more diverse than the Dragons on TV. Proportionately even more of them are men – about 98 in every 100, not 4 in 5! They have made money in all sorts of ways. Some are old and some are young. And, for every angel that invests occasionally, another will invest all the time. Then you would see how very different they all are. But it is not just in how they look, they are also different in how much they invest, what they invest in and how they go about their investment activities both before and after striking a deal. They are also extremely different in the amount of money they make.

Which type of private investor could you be?

As I have mentioned, the private investors I know are not looking for fame, and whilst they want to share their experiences with you through this book they do not want to reveal anything that could identify them. So I created a questionnaire for them to fill in, and here I have published the replies they gave me. There are lots of different profiles and you will see how very different investors are.

Why do you invest as an angel?	• for tax-efficient long term returns • for a balance of engagement and lifestyle • to diversify my investment portfolio • to have fun and make a large profit • to be involved closely in my investments • to support entrepreneurs • to make a lot of money
What is your background?	• accountant • full-time investor • part time advisor to entrepreneurs • retired from a family business after 25 years • entrepreneur • Venture Capitalist
How often do you invest?	• 1 to 3 new companies every year • when the right deals come along • when I successfully sell an angel investment • I have done 6 deals in 18 months but will now wait until some of these have exited • once or twice a year
How involved do you get?	• I like to be a non-exec director • I like to get involved when I think I can help • I look at monthly reports carefully

(continued)

	• Actively support investments as they need it • A lot of 'management by walking around'
What is your investment strategy?	• It is mostly about the quality of the management team • I look for a passionate team, a business which solves real problem and can make a lot of money, and a sustainable business good for people, profit and the planet • None • I stick to areas I know, are close, and I'm passionate about • I make many small investments
What investment tips would you offer potential investors:	• only invest if you are 100% happy with the management • avoid investments outside areas you know • be willing to support your investment through the inevitable twists and turns • only invest money you can afford to lose • diversify • invest alongside experienced investors to start with • hold funds in reserve for future investment rounds • Be patient • have a second motivation besides making money • take investment training class • choose large, growing and profitable markets • bet on the best teams • never panic • enjoy it!
Do you have any disastrous stories to tell?	• I have been cheated twice • shortly after investing we discovered the business was not ethical; we got out fast, losing everything • we fell in love with the technology and ignored management weaknesses; the company was unable to deliver

- a startup which needed follow-on investment within a month!
- turning down Innocent and Green & Blacks
- I lost £5,000 in a translation company
- the business worked well but the MD was incompetent, and the company went bust after not paying its bills on time

Ten important things to know about private investors

1. Private investors tend to keep out of the limelight; they may look just like you and me.

2. They are wealthy, but how wealthy, you may never know.

3. Business angels are not predictable. They do not necessarily invest in the same things or in the same way.

4. The majority of business angels are men (98%–99%), but women make pretty good investors too.

5. Most investors are older rather than younger, but not all of them!

6. They may invest in anything from 1 to 70 deals or more in the course of their career.

7. Some get actively involved in the businesses they back; others do nothing except invest their money and wait for the payout.

8. Some have day jobs too. They are not all hiding out on yachts in the Bahamas, although if you try to get hold of any of them during the summer holidays you may start believing they are!

9. Every one of them has a disaster story to tell. Not all of them (yet) have a success story.

10. Every angel will have their own different tip for making successful investments, but they all look for great management teams.

CHAPTER 19

We are the real dragons

'It is hard to be definitive on my investing experience when it is still on-going. I would consider myself to be midway through my first cycle of investments. The scorecard looks respectable, so far, with only one out-right loss and a number of investments that are progressing nicely with the potential to be investment multi-baggers. However, until the cash is exited, the final verdict is reserved.

'The real experience of investing over the last four years has honed my under-standing of the importance and interaction of the various components of invest-ing i.e. management team, commercial validation etc. Through my experience in making investment decisions, I have also learned to rely less on the opinion of others in making my own judgements and to incorporate my gut feel in the decision-making process. I now also insist on being an active investor in my investments. This role helps to spot and intervene in any issues early (i.e. be-fore the hat is passed round again) and to be better informed in making deci-sions on whether to follow on my investment in further rounds.

'I would consider that my angel experience to date has been enjoyable and rewarding and I intend to continue angel investing in the future.'

Of course all the Dragons on TV have done it because it has made them and their busi-nesses more famous. Duncan Bannatyne talks in his autobiography about how proud he is that everyone from people in the street to Gordon Brown now know who he is, but he has also said,

'I told them [the producers] I would be absolutely delighted if the show introduced me to new ways to make money.'

Other Dragons talk of different reasons for doing it, including Peter Jones who says he likes it because all the different business ideas make his imagination run away with itself. Any investor will tell you that even if they start looking at private investment just to make money there are many more reasons that keep you doing it for years, even if you have already lost some money at it.

I was intrigued to know why people became private investors in the first place and more importantly continue to invest. The answers I heard were as varied as they were interesting. My personal favourite is one told to me by a great investor I know. He told me that he liked to be a millionaire maker, helping others to get to a position where they can enjoy the benefits of the wealth he has. Another told me that after selling his business, doing up his house to perfection and having taken holidays to every place he and his wife had ever dreamed of going to, he was just plain bored! As you can see, there are many reasons people become a private investor, but in case you are not yet convinced, here are some more reasons people offered me.

Giving something back

'I want to "give back" . . . by helping to promote innovation and new jobs.'

It is really common to hear investors reminisce about how when they started out in business some kindly fellow (and it was a fellow in those days, not a woman), gave them a helping hand up the ladder. Now, decades later, they feel that they owe something to that long departed person and the best way to repay is to give help and support to a young entrepreneur today who needs that same helping hand.

Using your business skills

'[I am] very involved with one, having become finance director, otherwise [I] like to receive board reports and/or attend board meetings.'

Others tell me that they have proved to themselves they have really strong business skills, but having built their own business and sold it once, they do not want to become start-up entrepreneurs again. Instead they want to offer and then use those skills helping other entrepreneurs. So their motivation is to have the satisfaction of being able to continue using their skills, teaching others those same tricks of the trade and having the satisfaction of building another great business, but without quite the same levels of responsibility as they had the first time around.

Case Study: a gaming business

I have an investment in a gaming business. It works really well. The founders are first class performers and we support them as if we are non-executive directors, although we are not legally directors. We talk about the management every day and they are completely open with how the business is performing. We go with them to meetings and help them recruit senior directors. I get a nominal fee of £2,000 per month which covers my hours.

Testing your own self-belief

'I decided to become a business angel to make a difference, learn about new sectors and see if I could identify winners.'

What is your appetite for risk? At the end of the day, dragon investing is risk investing. It is one of the most satisfying ways of testing your own appetite for risk and your own confidence in your ability to judge an opportunity. Get it wrong and you may lose your money and have wasted a lot of time and emotional energy. Get it right and you will not know a greater sense of satisfaction. It feels good to be like Duncan

Bannatyne and to have the confidence to say that what represents a bad opportunity for him, might be perfect for someone else.

Investing your money in a new way

'[I wanted] diversification of portfolio, fun, to help others and make a profit.'

Years ago one wise investor told me he started investing because he had made a lot of money in property. Sitting on his riches, he had to decide what to do with them, so he started doing fantasy stock market investing with the intention of starting to invest seriously in quoted companies. Very quickly he realized that he was terrible at picking which quoted stocks would perform well, but expert at picking the ones where the share price dived! So he turned to dragon investing as he thought that it had the same characteristics as property investing, namely that you have to hold the investment for quite a long time before you make any money and you have to cherish the investment while you own it, spending time and money on it, just as if you have a property, which you have to refit and refurbish at regular intervals to ensure that it will increase its value.

Intellectual satisfaction

'[My strategy is to] investigate excellent people, [the] proposition .... And [the] plan.'

Some investors are very technical about their investments. They invest because they are attracted to the theory that, with the right investment strategy, they will get better returns on their money than if they invested in quoted companies or indeed other types of investment such as property or commodities.

Beating the odds

'We helped sell the investment within a year and I made a good profit ...'

Investors like nothing more than backing something that turns out to be a raging success, to the consternation of family, friends and colleagues. What could be better than to be able to pop into your local golf club and let slip to people that you were the person behind 'the next big thing' that they are all talking about or using? As Richard Farleigh often says, a small company has a much larger chance of doubling in size than a large company.

Occupying your time

'Angel investment offered me the right balance of engagement and lifestyle.'

Relatively few investors spend their whole time on their investment, though those who do will tell you that not only is it a great job, but it will also take up far more of your time than a conventional job would have done. Richard Farleigh is a pretty full-time private investor and it would not surprise me if his life is similar to the Dutch full-time investor I spoke to the other day. Like the UK-based angels I know, he complained that dragon investing has led him into 70- or 80-hour weeks and a wife who complains that she sees even less of him than when he ran his own business.

Being a full-time angel investor is one of the most varied jobs you can have. One day you may find yourself in a sales meeting with one of your investee companies, and then have to rush off to fire the production manager at another one. You will find yourself reviewing employee handbooks, testing budget projections, dealing with bank managers and other financiers, attending product launches and then going off to a meeting that evening where you can meet a whole crop of new investment opportunities!

There is another type of investor who does not get involved with their investments, but in all likelihood they will spend a lot of time watching investment pitches, thinking about which deals to invest in and what terms they should be negotiating when they do invest. It may not be a full-time job for them, but it more than fills their spare time. Theo Paphitis is a good example of this type of investor. He says that he has around 25 deals he is considering at any one time as well as running various retail chains.

There is also a third group of private investors. These are the people who are actually using the opportunity of making an investment to deliver themselves a real job in the company in which they have invested. Think of investor four in the previous chapter who describes how he has become the finance director of one of his investee companies. Even investors who did not intend it to turn out this way, tell me that sometimes they find they are the ideal person to take on the role of CEO, Marketing Director or even Finance Director and end up back with a job contract and a salary! Just one word of warning, if you do make an angel investment with the intention of getting a full-time job, be up front about this with the entrepreneurs. You may find that while the entrepreneurs want your money, they may not necessarily want you!

Case study: www.iammoving.com

Some years ago Eileen Rutschmann made an angel investment in a novel website business that would transform how home-movers updated their address details when moving. The business www.iammoving.com had an inexperienced management team which quickly showed that it could not deliver against the business plan and the targets that had been set. At one point the business almost went bust. When things became critical, Eileen moved in and with the support of the other shareholders took up the post of CEO at the company to turn it around. Under her guidance, various business models were trialled, new people were recruited at all levels of the business and a new business plan was put in place. Today www.iammoving.com has beaten off its competition and is the only online change of address service. It has a major strategic partnership with the Royal Mail in addition to the hundreds of national and local organizations that you can notify via the site that you have moved house. The business has expanded far beyond the original vision when Eileen invested. After putting in significant sums of additional money (10x the original sum invested), Eileen is still the CEO and hopes to realize an exit in the next two to three years as the company grows from strength to strength.

Building a portfolio of non-executive directorships

'A lot of "management by walking around".'

What better way to build your reputation as an expert and valuable business person than to be invited to be a non-executive director of a small growing company? Do a good job and you may find yourself being invited to join the board of much larger, even quoted companies. For some people, private investing is the route to achieve this objective. Tread carefully on this path and remember that if you are a director of a company that goes bust, it will be recorded at Companies House and if something dodgy went on (even if you were not directly involved) you may find that you are held responsible and could find yourself struck off from being a director of companies in the future.

Hanging out with new groups of great people

'In most cases I have created strong bonds with the entrepreneurs …'

Once you have started investing it all gets more interesting. Private investors get an almost unique opportunity to work with and support interesting and talented young people and also to influence the future. Investors find that young entrepreneurs think differently, have never-ending depths of energy and imagination and will often be impulsive, passionate and determined. It could not be more unlike backing the management team at a quoted FTSE100 company.

Dragon investing is not stock market investing where you will be lucky if you get to meet the management at the annual general meeting, or dry property investing (you can't talk to a building can you?). You will find yourself celebrating their successes and commiserating with them when things go wrong. There will be late night phone calls dealing with crises, but there will also be the enormous satisfaction of having supported and nurtured something into a great success having travelled the rollercoaster ride of being involved in a rapidly growing business.

The other investors can be pretty interesting too. Typically any business angel network or club will contain an amazing group of successful and interesting people to socialize with. Some will fly private jets, others will drive a Citroen 2CV, but they are generally some of the highest quality individuals you could possibly meet.

The social whirl of being a private investor is pretty much constant, except for long breaks over Christmas, Easter and the summer, when private investors disappear on their holidays. There are numerous networks of investors. They range from those where you are offered deals on a plate and only have to sign over a cheque, but where the networking opportunities are superb and give you a chance to meet some really famous business people and even celebrities, to those where all the hard work is up to you and you will meet investors who are very like you and me.

The common theme is that whenever investors are entertained, they are entertained well; amazing venues that you would be hard pushed to see any other way, delicious food and great drink. If you play your cards right, you can end up on a seemingly never-ending whirlwind of parties and networking events where you hang out with loads of other people interested in exactly the same things that you are.

Access to exclusive offers and opportunities

Becoming a private investor will also expose you to a whole new range of exclusive deals and relationships, discounted membership of luxury travel clubs, meetings where you will hear speakers from the cream of politics and business and even the chance to invest in deals that you would never get your hands on in any other way.

Making money – lots of money!

You might have noticed that the most obvious reason for investing – namely investing in a business that will take your investment of £10,000 or more and turn it into £millions if not £billions – has not been mentioned until now. Don't get me wrong, the one thing all the investors agree upon is that you are only one of them if you want to make a lot of money out of your investments.

As one investor put it to me:

'If we did not want to make money, but just to help, we would be doing charity work.'

Here are some examples of just how much money you can make out of angel investing:

- Andy Bechtolsheim and Ram Shiriram each backed Google in the early days with a few hundred thousand dollars. Those stakes are now each worth around $2bn – 9,300x more than they originally invested.
- Ian McGlinn who backed Anita Roddick's The Body Shop back in 1976 with less than £5,000 and sold his stake in 2006 for £137 million, a return of some 34,250x.
- Stefan Glaenzer invested 'a few hundred thousand' in Last.fm in 2004 and turned it into £22 million just three years later when the company was sold to CBS in June 2007.
- Maurice Pinto backed Innocent Drinks with £250,000 and has reportedly now got a stake worth over £20 million today, with the value growing all the time.

The reason making money is not listed as the most important reason for angel investing is that making that money is not easy. Private investment is a unique asset class, as you are usually investing in the passionate belief of just a few individuals, a great idea and a small overstretched business. Although statistics are hard to come by, the rough rule of thumb is that for every mega-success, there will be 12 or 13 angel deals that fail completely, giving investors back no money and probably quite a lot of time and trouble. Another 11 or 12 will give the investors their money back or up to 10x their money. So, to put it crudely, you have a roughly 50:50 chance of making any money at all and only a 2:50 chance of making 10x your money or more. It is not an activity for the faint-hearted!

What a real life investment profile looks like

This book will show you how you can become a successful angel investor and avoid the bad deals and back the good ones by analysing how it works in real life. Richard Farleigh has told people about his own successes and failures at angel investing in his book *Taming the Lion*. He reports that of the 52 companies he has backed:

- 3 have been sold to bigger companies;
- 13 have listed on the share market;
- 10 are still private but progressing;
- 10 are still private and not doing too well; and
- 16 have gone bust.

Therefore he has had 26 wins and 26 losses, which is about in line with the statistics that are usually reported on performance in this market. Some of those successes will have brought him incredible returns. One company he has backed, called IP2IPO, has been an incredible success. Even after it floated, IP2IPO saw its share price double in a year, although since then it has fallen back.

The information below provides a sneak peek into the usually secret world of private investment, by revealing real-life investment profiles. It will show you:

- the diverse range of businesses that private investors back
- the wide differences in how much they invest
- what returns they really get
- how long it takes to get them and
- some of the lessons they have learned.

As you can see, every investment portfolio is unique and none of the investors have particularly stuck to investing in fixed sectors or even stages of investment. Some investors also invest very different amounts of money depending on the type of investment they are making, whilst others stick more closely to putting a similar amount of money (at least first time around) into every business.

As I received these details, I was struck by how much they proved that every angel investor is unique and builds the portfolio that suits them and their interests. The most common theme is they are all smart enough to back businesses in the sort of sectors that tend to make investors a lot of money, such as medical technology, clean technology, IT, media, consumer goods, restaurants and retailing. Thinking of iTeddy, which Dragons Theo and Peter backed, it is clear why they liked it so much. Not only was it a consumer good (for kids), but it was also an IT business (it had an MP3 player with a video in the teddy's stomach) and also had a media angle as it played music and videos. They were backing a business which was operating in the top sectors that real dragons like so much.

Investor 1 – Investing for over 15 years

Investment number	Type of business	Stage when you first invested	Initial investment £	Total amount of all subsequent investment £	Current status	Proceeds £	Other comments
1	Childcare	Start-up	not disclosed	not disclosed	Sold	37% pa return	not disclosed
2	Drinks Brand	Early	not disclosed	not disclosed	Rapid growth	Value 40X	Partial exit
3	Childcare	Early	not disclosed	not disclosed	Sold to mgt	10% pa return	
4	Food mfg	Start-up	not disclosed	not disclosed	Sold	49% pa return	
5	Logistics	Early	not disclosed	not disclosed	Rapid growth		
6	Food mfg	Expansion	not disclosed	not disclosed	Growth		
7	Data provider	Early	not disclosed	not disclosed	Struggling		
8	Food retail	Early	not disclosed	not disclosed	Refinancing		

Investor 2 – Investing for less than 10 years

Investment number	Type of business	Stage when you first invested	Initial investment £*	Total amount of all subsequent investment £	Current status	Proceeds or current valuation and prospects £	Other comments
1	Medtech	Development	£150,000	£75,000	Still to prove itself commercially	£336,000 Potential value uncertain	Won't invest in Medtech again – too opaque!
2	Modified Wood Manufacture	Commercialization	£100,000	£100,000	AIM Floated/ Commercialization still at an early stage	£500,000 10x plus potential from here	Initial lack of management team/ funding held co. back
3	Pre-fabricated Buildings	Expansion	£50,000	£30,000	Bankrupt	£0	Management split and set up new but similar companies / did not invest
4	Agricultural Technology	Commercialization (but actually was development!)	£25,000	£100,000	Has struggled, but now gaining traction	£100,000 10x plus potential from here	Even simple products can be technically complicated!

(continued)

Investor 2 – Investing for less than 10 years (continued)

Investment number	Type of business	Stage when you first invested	Initial investment £*	Total amount of all subsequent investment £	Current status	Proceeds or current valuation and prospects £	Other comments
5	Location-Based Services	Proof of Concept	£33,000	£0	Commercialization/ generating lots of interest	£112,000 10x plus potential from here	Exciting technology at a low initial valuation!
6	Fuel cell technology	Development	£50,000	£0	Commercialization/ undergoing trials with most key customers	£200,000 10x plus potential from here	Exciting technology at a low initial valuation!
7	Modified Wood Manufacture	Commercialization	£30,000	£0	Commercialisation	£30,000 10x plus potential from here	Invested with co-investors in a similar company – Investment 2

Investor 3 – Investing internationally for over 10 years

Investment number	Type of business	Stage when you first invested	Initial investment £	Total amount of all subsequent investment £	Current status	Proceeds £	Other comments
1	Telemedicine	Early	80,000	–	Struggling	£0 < multi £M	Needs unplanned 2nd round funding
2	Sports/Leisure goods	2nd round	50,000	–	On point of failure	£0	Failed to achieve sales targets
3	Electronic Microscope	2nd Round	50,000	–	Entering unplanned 3rd round (down round)	£50,000 – £200,000	Teetering on the point of cash break-even. Needs more funds for future development
4	Modular 'eco' housing	Early	50,000	–	Successful 3rd round – sales behind target	£0 – £100,000	Very poor information flow, despite an investor director on board.
5	Medical diagnostic device	Early	12,500	12,500	Achieving targets so far.	£25,000 – £100,000	Plan includes future fund-raising, may participate if funds are available
6	Publisher/video producer	Early	40,000	40,000	Cash is tight, but managing to generate sales growth after false start.	£0 – £200,000	I am finance director of this company, work (unpaid) two days a week.

Investor 4 – Investing for less than 5 years

Investment number (in chronological order)	Type of business eg food manufacturer, computer software company	Stage when you first invested	Initial investment £	Total amount of all subsequent investment £	Current status e.g. sold, bankrupt, profitable, struggling	Proceeds (either amount or comment – please include expected return if you have not yet exited) £	Other comments if relevant (e.g. company failed but management went on to build another business)
1	Alternative energy – hydrogen	Early	£15,000	£5,000	Bankrupt	£0	Management issues (CEO replaced) and basic technical error in original proposal
2	Computer Games	Early	£2,000	£8,000	Major funding round	£50k hoped for	Very slow start due funding issues
3	Retail	Early	£5,000	£0	Building up sales but still delicate	£15,000 hoped for	Very dubious manager but seems better now a fund has become involved
4	Biotech vaccine delivery	Pre sales	£21,000	£0	Progressing but at least 1 year behind schedule due to technical problems	£40k hoped for	

Investment number (in chronological order)	Type of business eg food manufacturer, computer software company	Stage when you first invested	Initial investment £	Total amount of all subsequent investment £	Current status e.g. sold, bankrupt, profitable, struggling	Proceeds (either amount or comment – please include expected return if you have not yet exited) £	Other comments if relevant (e.g. company failed but management went on to build another business)
5	Alternative Energy – wind turbines	Early	£10k	£0	Major problems due to design proposal flaws, corrupt MD and death of founder	£2k – well anything would be a plus!	Company trying to restart almost from scratch with new design team and management and very little money.
6	Fuel Cell components	Pre sales	£10k	£10k	Progressing to plan and samples out with customers	£100k hoped for	
7	Video software	Early sales	£10k	£5k	Sales of basic product OK but major cost and time over runs on 'blockbuster product'	Doubt I will see my money back but possibly about £7k	Company struggling re cash flow but unlikely to go under – I hope

(continued)

Investor 4 – Investing for less than 5 years (continued)

Investment number (in chronological order)	Type of business eg food manufacturer, computer software company	Stage when you first invested	Initial investment £	Total amount of all subsequent investment £	Current status e.g. sold, bankrupt, profitable, struggling	Proceeds (either amount or comment – please include expected return if you have not yet exited) £	Other comments if relevant (e.g. company failed but management went on to build another business)
8	Medical device	Development	£10k	£10k	Testing phase but initial failures mean major cash flow crisis	£5k perhaps – would need a major recovery to get my money back	Trying to raise money to keep going long enough to qualify for grants already awarded
9	Dental treatment device	Early	£10k	£6k	Marketing	£50k hoped for	Looking good
10	Superconductors	Development	£10k	£0k	Still in development. Making progress but perhaps 12–18 months behind schedule	£100k hoped for but definitely under high risk/ high reward	Seem to keep managing to raise more money without too much problem
11	Internet data collection to aid brand managers	Early tests with customer	£10k	£0k	Good progress although sales were behind schedule	£50k hoped for	Looks promising

Investment number (in chronological order)	Type of business eg food manufacturer, computer software company	Stage when you first invested	Initial investment £	Total amount of all subsequent investment £	Current status e.g. sold, bankrupt, profitable, struggling	Proceeds (either amount or comment – please include expected return if you have not yet exited) £	Other comments if relevant (e.g. company failed but management went on to build another business)
12	Atomic clock replacement	Early development	£10k	£0k	Technical progress 6–12 months behind schedule	£50k – hoped for but high risk	Breaking new ground and so could still fail to produce a product
13	Medical – flu and HIV vaccines	Development	£5k		Very secretive but believed to be making good progress	£25k hoped for making good progress	
14	Medical scanner for cancer	Testing	£5k	£5k	Good progress and positive response from users	£50k hoped for	Lost a few months due to funding delays
15	Video manipulation for advertising	Development	£5k	£0k	Looking good but a big sale still proving hard to close	£25k hoped for	

(continued)

Investor 4 – Investing for less than 5 years (continued)

Investment number (in chronological order)	Type of business eg food manufacturer, computer software company	Stage when you first invested	Initial investment £	Total amount of all subsequent investment £	Current status e.g. sold, bankrupt, profitable, struggling etc	Proceeds (either amount or comment – please include expected return if you have not yet exited) £	Other comments if relevant (e.g. company failed but management went on to build another business)
16	Biotech – antibiotic alternative for c-diff and MRSA	Development	£5k	£0k	Tests are promising but still a long way to go re regulatory trials etc	£25k hoped for	
17	Cosmetic	Early sales	£5k	£0k	Sales rising	£20k hoped for	Trying to expand sales overseas
18	Medical device	Testing	£10k	£0k	Awaiting result of approval applications	£50k hoped for	
19	Biotech – C-diff treatment	Development	£5k	£0k	Tests look promising	£25k hoped for	As with number 16 a long way to go re regulatory approvals and safety testing.

Investor 5 – Investing for over 10 years

Investment number	Type of business	Stage when you first invested	Initial investment £	Total amount of all subsequent investment £	Current status	Proceeds £	Other comments
1	Telecom consumer products	Start-up	50,000		bankrupt	0	
2	Distributor	Expansion	20,000	1,000,000	profitable	None yet	Worth approximately what I have invested
3	Restaurant	Start-up	20,000		profitable	None yet, none visibly imminent	
4	Interactive language publisher	Start-up	25,000	25,000	sold	Minimal in a trade sale	
5	Website publisher	expansion	38,000		struggling	None yet	
6	B2B telecoms publisher	Start-up	100,000	15,000	Very profitable	None yet, expect 10x return	

(continued)

Investor 5 – Investing for over 10 years (continued)

Investment number	Type of business	Stage when you first invested	Initial investment £	Total amount of all subsequent investment £	Current status	Proceeds £	Other comments
7	Retailer	Start-up	1,000,000	2,000,000	Breaking even	Expect 3x return in 3–5 years time	
8	Retailer	Expansion	250,000		Struggling	Anticipate trade sale at cost	
9	Mail order	Expansion	50,000	350,000	bust	Total loss	Company management then restarted the business which is now working
10	Software (B2B)	Expansion	50,000		unknown		

Top reasons to become a private investor

① You will never be bored again.

② You can build a tailor made investment portfolio to suit you.

③ You can back what could be one of tomorrow's major businesses.

④ It can be great to take friends to 'your restaurant' (bar, cafe, etc. . .).

⑤ You meet whole new groups of interesting and exciting people.

⑥ It is a great way to use your skills.

⑦ You will have great stories to tell your friends, family and colleagues.

⑧ You will be exposed to deals and opportunities beyond your wildest imagination.

⑨ You will get to go places the public can't visit.

⑩ Maybe, just maybe, you will back the next big winner and make a fortune along the way!

⑪ But beware:

    ① It could take over your life.

    ② It could cause you serious stress.

    ③ You could lose all your investment.

CHAPTER 20

Feeding a dragon's hunger

Dragons get fed on the deals they do. So when you become an investor where should you go to get fed? First of all, let me warn you that if you tell anyone that you have money to burn in your pocket for investing, I guarantee that before you have had a chance to turn around, people will start telling you about businesses which are looking for money. Before you know it, if you are not careful, the trickle will turn into a flood. Look at how many people apply to win investment on *Dragons' Den* and the many crazy ideas amongst them.

In the early days it is best to keep quiet about your desire to invest. Approach a few groups or business angel networks to get a feel for what the market is really like and bear in mind that as your experience of investing grows, you may find you want to change the groups or networks to which you belong.

Probably the best place to start is the back of this book, where I have listed many of the business angel networks and clubs across the UK. You can also try the British Business Angels Association website www.bbaa.org.uk so you can see who their members are. You can also contact your local regional development agency who should be able to provide you with a list of local business angel networks and groups. If you are working, it may also be worth asking colleagues, customers and suppliers if they know of any groups you could approach.

Several business angel groups run investor readiness training programmes, which are a good place to start as you will meet advisers and other people who already know a lot about angel investing, as well as new investors like yourself. Usually these programmes will either be subsidized by the government or will be offered free of charge by the people managing the group. After all, it is in their interests to start you investing!

Business angel networks vary in the types of deal they do and the levels of service that they offer to investors. How confident you are and how much you like to be supported will affect where you are happiest.

When starting to invest you may not be familiar with the costs you will incur when you make an investment. Occasionally membership of a network is free for the first year or even permanently but, typically you will find yourself paying a membership fee to the organization showing deals to you: this could be a few hundred pounds a year. You (or the company you are investing in) will probably also pay commissions on the money you invest. In addition to these sums you may also have to bear the costs of actually doing the deal, for example, the fees you will incur in getting a lawyer to ensure that the deal you think you have done is the deal set out in the paperwork you end up signing. Even the Dragons will be paying advisers to help them strike deals.

An important point to note is that business angel investing is an activity regulated by the Financial Services Authority. If someone is promoting deals to you as an investor, it should be set in the context of the regulatory environment. So when you are checking out the various organizations, make sure you understand their legal duties and responsibilities towards you.

Matching services (especially online)

There are several businesses in the UK that invite entrepreneurs to send in or post to a website their investment proposition. They then send out summaries of these propositions to the investors on their database, and the rest they say is history! Some great investors never use any other source for their deals, so do not ignore these just because they do not offer you much support. If necessary, find yourself a good lawyer and accountant who can help you negotiate the deal further down the line. You can find lawyers and accountants interested in helping you via the BBAA. They are listed as Associates on the BBAA website.

At the time of writing there are at least four new websites that are planning to start up by the end of 2008, which will host videos of entrepreneurs pitching for money. It is very unlikely that you will be charged money up front to see these deals, because they will be charging the entrepreneur to put up the video. Therefore, quality control might not be as high as you could hope for because they will want as many entrepreneurs as possible to put up their videos. You should also check out the small print as you or the entrepreneur may have to pay commissions on the funds raised. This can be between 5% and 10% of the money you invest. These fees may be billed as payable by the company, but the whole reason the company is fundraising is that they have no money, so inevitably, the real result is that your money will be used to pay the fees.

Generally speaking, however, if you are looking for really high volumes of deals, head for these websites.

Angels Den www.angelsden.co.uk

Beer & Partners www.beerandpartners.com

There are also a number of new matching services which are based on entrepreneurs pitching via online video which you can access. Examples of these are www.cmypitch.com, www.inbizvest.com and www.mydealmaker.com.

Business angel networks that arrange presentation events

Some business angel networks help investors to meet entrepreneurs by arranging events where you can come along with a lot of other investors and watch investment pitches. These are a lot more enjoyable than the nerve-wracking pitches you see on TV. Often these networks are subsidized by a parent organization (or government) because of the good they do in helping local economies grow or because indirectly they benefit another part of the parent company's business. HM Government likes private investment because it helps to create companies that employ people and pay taxes. Therefore, one way or another you will find that most of these groups have received government funding either directly or indirectly at some point.

Typically these networks will give you a bit of support in negotiating the deal, but see their main role ending once the investment presentation has been made. The people who run these networks are a great resource. They will try to find the best deals they can to show you and will happily put you in touch with other angels and advisers who can help you close your deal.

Bear in mind that most of these networks charge an annual subscription fee of perhaps £200 and will also take commissions on any funds they raise for the company. Fees are usually 3%–5% of funds raised.

Typically these types of networks are very well established and know what they are doing. There is no commitment to invest and so you can wait and see until you are ready to step forward. You will also meet lots of other investors to network with and you may find that they start to bring you into other deals they are doing outside the network where you met them. These angels will also know where the best hunting ground for deals is at the moment, so it pays to make friends with them.

Some of the best angel networks in this group are:

Advantage Business Angels www.abangels.co.uk

Central England Business Angels
    http://centralenglandbusinessangels.angelgroups.net/

Creative AAS Investment Network www.cainuk.com

Envestors www.envestors.co.uk

E-synergy www.e-synergy.com

Entrust www.entrust.co.uk

Great Eastern Investment Forum www.geif.co.uk

Kingston Business Angels www.kingstoninnovation.org

London Business Angels www.lbangels.co.uk

Oxford Investment Opportunity Network www.oion.co.uk

NorthWest Business Angels www.nwbusinessangels.co.uk

South East Capital Alliance www.financesoutheast.com

South West Angel Investor Network (SWAIN) www.swain.org.uk

Thames Valley Investment Network www.tvin.co.uk

University of Warwick Science Park www.minerva.uk.net

Xénos, the Wales Business Angel Network www.xenos.co.uk

Yorkshire Association of Business Angels www.yaba.org.uk

Investor clubs that provide a full service proposition

There are now about half a dozen investor clubs in the UK that operate as profitable businesses that offer a full service business model to private investors and to entrepreneurs. This means they will find deals, negotiate the terms and then send out an information memorandum to the investors inviting them to buy some shares on the terms stated.

They typically charge a subscription of £2,000–£5,000 per year and some also charge a joining fee. When they offer a deal to their club members, they will usually have a management presentation so you can meet the team you are backing, but you will not (except in exceptional circumstances) be expected to get involved in the deal, either before it has been negotiated or after the investment has been made. In return for the work they do, these organizations will also charge commissions on the funds raised, but often at a lower rate, for example, 2%–3%. From a legal perspective, when you join these clubs you normally become their client. You will be asked to sign documents setting out their relationship with you when you join. This will give you some protections in the law in respect of the way they treat you. It also means they can show you very interesting and unusual deals.

As well as offering deals these networks also arrange great networking events for their members with famous speakers and will also arrange lunches and dinners for members to meet each other.

Typically these networks are extremely good at finding deals that make their investors money. Look at the subscription as an investment, not a cost!

> **The best networks of this type are:**
>
> Archangel Informal Investors www.archangelsonline.com
>
> Braveheart Ventures www.braveheartventures.co.uk
>
> MMC Ventures www.mmcventures.co.uk
>
> Octopus Ventures www.octopusventures.co.uk
>
> Pi Capital www.picapital.co.uk

Other types of networks

There are a number of other groups where you can find deals, which do not fall into any of the standard categories of business angel networks. These are some of them.

Hotbed www.hotbed.uk.com

Hotbed does not charge investors subscription fees, but it does pre-package the deal and offers investors the chance to invest in £25,000 units for shares in each business.

It charges commissions on funds raised and sometimes takes options for itself in the business. It does post-deal monitoring for the investors. It is a great group to join if you want to have the fun of investing in exciting young businesses, but do not want the hassle of negotiating deals.

Private clubs of investors

Did you know that Doug Richard helped to set up a special private club of angel investors, called Cambridge Angels? Around the country are a number of private clubs like this which are effectively run by the members for the members. Many of them are invitation only, so you cannot join unless someone who is already a member proposes you. They are often in hubs of entrepreneurial activity, for example, in university towns. Many of these networks do not publicly advertise, but you can find out more about them if you contact them via their websites.

LBS Enterprise 100 (email: jane.khedair@bizplans.co.uk)

Cambridge Angels www.cambridgeangels.net

Cambridge Capital Group www.cambridgecapitalgroup.co.uk

Eden Ventures www.edenventures.co.uk

There may be a private club of investors near to you. Try asking your local accountants, lawyers and other advisers to see if they know of one near you.

Other places to find deals

These are some of the other places you can find out about deals.

Friends, family and colleagues

Once you are ready to tell people about your desire to be an investor, start letting friends, family, colleagues, customers and suppliers know about your interest.

Remember that deals passed to you by friends, family and colleagues can be fraught with difficulty. Ask yourself if you will be prepared to turn down your best friend's son, or your boss's niece?

So, before you go public in this way, decide what message you are going to put out. For example, if you only want to invest in hi tech deals, make sure you tell people this or you might find yourself being approached by every type of entrepreneur under the sun. If you are only going to invest occasionally, don't send out a message implying you are going to be a full-time investor. Alternatively, if you have specific skills to offer, let people know.

It is also worth deciding how you want to be approached. Do you want entrepreneurs to ring you first, send you a summary of their business plan by email or put the full business plan in the post? If you are planning to become a full-time angel investor, it may even be worth setting up a website through which entrepreneurs can submit proposals to you. Two investors I know have one – www.avonmoredevelopments.co.uk which is a good example to follow.

Venture capitalists

There are several venture capitalists who like to have strong relationships with angel investors. Usually this is for two reasons. First, they like to work with experienced business people who can provide resources to support the management team either by taking a management role or becoming a director of the company. Second, when they see deals that are attractive and might be suitable for investment when they are at a later stage, they like to have a safe pair of hands to which they can pass them for 'babysitting'.

So, if you know any venture capitalists, it may be worth telling them of your interest in investing.

Hedge funds

Some hedge funds are starting to invest in venture capital deals. As with venture capitalists, talk to anyone you know who works for a hedge fund and see if they have any deals they can pass to you.

Private banks

There are lots of banks these days which cater for wealthy people. Some of these banks have taken a special interest in the UK's pool of entrepreneurs, from which they believe they will draw their clients in the future. If you know anyone at a private bank, or if you are already one of their clients, talk to the managers to see if they can help you find great entrepreneurs to back.

Financial advisers

These days there are dozens of accountants, lawyers and corporate finance advisers who specialize in working with and for entrepreneurs and other management teams at smaller unquoted companies. You can find many in the directories on the BBAA and BVCA websites. Many years ago my own lawyer approached me because he knew an entrepreneur who wanted finance, so it's always worth talking to your own advisers.

Entrepreneurial networking events

Across the country there are groups big and small where entrepreneurs get together to network. As a known investor you are likely to be guaranteed an invitation by the organizers of these events, as nearly every entrepreneur at these events will be looking to raise money. So if you think you might like to come along to one of them, just get in touch and introduce yourself.

Some of the big entrepreneurial network events are organized by the following groups:

Mashup* www.mashupevent.com

Second Chance Tuesday http://www.theglasshouse.net/content/sctlondon

Talk to entrepreneurs, other investors and advisers you know to find out which are the good smaller networking events. Many of the best ones are kept relatively low key to ensure that the quality of the attendees remains high, so you are most likely to find out about them by word of mouth. You might even like to come along to one of the AngelNews events which are held from time to time. You can find out about these on www.angelnews.co.uk.

Being proactive

You can wait for deals to come to you, but sometimes the best deals are the ones you find for yourself. If you meet a great entrepreneur or see a business that you would love to have a stake in, don't be afraid to ask if they are looking for investment. You never know, and even if they say no, they are likely to be pleased to have been asked.

Ten top tips for finding the best investments

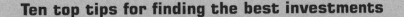

1. Before you tell anyone that you are going to be an investor, decide how you might like to invest and what you may want to invest in.

2. Then decide how much you are going to tell other people about your investment strategy and objectives.

3. Different networks and groups offer different levels of service to investors. As your own experience grows, you may find that you want to change your sources of deal flow, so do not feel that you have to stay with one group forever.

4. Time spent in reconnaissance is seldom wasted, do your research by meeting lots of different networks before making a decision as to which one to join.

5. The fees vary significantly and can be up to 10% of the funds you invest.

(continued)

6   Understand whether it is you or the company you are investing in that is the legal client of the organization showing you the deal.

7   Make sure you understand your own legal relationship with the people showing you deals. Are they liable if they show you a deal that goes badly wrong?

8   Talk to friends, family, colleagues, customers, suppliers and advisers about whether they know of any good investment opportunities.

9   Get out into the market. Attend networking events where entrepreneurs are known to hang out.

10   Be proactive; approach people you would like to back. Even if you do not end up investing you may make a useful contact.

CHAPTER 21

I'm in!

Let's be frank, it can be pretty easy to make a dragon investment. Look at how easy it appears to be on *Dragons' Den*. In theory you just agree a deal with an entrepreneur, shake hands, write a cheque, receive a letter or share certificate confirming that you have bought shares in return for the money you have handed over and then wait for the riches to come rolling in. Indeed the first time I ever came across an angel investor it was a man who had done just that – well in fact, not quite. He had handed over the cheque and did not get the letter or certificate in return. He had been done over and ended up having to threaten the entrepreneurs (who turned out to be serially dodgy) by letter and in person in order to get his investment acknowledged. Then he had the agony of watching them ruin the business and then go bust!

So there are ways to do deals and ways not to. Here are some good rules to follow. None of these will guarantee financial success, but they should limit the chance of losses and will definitely remove much of the anguish you will feel if you ignore them.

Investment Strategies

As you will have seen in the earlier chapter, investors back all sorts of businesses at all sorts of amounts. Every day they compare the risk of handing over their money with the chance that they will get it, and more, back again one day. And for the Dragons even if they intend to hand over the money when they appear on the show, once they really look into the deal, they often draw back. When they do invest they like to get back a really large sum. The Dragons now vie with each other about who has backed the most successful company. From reports it appears that Igloo Thermo Logistics and Goldgenie are currently competing for the top slot!

Investors are bright people and they know it is a good idea to have a strategy before you start investing. With the right strategy you have a better chance of making money. If you read the books published by the various Dragons, especially Richard Farleigh's *Taming the Lion*, you will see just how logical you can be when forming your own strategy.

I have watched investors over the years and this is my guide to how to set up your personal investment strategy:

1. Decide how much money you want to invest each year and in total.
   Typically you should not put more than 5% of your free assets (i.e. after your main home, living costs and pension) into angel investing.

2 Decide what sort of investment approach you want to take.
Do you want to invest small amounts in lots of businesses, or do you want to invest in far fewer and get very involved, or something in between?

3 Decide how much money you want to invest in each business.
Generally speaking, the larger the stake you have, the more influence you can command over the entrepreneurs.

4 Decide your investment criteria.
Do you only want to invest locally or will you invest in great deals even if they are overseas? What sectors should you choose — ones you know well or completely different ones? Will you only look at really young companies or would you prefer to invest in later stage businesses which are already up and running? Do you want to invest in businesses with very high profit margins, but lower sales or those with low margins, but high volumes of sales? Do you want to invest alone, lead deals or hand over a cheque and cross your fingers?

5 Decide where you are going to find deals.
Are you going to use online services offering deal flow, one or two business angel networks/clubs or just ask your contacts?

6 Decide what you are going to do with your profits if and when they come.
Are you going to reinvest them in more deals or not?

Having decided your strategy the next thing to do is give yourself this warning.

If in doubt – out!

The regular cry of all investors who have backed deals that went badly wrong is that they should have listened to the doubts they had before they invested. Maybe the doubts were about the business plan, the market, the terms of the deal or the management team, but the excitement of the proposition overwhelmed their worries and they put their money in anyway.

Many of the Dragons have got caught in a similar way with their *Dragons' Den* deals. A good example is Doug Richard and Rachel Elnaugh who got caught out with Grails — the money they invested went immediately to pay off existing debts, not grow the business.

No-one likes losing money, especially if they realize that they knew at the start they probably should not have invested. In fact, no-one likes losing money even if they can afford it. The fact that it may only have been a small amount does not matter. Money lost on investing in the wrong thing is money wasted, as it could have been put into something that did make money, or even on a good holiday!

If your gut instinct tells you that you should not do the deal, then don't!

Spotting the good and bad signs

Now you are ready, it is a good idea to think about the signs that will tell you whether the deal you are looking at is going to be a roaring success or a disaster.

I could write a whole book on this issue, but here are the key things to look out for. Remember though that whilst these rules will hold true for the majority of cases, the nature of entrepreneurial deals is that there will always be one that breaks the rules.

The team

'Only invest in a company if you are 100% happy with the management.
Any doubts, don't invest.'

The team is the single most important thing to consider when investing. They will be the people who make or break the opportunity. Every investor will be able to tell you a story about what went wrong with the people, from suicides to fraud and everything in between. One of the biggest things to worry about is how they will communicate with you as an investor once you have handed over your money and it is vital to get a handle on this before you invest. You will have to make a judgement call about how you will get on with an entrepreneur post investment. This is for several reasons, not least because they will be being exceptionally nice to you whilst you are deciding whether to invest, so you are unlikely to be shown their bad side.

Entrepreneurs need to be a bit bull-headed to get to a stage where their business can be invested in by a stranger. Many people along the way will have told them not to bother or to give up, so you can expect them to be used to acting alone; sometimes in the face of real opposition. Post investment they will have to switch out of this mentality in terms of how they deal with you, whilst keeping it when dealing with taking the business forward. This means the entrepreneur will have to have high levels of emotional intelligence and also accept that you are now on their side, but need to be respected.

> **Case study: online media business**
>
> One of my investments is in an online media business. It is a basket case. The MD is over-confident in her abilities and will not take feedback on her actions. She does not send financial performance figures to me regularly and if stuff does come it is via her P A so I never talk to her. I don't get updates on latest trading or how tweaks to plans are working. She does not invest time and effort in me, but the time will come when she needs more money and I won't be investing again. It's a vast contrast to another of my investments which is in a high tech microscope business where there is incredible trust between the entrepreneur and myself. They are great at sharing information with me. You cannot beat this as a good investment.

Bad signs in the team include:

- The team has no experience in the market they are intending to enter.
- The team is a one man band or is missing people performing key functions, such as in sales.
- The team has not proved it can perform the key functions such as sales.
- The team does not understand that one or more of them will, one day, be replaced by someone who is more expert than they are.

- Individuals cannot provide consistent CVs, references and fail credit checks.
- The atmosphere of the team is 'childishly' enthusiastic.
- The team does not respect and involve the shareholders.
- The team whom you are not confident will listen post investment.

Good signs in the team include:

- The team is calm and has already achieved notable goals. They get up each day and go to work, broadly following the plan that is in place.
- The team enters enthusiastically to creating a professional (it can also be fun!) business culture and establishing consistent repeatable business processes.
- The team has failed before, but has learnt from and overcome the challenges they faced.
- The team has a good mix of business skills.
- There are a team of bright enthusiastic people at the second level or in junior management who can grow to lead the business when the first team you back move on.

The vision

'It is a combination of an idea I like and a sensible financial projection.'

As well as backing the people, you will also be backing the vision for the business. This is not just the idea that it will be the biggest and best in its market, but also all those harder things that support the vision, for example, the brand, the corporate philosophy, the structure once the business is established and the profit margins etc.

Bad signs in the vision include:

- A vision that is a copycat of an existing business without any major strategic difference.
- A vision that is totally fixed without room for change.

'One of the best plans presented to the Dragons was Huw Gwyther of Wonderland magazine whom Peter Jones backed. As Peter says 'He was concise but precise, well presented in all senses of the word, had confidence in his figures, had taken substantial action to get to this point and had a clear vision and plan of how he intended to reach his goals.'

- A small vision or a vision for dominance of a sector that is small or dying. A good example of this is someone who wanted to pitch a business that specialised in printing personalised cheque books, at a time that most people are moving towards using debit cards.

Good signs in the vision include:

- A simple vision that can be understood by many if not everyone.
- A vision to change the world or make it a better place.

- A vision that is commercially feasible i.e. one day either a lot of people (or businesses) will pay a small amount for the product or services, or a few people (or businesses) will pay a lot of money for the same.

The business plan

The business plan is the written explanation of the vision for the business and how it will be executed. Therefore it is a vital document. But remember that not all business plans come in the form of a lengthy, wordy, number-filled document. It is rare, but these days the business plan may come in the form of a presentation or even a video! Length of a business plan is no guarantee of quality. Often the better the opportunity, the simpler the proposition will be, and therefore there will be much less need for the business plan to absorb hundreds of pages!

Bad signs in a business plan:

- The plan is too long or complicated.
- The plan does not include a short (i.e. one to two page) summary at the front.
- There are spelling or grammar mistakes (there is no excuse for this with word processing software).
- The numbers do not add up (there is no excuse for this with spreadsheet software).
- Key parts of the plan are weak or missing, especially details on the market, competitors, management and business model.
- There are assumptions of turnover rising at an exponential level without sufficient explanation about how such growth will be achieved.

Good signs in a business plan:

- A succinct summary that makes you want to read more.
- You can understand and are excited by the business within one reading of the plan.
- Lots of information on the competitive landscape and the issues the business will face as it grows and expands.
- Strong management profiles.
- A contingency in the financial projections to allow for costs to rise ahead of the projections or for revenues to grow more slowly than forecast.

Intangible value in the business

On *Dragons' Den*, the Dragons are always talking about patents and brands. They have a good point. When Nova-Flo presented, the Dragons got very excited about their patent and, as they did not own it, but had a licence to exploit it, whether the owner would sell one day.

Much of the value in today's businesses is in the non-physical assets the company owns. These may vary from patents over the technology the company has developed to a brand which has values appreciated by customers and enables the company to secure a profitable position in their market. There are many other intangible assets in a company. Take the staff, for example. All employees are replaceable, but there may be a devastating loss of value if the key salesman departs for a job at the company's main competitor. Another important intangible value is know-how, i.e. the knowledge held in the business about the processes used to make sure that its profits exceed those of the competition.

It is critical that you understand the intangible assets in the company you want to back. Even though there may not be much value in them today, sure as anything you will want a high value to be placed on them when people start wanting to buy the business in a few years time!

These are some general rules to follow.

The more technology-led the company, the more importance you should place on the patents behind the technology. Also think about design rights. If a company is relying on trade secrets to protect their technology, make sure that the control mechanism is in place to ensure that they do remain secret. But also make sure the trade secrets are not just in the heads of the senior management. As an investor, you will want to know that other people can get their hands on them if something terrible happens, like all the team dying in an accident.

If the company is creating software, make sure that you know what code they own, which they will have copyright over, and which is open source and where they might have to share ownership with others. Remember that if they have outsourced the code it may be that the person they outsourced it to has copyright over it.

The more consumer-led the company, the more you should look into the trademarks they own or might be able to apply for. This will also be true for some B2B companies especially in very competitive markets. Have a look also at who owns the copyright over the designs for their brands etc. You might find that the individual who designed the amazing logo, or the website, owns the designs, not the company using them.

In all businesses, all employees should be signed up to modern employment contracts with proper confidentiality and non-compete clauses.

Lastly, check out the company's different insurances. In particular, check their loss of profits insurance. Many companies skimp on this, but if the head office or the factory burns down it normally takes at least 18–24 months for the business to get back to normal operations. Will the insurance pay up enough for the business to move and re-establish the office? Whilst you are looking at this, check out the current lease on the office they are renting. Could they find another office for such a good price nearby in a hurry? Make sure that the company has appropriate levels of key man insurance for each key member of the management team. Remember that if the business would fold if one of the team dies, you will need to make sure that the insurance monies should also provide sufficient compensation to the investors once the business has been closed down.

Bad signs for the intangible value of a business:

- Management have little understanding of the importance of the intangible value in a business and does not have a strategy for protecting it.

- The company is skimping on its investment in intangible value protection, for example, it is not applying for patents or trademarks when it should be.
- The company does not have anyone advising it on intellectual property protection.
- The company does not have clear contracts with suppliers and employees.
- And, worst of all, the founders or the third party designers own the business's patents and trademarks, not the company.

Good signs for the intangible value of a business:

- The company has an intellectual property strategic plan and owns its intellectual property.
- All contracts between the company and third parties, including employees, are up-to-date and clearly define the relationship.
- Employee contracts have appropriate non-compete and confidentiality clauses.
- The company has really thought through what insurance it needs.
- The company has a strategic plan B in case unforeseen disaster strikes.

The financial model

'I look at the investment as to how much time it gives the company to prove its business model or enhance the value prior to subsequent rounds.'

There are really three types of financial model:

1. Lifestyle businesses, which are run to give the owner and his family as much money as they can possibly get, but which are very unlikely to ever pay back any other investors any money. For example Joanne Morrison and Emma McPherson's fashion business which pitched in Series 1.

2. Businesses that make a large number of one-off sales, but have to resell the product or service they offer every time. For example, someone who builds houses!

3. Businesses that sell the same thing over and over again to the same customer and can also sell it over and over again to all sorts of other customers. For example, Reggae Reggae Sauce.

As an investor the best financial model is type three, especially if the profit margins on the product or service are very high. Sometimes, it is worth backing businesses with the type two financial model. And the very best type of business to back is one where you have both type two and type three financial models together. For example, a great business to back would be a business that sells an enormous, expensive machine to say, a hospital, and then every time the hospital has to use it they have to insert a new disposable part, which (of course!) can only be bought from the company that sold them the machine! A good Dragons' Den example is the i-Teddy, which had a model that meant that customers would have to come back to buy more movies etc to play on the i-Teddy machine. It has been so successful that it made £1m in sales in its first year and is now selling in 40 countries across the world.

Check out the 'gearing' of the business – does it have to spend a lot of money on fixed costs before it can turn a profit, or does it only have to spend a little money on fixed costs, but has high variable costs such as advertising, in order to make the sale? Ideally the business should have low fixed costs or these costs should be outsourced e.g. they pay someone else to do the manufacturing of the product and spend their time and money on product development and sales and marketing.

It is worth looking hard at salaries too. In the early days many people will work for much less than they would if they were being employed in a bigger company. When you look at the financial model, assess what would happen if all the employees suddenly had to be rehired at market rates?

'Turnover is vanity, profit is sanity but cash is king.'

Profit margins are still one of the quickest indicators of a good opportunity. As a broad rule of thumb take a look at the gross margins. The higher they are the better. The reason for this is that small companies face two main issues, customers who want to pay less or suppliers who want to charge more. And often there is very little the company can do about it! Therefore you need a high margin to give you room for sales to fall and costs to rise and there still to be a profit around to pay for all the costs like salaries, bank interest and marketing etc.

Look also at profit before interest and tax – that is the one the bank will look at, and also profit after tax (out of which [maybe] you will get any dividends paid), which will be the one that any buyer of the business also looks at!

Check out the cash flow model too. How long does it take for the business to collect the money for the sales they have made? Do not ignore businesses that will take three months to get their invoices paid if, in fact, all their customers are A grade, such as governments or global companies. If this is the case, maybe the company should look at factoring its invoices so that it gets the money into the business earlier? Factoring is when a company borrows against the invoices it has raised for sales it has made, which have not yet been paid by the customers. If you find a business that has a very short cash collection cycle – for example, an online business, which takes payments by credit card – make sure the financial model takes this into account and has a deposit account so that it can earn some interest on the money! Beware of businesses where all the cash generated goes into creating more stock.

Bad signs to look for in the financial model:

- The founders and senior management will be earning a fortune but there will be no money for the investors.
- Each sale is unique and cannot be repeated easily.
- Lots of money needs to be spent on fixed costs rather than on variable costs.
- Salaries are much lower than true market rates so it would be very expensive to replace the current team with new people.
- Profit margins are not high enough.

- The company does not understand the importance of how quickly they will collect the cash and once the business is successful how they will make that cash work positively for the business.

The worst possible sign is an entrepreneur who does not even understand that the financials are a core part of a business. A great example from *Dragons' Den* is Alex Hall of The Big O who was asked by the Dragons what her turnover had been to date. She asked them to clarify what they wanted to know, and then refused to answer because she felt her turnover statistics were not relevant and did not reflect her business potential. The Dragons were angry and said they would never invest in a business that would not reveal financial information to them. Compare this with Huw Gwyther of *Wonderland* magazine whom Peter Jones backed. As Peter says, 'He was concise but precise, well presented in all senses of the word, had confidence in his figures, had taken substantial action to get to this point and had a clear vision and plan of how he intended to reach his goals.'

Good signs to look for in the financial model:

- Repeatable sales of the same product to the same (and lots of other) customers.
- High profit. A great example of this type of financial model is Duncan Bannatyne's investment in Razzamataz Theatre School.
- High levels of cash generation.
- A strategy for making the cash generated work well for the business i.e. it does not just go into building up stock levels.

The financial projections

Ah, the financial projections. A very smart investor regularly tells people that in their view the problem with Microsoft having developed Excel spreadsheets is that nowadays all financial projections are perfect! Entrepreneurs have no excuse to producing anything other than a spreadsheet of perfect financial projections. In fact as the Dragons are always saying on TV, any entrepreneur who does not know their numbers back to front and upside down does not even deserve the right to pitch to them. When you see financial projections they should be perfect and the entrepreneurs should also know all about them. Ideally they should be printed off and included as an appendix to the business plan, but also available as a spreadsheet.

Good financial projections should be prepared so it is easy for another person to take away the spreadsheet and play with the numbers to see what happens if things go better or worse than expected. One of the most important tests of a good set of financial projections is that they include a profit and loss account, a balance sheet and a cash flow projection which are linked together so any changes you make to the profit and loss will flow through automatically into the balance sheet and cash flow projection.

Financial projections should be based on several, but not a ridiculous, number of assumptions. No one size will fit all, but in general the bigger the number, the more important it is that there should be good assumptions behind it. For example, every financial projection should have a number of assumptions for the sales projection. Ideally this will be flexible enough to accommodate changes in numbers of customers, volumes of product and varying prices. A manufacturing company should have similarly strong assumptions behind costs of production, whilst a retail shop will need to have good assumptions about the cost of leasing new premises. If a financial model has an assumption behind the cost of stationery, it probably means that the financial model is too complicated!

Whether you are a venture capitalist or an investor you will very quickly get used to seeing projections where there is a J-curve in profits and cash generation. The J-curve is the shape made when you display the profits on a graph. Typically you will see a graph that looks something like this:

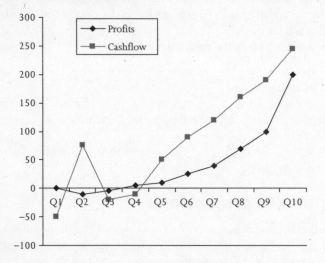

The peak in cash flow in Q2 reflects the cash you will be investing in the business.

Although the timeframe will change (the Quarters may be years, for example), as will the numbers on the left-hand column, the picture won't! The reason for this is that in order to get their hands on your money, the entrepreneurs have to show why they need the money (for example they will be making a loss in the early days) and also that you should hand over your money because the opportunity is going to make so much money (for example, they will be making enormous profits and generating loss of cash within a very short space of time)!

As you start seeing more sets of financial projections you will start to see a pattern emerging, and the trick is to look behind the numbers to see where they are different from the norm for a young company and compared with the normal pattern in the sector in which the business is trading.

The outstanding example of someone getting their financial projections wrong is, of course, Levi Roots who enormously miscalculated the size of the order for his Reggae Reggae Sauce. It did not stop him getting investment though! Maybe this would have been true in the real world as well because Levi is such a great person, but if most entrepreneurs get their numbers wrong it is a real sign to make you worry.

Bad signs in the financial projections:

- The numbers do not add up – this is just incompetence.
- The growth rate is just ridiculous – only one or two companies a year will achieve crazily high levels of growth.
- There are no proper assumptions behind the numbers, and importantly the spreadsheet model is not based on assumptions, so you cannot easily test it to see what happens if sales collapse or interest rates go up.
- No balance sheet and, especially no cash flow projections.
- The projections are totally different from other similar companies, for example, the profit margins are too high or the salaries are too low.
- Gross margins rise as the business grows (in the real world they normally fall off a bit).

Good signs in the financial projections:

- A simple clear set of projections on a spreadsheet with assumptions that can be easily changed so the projections can be tested.
- As time progresses the costs take into account inflation and salary increases etc.
- The profit and loss account, the balance sheet and the cash flow projections are all automatically linked to one another.
- The numbers show high levels of growth, but costs rise accordingly.
- There are step changes in the numbers as the business grows and invests in expansion. Crucially at these points, you will see costs grow ahead of another big increase in sales.

Ten baggers

All of us want to back the Googles, Body Shops and other businesses that become enormous successes. These are known as '10 baggers' based on the concept that investors will 'bag' or get back 10x the money they put into the business when their shares are sold. Without a doubt you must try to back this type of business.

Bad signs for a 10 bagger:

- Niche sector or geographic region as target market.
- Declining sector, however big!
- Large consultancy/service-led business model.
- Complicated 'sell' when in front of customers.
- Seemingly limitless capital expenditure requirements.

Good signs for a 10 bagger:

- Businesses in areas where there is global demand and a real need for the same or a very similar product, for example, healthcare, internet or mobile telephony.
- Simple concept and simple, replicable product or deliverables.
- A revenue model that can be adopted by customers quickly and easily – such as Google Adwords.

- High profit margins.
- Management team who show top rank skills at implementation and execution.

Paperwork, paperwork

The first time you make an investment you will be staggered by the amount of legal documents that are needed.

For a start, it is vital that you invest your money in the business you think you are investing in and not in something else, particularly if that something else is the individuals behind the business, who might just bank the cheque and run away! Handing over a cheque addressed to an individual is a risky activity, so don't do it. So you need to be investing in a properly set up company.

Make sure therefore that the company has been set up properly and that all its legal documents are in order. Unless you are experienced in this sort of thing, get a lawyer to help you with this. And make sure that when you do hand over your money, you receive a document in return (sometimes a letter and sometimes a certificate) that shows what you have bought with that money.

The days of just writing a cheque in return for shares and relying on ordinary company law or common law to protect you as a shareholder are long gone. If you read a standard company memorandum and articles of association you will see that usually they leave the people running the business pretty free to do what they like without telling the shareholders anything or involving them.

It is vital therefore that when you invest you have various legal agreements setting out your rights and obligations, especially a document called a Shareholders Agreement. It is equally vital that unless you are very experienced you employ a lawyer to check that all these documents are saying what you think they are saying. The general rule is the better the investor, the better the lawyer behind him or her.

The vital document

The Shareholders Agreement is a document signed by all the shareholders in the company (both existing and new) and by the directors of the company or their representative. It sets out all the rules governing how the company will be managed after the investment has been made. It is a document that is confidential. Typically only the other signatories have a right to see it. It will detail lots of different things, of which the most important are:

1. The terms of the deal.

2. The roles and responsibilities of the signatories, especially the management team.

3. The warranties and indemnities provided by the management and the existing shareholders and the penalties the new investors can demand if the warranties and indemnities are breached.

④ The rules governing what happens in the event of a shareholder wanting to remove themselves from the investment.

⑤ The rules governing what happens if a founder or employee shareholder leaves the business (known as good and bad leaver clauses).

⑥ Restrictions on how the company spends the money that has been invested.

⑦ The rules governing what happens in the event of a sale of the business, known as drag along and tag along rights.

Sometimes in a deal whole new sets of documents will be produced; in other deals you will be adding your signature to an existing document.

You may have other documents, for example if you decide to lend the company some money as well as buying shares you also may have a loan agreement which sets out the interest and repayment terms.

Other legal documents you will see will be employment and management contracts, major customer and supplier contracts and much more. Good legal documents will not be too long and will be worded in plain English, not lawyer speak, but even so they can be quite a maze to get around, which is why, yet again, I suggest that you must employ a lawyer to look after your interests. The lawyer should be experienced in negotiating private investments – you will be unlikely to find him or her in your average high street law firm.

Bad signs in the legals:

- You do not have a lawyer to look after your own interests.
- There are problems with the legal status of the business you are backing.
- The documents you see are patchy and poorly prepared or are very out of date.
- It is all too much of a rush job.

Good signs in the legals:

- Everyone around the table has a sensible lawyer advising them.
- The company documents including the shareholder register and the memorandum and articles of association are in good order.
- The company keeps its legal documents in good order – for example, copies properly filed in their office and all records kept up-to-date elsewhere, for example, at Companies House.
- Either you or your lawyer is confident that the deal documents are based on up-to-date best practice.

Valuation

We will talk in greater length about the valuation in Chapter 22. However, bear in mind the following.

Bad signs in the valuation process:

- The entrepreneurs have set a wildly high valuation based on totally improbable financial projections.

- The entrepreneurs show you lots of slides of other deals in their sector where the businesses sold out for mega-bucks only two minutes after getting started.
- The entrepreneurs value the business highly AND want to take out a big salary.
- The entrepreneurs do not understand or are resistant to having an open discussion about valuation and, if relevant, insist that the company's Enterprise Investment Scheme (EIS) status means you should pay more for the shares.

The worst sign in a valuation discussion is when the entrepreneur believes his or her business is worth enormously more than it really is. As James Caan always says, 'You value your company at £1 million. What planet are you on!?' Graham Whitby and Barry Haigh of Baby Dream Machine stunned the Dragons when they asked for £100,000 for 5% of their company. Duncan Bannatyne has talked about how amazed he was that they could possibly have believed their business would be worth more than £600 million in three or four years' time.

Good signs in the valuation process:

- The financial projections have valid assumptions behind them so that you are reasonably confident that you can judge what will happen if things go well and if things go badly.
- The entrepreneurs understand valuation issues and come to you with a sensible valuation in the first place.
- You are allowed full and free access to the financial projections and they are easy to 'play around' with on a spreadsheet.
- You can create a deal which may have a mixture of equity, loans, convertible loans, options or ratchets to suit the nature of the deal you are doing and the people involved.

Investing in the right sectors, at the right stage, and alongside the right people

Right sectors

Investing in the right sector is one of the biggest tricks to successful investing. Some sectors seem ready made for young companies to grow quickly and make big returns for their investors. Companies in other sectors always seem to find it harder. If you don't believe me, take a look at the investment portfolios of the various venture capital funds.

There is a reason why venture capitalists and clever dragon investors look for their opportunities in some sectors and not others. They are sectors where normally the set-up risks are lower and it is much quicker to find out if there is real market demand for the new products and services, before you have to gear up all the costs!

Below is a list researched from many private investors of what they invest in and what they avoid.

Bad sectors:

- Biotechnology – you will face a seemingly never-ending call for more money.
- Heavy manufacturing where you may have to invest in lots of machinery before you can make and sell any products. This includes parts of the environmental sector.
- Services businesses which can easily turn into lifestyle businesses or where the primary assets of the business (the staff) walk out of the door each night and may not return! For example, design agencies, PR firms etc.

Good sectors:

- Computer software and Internet businesses.
- Wireless technologies and businesses changing the way we communicate.
- Medical devices.
- Creative media.
- Parts of the environmental sector where there is an identifiable **compelling financial** need by industry or people for the technology or product.
- Fast Moving Consumer Goods, especially those with a brand.
- Retail (provided there are already a couple of outlets or a mail order business that is trading successfully).
- B2B businesses.

Right stage

'Choose large, growing profitable markets.'

We could spend many hours discussing the merits of investing early when deals are at their most risky, versus investing in businesses only when they are up and running, but the valuation has gone up a lot.

The trick to investing at the right stage is to understand three major things:

1. Is this business at the right stage in its own life to accept my money?

2. How long is it likely to be until this company will sell out and you will recoup your money?

3. How many more funding rounds will there be before that exit happens?

Some investors love to invest in really young businesses, almost as a gamble, because it will be such an exciting experience along the way. They may also back a really early-stage business (like the usual ones that appear on *Dragons' Den*) because they can buy the shares for such a less price that if it does succeed they will make a really enormous amount of money. A good example of this is Ian McGlinn who backed Anita Roddick when she wanted to open only her second The Body Shop in Sussex in 1974.

Others want to wait for a bit more certainty that there is actually going to be a business that will grow quickly, before they invest. They look for signs such as the product working, real customers using the product and the company already making sales before they will invest.

The trick to investing at the right stage is also not to invest too late. Some companies look for funding only when the business has already gone off the boil. They will not tell you this of course, so you have to look for signs in the history of the business – check how long it has been going and also what the sales and profits history has been. Remember, though, that Theo Paphitis has made several fortunes backing ailing businesses such as Rymans and La Senza so a tired business can sometimes be a bargain, but it will probably need a new specialist turnaround management team!

A big warning sign that it can be too late to invest is if a company that has had venture capitalist backing comes to you saying they need money. Always ask yourself why the existing venture capitalist (who probably has much more money than you for this type of investment) is not continuing to back the business. It may even be worth ringing the venture capitalist to find out why.

Bad stages to invest in a business:

- Businesses with no sales and an incredibly long time (i.e. years) until you even know if the product works!
- Businesses which are up and running, with sales and profits, that could get the money more cheaply from the bank and which are therefore valuing themselves very expensively.
- When the business has seen sales start to fall off after a spurt of growth, which was not actually real because it was only customers paying to test the product or service.

Good stages to invest in a business:

- As early as possible if you really believe this business could be the next Google.
- Businesses which need relatively little money to get to a position where they are generating enough cash to support themselves.
- Businesses which have already proved the market opportunity, by winning real customers, for example, where they have sales (even if they do not yet have profits) and need the money to invest in growing the sales.
- Businesses due to float on a stock market within the next 3–6 months.

Alongside the right people

'Start alongside [an] experienced angel and see what they do.'

It took until the very end of series five of *Dragons' Den* for all the Dragons to agree to invest in the same deal. Here is the story of what happened.

Case study: Amanda Jones and James Brown

Amanda Jones and James Brown appeared in episode nine of series five of *Dragons' Den*. Their product was a reverse-osmosis sanitation system called Ross. They had designed it as a result of a university project to investigate problems faced by Water Aid in third world countries. The systems allows communities to carry water from the nearest source (which is normally a lot closer than the nearest clean source), and it purifies the water as it is pulled along by the turning motion of the wheels. They were looking for a £50,000 investment in return for a 10% stake in the device.

Amanda and James pitched really well and answered the questions brilliantly. Their only problem was they didn't have a working prototype. James Caan did not care as he had worked in a disaster area. He offered them half the investment, in return for a 10% stake. Duncan Bannatyne then matched him, so they could have the full £50,000 for a 20% stake. Then Deborah Meaden offered the full £50,000 for a 20% stake, followed by Theo Paphitis who offered the full £50k, but didn't know what percentage he might like. Finally Peter Jones was also interested, offering them the exact terms they had pitched for.

Theo then engineered a deal whereby all five dragons would invest at that rate, each taking just a 2% stake for £10,000. Deborah Meaden then organized all the investors so that the deal would actually get done rather than them all arguing with each other over the detailed terms of the deal once they were off air.

Amanda and James walked away with the best deal ever seen in the Den – all the Dragons as investors and the terms they originally wanted!

The quickest way to find out which deals you should and shouldn't do is to watch what other experienced angel investors are doing and to follow them or copy them!

If you are new to the industry, you are most likely to meet them at angel network meetings which are run by various organizations all over the country (see Appendix for details). Go to a few of these meetings and look out for familiar faces and the people everyone else is turning to for an opinion. If you are nervous, watch from afar at first, but quickly try to engage with these people. They will generally remember that they were in your shoes not so long ago and will be friendly. Perhaps you can get to know them better by going out with them socially as well, for example, over a game of golf.

The other people to watch out for are industry veterans. You might find these people at network meetings, but you will also find them by trawling the senior management teams of the leading companies in the sector. Tell yourself that if they won't back the next big thing in their sector, why should you know better?

The people to watch out for are twofold. One group is the people who invest just to make a splash – they usually drown! The other group is formal venture capital funds. This latter group are a very interesting species and the thing to remember is that they are motivated by different things to you.

Firstly, they are usually employees of someone else and are not spending their own money. Therefore, even if they see the same facts and figures as you (and even like, respect or agree with you) they may act differently because that is what their bosses or investors tell them to do.

Secondly, they have to think about the overall performance of their portfolio and to set each deal in that context. They will want to back their winners and 'get rid' of their losers in order to show that the overall performance of their portfolio and funds is as high as possible. They do this to make money, yes, but they also do it because they have one eye, all the time, on whether they can do well enough to raise another investment fund in the future. This means that if there is a company in their portfolio which is underperforming relative to all the others, at best they may drop their support and at worst they may try to kill it off, by selling it off cheap or even effectively putting it out of business by insisting it follow a strategy that is likely to prove fatal! (Note: I have seen this happen, by the way!) This may seem bizarre, but when it comes to portfolio investing it can be the right thing to do from their position. However, it is likely to be very bad news for you if you are also invested in the business.

Most venture capitalists are not like this, despite what people may say, and most of them are great to invest alongside. The most sophisticated venture capitalists these days even try to help angel investors by buying some or all of their shares from them when they first invest in the company.

If you can offer something to the deal as well as money, such as being a director of the business, venture capitalists will respect you more, especially if they decide they will really need you to make the business succeed. If this is the case, the tables will be turned and you will find that they believe you are the right sort of person to invest alongside rather than the other way around!

When it comes to investing alongside other private investors, you have to remember that not all of them are the same and others may start out the same but will then change because their own circumstances make them do so. There are countless cases where investors have fallen out with each other and with management teams, just because they do.

Investing alongside other people is therefore part of the game you play. Some investors are so wary that they refuse to invest alongside anyone else or will only invest with people they have known for a long time and who have proved themselves to be both reliable and consistent in their investment approach. Others go for safety in numbers and only invest in a pack. Another group will spend time snuggling up to the management team so they always have the inside story and therefore an edge over their fellow shareholders.

One major point to sort out is whether you will invest alongside other people, at the same time, who may be investing on better or worse deal terms than you are. Decide what your personal policy will be up front or you will spend hours arguing with your fellow investors as well as with the entrepreneurs and their advisers about this issue. Bear in mind that if other investors do have better terms, especially if this is through a grant of share options, you may find that your stake is diluted further than you thought one day when the options are exercised and this will affect how much money get on exit. Watch out also for terms that give other investors a predetermined payout of money at exit before any other investor receives their money. This is often referred to as liquidation preference. The name is misleading. It applies just as much to a successful exit as to an exit when the business has gone bust.

Aim to get to know the people you will be investing alongside before you sign anything or hand over your money. If you have a good relationship, it can be possible to negotiate different terms with the management and end up getting priority in terms of paying out the money when there is an exit. Not only will you literally get your money back first, but you may also be paid out more cash than the other investors. I have also heard of deals where the 'favoured' investor and the management team club together to spin-off the best bit of the business and before other investors realize, they have been left owning the less valuable portion, plus only a tiny stake in the new exciting business the investor and the management team are now running together!

The wrong people to invest alongside:

- Investors about whom you know nothing and who remain secretive when you try to get to know them.
- Investors whom you instinctively do not trust or who have a bad reputation in the market.
- Anyone with different investment objectives to yours.
- Sometimes, people who may have a wildly different amount of money to invest than you. If you are the bigger investor, it will be annoying that they cannot match you in terms of money and if you are the smaller investor, you will find that you do not have as much influence as they do, whatever the legal documents might say!
- Venture capitalists, unless they are known to work well with private investors or you are going to be a core part of the management team.

The right people to invest alongside:

- People you already know and trust in your other life, for example, in business, as old established friends or trusted members of your family.
- Well-known people who have a good reputation of honourable investing.
- Those who agree to act as a lead investor and represent your interests alongside their own.
- Those who have very similar investment objectives to your own.
- Venture capitalists known to work well with angel investors.

And last, but not least, gut instinct!

There is a simple rule to follow. If, at any point, your gut instinct tells you that you should not be investing in the business, then don't.

Likewise, even if the numbers don't add up, the team isn't perfect or the market isn't proven, if your gut instinct tells you that you must invest, then do!

Ten top tips for which deals you should do:

1 Deals which have a sound business plan, financial model and financial projections.

2 Don't just back a great idea, back a great management team.

3 Back deals with explosive growth potential that may give you a 10x return on your investment.

4 Back businesses which are properly organized in terms of legals, as well as day-to-day operations.

5 Deals other investors want to do; although not all the time, beware of pack hysteria.

6 Deals that are properly valued for where they are in their life.

7 Deals where your lawyer has assured you that all is in order.

8 Deals where you trust management and the other investors and where all your interests are aligned.

9 Deals where your interests will be looked after post-investment.

10 Deals which you feel happy with and when your gut instinct demands you go for it!

CHAPTER 22

Striking the deal

Once you have found the deal you want to invest in, it will usually be in one of two states.

Types of deal

Pre-packaged deals

Pre-packaged deals are deals where all the hard work has been done. Very few of the deals on *Dragons' Den* have been properly organized before they get onto TV and few have been properly pre-packaged. Usually the nearest the entrepreneur has got to this is having an adviser who insists they stick to a valuation regardless of what the investors say.

If you find a deal through a club or group that specializes in offering pre-packaged deals, you should find that all the terms of the deal have already been agreed and that you just need to write a cheque to buy some shares. Even with these deals, I would recommend that you try to meet the management team and hear about the opportunity from them. Also, if you are planning to invest a large proportion of the funds raised it is worth talking to the management and their advisers to see if you can get a discount on either the price you pay for the shares or the commissions you will pay the advisers, despite the fact it is pre-packaged. In the private investment world it is nearly always possible to renegotiate right up to the last minute.

All other deals

Most deals will not come pre-packaged and it will be up to you and your advisers to negotiate the terms with the company and its advisers. This is one of the most interesting parts of private investing, so enter into the negotiation with a sense of optimism and interest!

What you must achieve before you hand over your money

There are various things it is vital to achieve before you invest. These are:

1. A sound business plan that will be implemented post-investment, including your role in the business if relevant.

2   A valuation which you agree with.

3   An investment structure that protects your investment and gives you the best chance of making a profit.

4   Solid legal documents that protect you as an investor.

5   Warranties from the entrepreneurs that there is nothing that they should have disclosed to you and have not, and that everything they have told you is correct.

As a rule you will negotiate the first three things with the entrepreneurs and, if they have one, with their corporate finance adviser. You may also get advice from your accountant about point three. The last two will be negotiated with the entrepreneurs and both your lawyers and theirs.

Investing at the right valuation

One of the knottiest problems in investing is deciding what the correct valuation of a business should be at the moment you invest.

The valuation discussion is the one that, rightly, the Dragons focus on most on the TV show. Do you remember the case study from Nova-Flo at the end of Part One? James Barnham managed to beat the Dragons at their own game when it came to the valuation discussion. But he was unusual; great chunks of every pitch are always devoted to the valuation discussion and it is the one area where the Dragons, almost without fail, come back at the entrepreneurs saying they are crazy because their businesses simply are not worth the valuation that has been put on them! The cheaper they or any other investor can buy the shares now, the more money they will make when they eventually sell them. As an investor you are quite likely to be invested in a business for between three and seven years (and sometimes longer) so you will need to have a chance to make a return which would be much higher than if you invested in something which you could sell for a profit more quickly.

Added to this time risk, is the risk that the company sells more shares in itself to raise more money sometime before you can sell your shares. If this happens and you do not reinvest, your shareholding will be diluted to a smaller percentage of the total shares in issue. Therefore you will receive a smaller share of the proceeds when the business does sell.

It is vital, therefore, to get enough shares so that you do not find that when you do sell you only get a tiny return and everyone else has made more money than you!

The corresponding pressure on this negotiation is that the entrepreneurs want to keep as much of the company for themselves as possible so that they too will make a lot of money. You need to make sure that they continue to own enough shares or 'have skin in the game' which is the industry term, so that they have enough incentives to make themselves money and you too. If the entrepreneur's shareholding gets too small, they will no longer feel they own it, and their desire to get the business really big and profitable may decline.

Anecdotally both investors and entrepreneurs reveal that in the first round of an investment roughly + or − 25%–30% of the shares are sold in exchange for the investment made, regardless of how much money is being invested! So in this sense the Dragons are often not far off when they are negotiating with the entrepreneurs.

When it comes to valuation the first thing to be aware of is that there are two types of valuation discussed in an investment round. The first is the 'pre-money' valuation which is the value of the business before any new investment has been made. The second is the 'post money' valuation which is the valuation after the investment has been made. If you are investing, your shareholding will be calculated on the percentage of shares you own based on the 'post money' valuation. Bear in mind that this percentage may be a percentage also of the type of shares you buy. For example, if the deal includes both ordinary shares and preferred ordinary shares, and you only buy ordinary shares, you could end up with x% of the ordinary share capital, but this may be a smaller percentage of the total equity of the company as the preferred ordinary shareholders will have a stake in the equity too. So your belief that you own 10% of the company may in fact be only 5% of the total if the preferred shareholders own 50% of the total equity.

You can be very technical in your valuation methodology. It is always worth looking at the turnover, profit and cash flow projections to see what the likely value of the business is today, and also what it might be at the time you are likely to sell. It might be that it is better for you to take 35% of the business now in return for your investment or it might be that the story is so exciting that you want to give incentives to the entrepreneurs to outperform and therefore you will be happy to leave them with 80%.

Some people will advise you to look at the future profit and cash flow projections and perform a discounted cash flow valuation to get to today's value. The trouble with this technique is not so much that you cannot make projections and then discount them back to get a value of what the business might be worth today, but is that the assumptions anyone makes to get the projections (yourself included) are likely to be pretty wild and woolly. The business is quite unlikely to have a past history of trading upon which you can base future projections. It is very unlikely you will see another business of the same type at the same stage any time soon, so there will not be many examples to compare it with. So valuing the business based on the future is best left as just a small tool in your kit of valuation methods.

If a business is small and unquoted (so you cannot sell the shares easily) AND you will only have a minority stake in it, so you cannot just barge in if necessary and take over, then the stake you are buying is going to be worth much less than if you invested in a large, quoted company. In the old days in the City of London, people valuing a small company would do the following. It's a good extra check to use when you are valuing a deal.

1. Find an equivalent large company (perhaps one in the same sector) and find out its value as a multiple of its net profits. This is the price/earnings ratio, the 'PER' (share price/earnings per share).

2. Take the PER and knock 30% off to take account of the fact that the company you are valuing is small.

Take off another 30% if you will only have a minority stake post-investment.

 This reduced PER multiple can then be multiplied with the net profits of the small business to get the valuation.

I bet you will find that doing this will bring the valuation (and you) down to earth with a bump!

However, at the end of the day negotiating the valuation is about a trade-off and if you are too mean with the valuation, the entrepreneurs, if they have any sense, will walk away. Bear in mind that if your investment ends up generating you 10s of £ millions will you really care that you only owned 28% rather than 29%?

Structuring the deal to get the best return you can

Before you agree to invest, take a look at the different investment structures you can use.

It is normal for private investors to invest in ordinary shares, preferred ordinary shares, loan stock, convertible loan stock and even share options. So do not necessarily just agree to ordinary shares.

The only reason why you should not think about these structures is if you know that the company will quickly raise a large amount of new investment (especially from a venture capitalist) as it is likely the agreement will be torn up by the new investor who will impose their own terms. Unless you can match the money they are offering, you will have little room to argue.

The reasons investors use all these different structures are threefold.

1. To increase the chance of getting their money back quickly.

2. To give them a chance to get a much larger return on their investment.

3. To protect them from being diluted when new investment is made, though this does not always work.

The advantages of preferred shares

Preferred shares give their owners extra advantages over ordinary shareholders. These can include:

- extra voting rights in shareholder meetings
- rights to a seat on the board
- a fixed or higher dividend than the ordinary shares might be entitled to
- liquidation preference (i.e. if the company is dissolved or sold these shares get paid back first). Sometimes the shares have the right to an extra share of the proceeds of a sale, before any of the ordinary shareholders receive any money.

The one major disadvantage of preferred shares is that they are unlikely to be eligible for a tax break under the EIS scheme.

The advantages of loan stock and convertible loans

When you value a business, don't ignore the benefit of investing some of your money in the company via a loan or even a convertible loan. The advantages of lending the company money this way include:

1. receiving interest on the loan

2. getting the capital repaid either regularly over time or in a few big chunks as soon as the company can afford it, but long before the shares will be sold

3. if it is a convertible loan, having a chance to convert the loan into shares in the future, if the loan cannot be repaid by the company.

The key effect of investing in loan stock is that you will still get the shares you wanted but at a lower price per share. This will increase your chance of getting a higher return on the investment when the shares are sold.

Share options

Share options give their owners the right to buy shares at a price fixed today at some point in the future. They are a great way of motivating people to grow a business. Other advantages are firstly that until they are converted into shares ('exercised'), the option holders do not have shareholder rights and secondly when the options are exercised, the option holders must pay the company for them so the company gets a boost of cash.

If the company does not increase in value by the time the option is ready to be exercised (i.e. converted into shares) then the option holders will not bother to buy the shares and will let the option expire.

Lots of people talk about share options for management, but they can also be a very good thing to invest in if you are an investor. Essentially you will pay a small price to buy the options, say 1p for each option you buy over a share and you agree, one day, to buy those shares at a fixed price based on today's valuation. If all goes well you will end up owning another chunk of the company for the price you would have paid anyway, but today you have only had to pay for the option.

Ratchets

Some investors and entrepreneurs who cannot agree a valuation do the deal by including something called a ratchet. This mechanism is used to bridge the gap between the valuation the investor believes and the valuation the entrepreneur wants. With a ratchet, the entrepreneur agrees to hit certain targets in terms of growing the business, in return for you transferring a percentage of the shares in the company to him or her when they have been hit.

It is quite a technical thing to use. And it is something you never hear mentioned on *Dragons' Den*, but it would not surprise me to hear that after the show when the serious negotiations get going it does sometimes get raised.

In theory, this gives the entrepreneur incentives to work extra hard, but if they fail then you get to keep your bigger stake. You will not mind them doing well, because if the right targets have been set, and are achieved, the business will be worth lots more, so your stake though smaller will benefit accordingly.

Ratchets can be great, but more often they become a nuisance. Firstly, if things don't go well, the entrepreneur will miss the targets and could become even more de-motivated than they would otherwise. Secondly, it is very rare that things stay stable in a fast growing business, so the targets set 12–18 months ago could be the wrong ones. The risk is that the entrepreneur may head for those targets (even if they are wrong) so that they get their shares, even if this is not the best route for the company now to follow. A similar effect happens when share options are used as the motivator.

Ratchets (and share option schemes) can also work the other way around. The entrepreneur agrees to give up shares to you if he or she fails to deliver the results promised. Similar problems to those described above tend to arise if the right targets are not met. In the worst case, you may end up controlling the company and having to run it yourself!

The knotty question of tax breaks for investors

The UK has a tax break scheme called the Enterprise Investment Scheme. It is designed to give income and Capital Gains Tax breaks to investors who invest up to £500,000 a year in small risky companies that qualify under the Scheme. There is a whole section on the EIS Scheme which explains all about it and how you can take advantage of it.

However, in the context of valuation, EIS can become very important. Many entrepreneurs (and even others) will argue that because HM Government is giving you, the investor, an upfront income break of 20% when you invest (and this means that you will actually receive a real cheque for 20% of the money you invested in due course from HM Revenue & Customs, provided the forms are filled in correctly), then you should be prepared to pay more for the shares when you buy them. This is rubbish!

The issue of your tax bill is between you and HM Revenue & Customs. There are many examples of cases where companies have started out as EIS qualifying, but for one reason or another, the Revenue has then withdrawn their qualification. The effect of this on the company is nil, but for the investors it has meant they got a letter from the Revenue politely asking them to send back that cheque for 20% of the money invested and also to send interest on the money too! So the lesson is: don't allow for the benefit you might or might not be receiving under EIS to be taken into account when valuing the shares you are about to buy.

The negotiation process

Setting up the negotiations

The trick to a successful negotiation is to set up everything in the right way from the start.

Your attitude

You will be keen to get a good deal for yourself. To do this you need to get into the right mind set.

The deal negotiations are about achieving a win for you and a win for the entrepreneur.

You may also have to achieve a win for other investors who are already invested in the company and for those who will be joining you as a new investor.

This is something that *Dragons' Den* really shows up in a bad light as usually the Dragons are as greedy as possible and are really tough on the entrepreneurs. The only case where this wasn't seen was with Amanda Jones and James Brown and their 'good for the world' water purification system.

If you enter into the talks with an attitude of winner takes all, it is likely that the deal will fall through and you will have ended up wasting your time and possibly your money. Even if you do win, you may find yourself invested in the business where everyone else dislikes you and thereafter you will find it a frustrating experience.

Remember you will need to sell yourself to them and win their trust and respect, just as much as they need to win yours.

Understanding the attitude of the other parties

Investors tell me that the time entrepreneurs are at their nicest and most helpful is during the negotiations and up until the point when they have cashed your cheque.

So they are likely to appear very willing whenever you talk to them. Just remember that they are after your money, but they may also be after other people's money too, so they could be juggling your demands with those of several other people. As a rule they will be as nice as is necessary to get your money. But they will also be nice to everyone else too!

Meanwhile they are trying to keep their business running so it does not go bust before the deal is closed. If they are not doing so already, try to encourage them to put one person full-time onto the deal negotiations. If they cannot spare someone from the team, encourage them to seek help from someone else – possibly their lawyer or their accountant.

This is probably the first and possibly the only time they will raise investment, so expect them to get things wrong. Just make sure it is not too wrong. You should only be investing in them if they are really competent.

It is reasonable to expect total honesty from the entrepreneur. For example, they should tell you if they are negotiating with more than one person, even if they will not tell you who it is and they should give you regular reports on how the business is performing day to day.

Here is a guide to approaching the negotiation so the outcome is successful.

Before you start negotiations

Step One – Review what you know

Read all the paperwork, for example, the business plan, and thoroughly familiarize yourself with the deal. The Dragons spend a lot of time when filming looking at the paperwork the entrepreneurs supply, even though you do not see this when the show is televised.

Step Two – Record what you still need to find out

Write down all the things you still don't know or have questions about. Some of the questions may be about commercial issues, such as the competitive landscape, others might be about things like the terms of the deal. You will probably also have questions about practical issues such as whether the company is eligible for EIS relief.

Step Three – Decide how much to invest and what your role could be

Decide roughly how much money you will be prepared to invest and what sort of terms you want. Do you want to just invest in shares or do you want part of your money to be invested as a loan?

Decide if you want to be a leader in the negotiations and control the process or whether you will be passive and let the company, their adviser or other investors be in charge.

Decide whether, post-investment, you want an active role with the business or to be a passive investor.

Step Four – Decide what issues are deal-breakers

Have a think about the key things which must be agreed if you are going to invest. These are known as the deal-breakers. Then decide which issues you are prepared to compromise on and those which you really do not mind if you lose. Write everything down and keep the list in your back pocket.

Step Five – Set aside plenty of time

Block out chunks of time in your diary for phone calls, meetings, review of the documents and thinking time.

Entering into the negotiations

Step One – Setting up a process for the negotiations

Private investment deals are notorious for taking ages to complete. It is not unusual for a deal to take up to six months to close, but there are some simple tricks that can speed up the whole process.

- Choose who will lead the deal and be responsible for the negotiations and 'making the deal happen'. This could be you or it could be the entrepreneur or their adviser. Sometimes it will be another investor.
- Prepare a timetable for the negotiations. Start the timetable at the date you plan to close the deal and then work backwards to today, putting in all the key things that must happen during that time, including
  - meetings with the management team to discuss the deal
  - due diligence meetings to discuss the facts and figures

- meetings such as board meetings and shareholder meetings
- when various drafts of the legal documents will be circulated and when comments on those documents must be sent back
- holidays when people are not around to make decisions.

When the timetable is ready, circulate it to everyone.

- Prepare a list of all people involved in the deal, what their role is and all their contact details, including phone numbers, email addresses and physical addresses.

When this contact list is ready, circulate it to everyone.

- Get the entrepreneur to prepare a due diligence pack with every single document that is relevant to the deal, including:
  - the business plan
  - the documents supporting the business plan, for example, the marketing plan and the financial projections
  - legal documents such as those from Companies House and HM Revenue & Customs
  - historical sets of accounts, the company's memorandum and articles of association
  - the management accounts
  - employment and other contracts, such as the office lease
  - customer contracts and references
  - supplier contracts
  - details of any pending, current or suspected litigation.
- Start to get the entrepreneurs to think about the warranties they will be expected to sign.

Step Two – Starting negotiations – tactics

Closing the deal will involve lots of answers from all sorts of people. Some things will be dealt with in formal meetings and others will require a quiet chat over a drink. Typically, the more sensitive the issue, the more likely that it will be dealt with over a drink!

If you have an adviser leading the deal, you will find that the process will move forward fairly smoothly and you will be told what to do and when. If you are leading the deal, you will have to take on this role and direct the others; make sure, therefore, that you are available to deal with anything that might take the deal off track or your life will become chaotic.

I have acted as the adviser on various deals. It is a bit like being a nanny in charge of small children! You have to take care of everyone and try to be even handed, but you will also have to listen to, and deal with, all the moans and groans. If you are the sort of person that gets wildly annoyed by other people's inefficiency, it may be worth taking on the role yourself so you stay sane. Another good reason to be the lead is that the person who controls the deal normally wins more points in the negotiations than the person who does not!

Step Three – Moving through the negotiations (see also Step Four)

Depending on how you like to approach negotiations and how much competition there is for the deal, you may find that the negotiations proceed smoothly with an offer only being finally agreed when everyone has all the information they need, or sometimes you may find that they lurch along as different people get involved. Sometimes a rough price is set at the start and then it is adjusted during the negotiations; other times it will only be negotiated after all the due diligence has been completed.

Try not to rush the negotiations and stay flexible. Small risky deals need plenty of air around them so everyone has time to get to know each other and judge the risks and opportunities.

These are the main things which should take place in the negotiations:

- Meetings to review the business plan and the financial projections and agree the final plan and the projections which the business will implement post the investment.
- Meetings to discuss your role and rights in the business post-investment.
- Due diligence meetings to verify all the facts. Note: *some of these may be virtual meetings, for example, when the lawyers review all the contracts for you.*
- Site visits, so you can see in what you are investing.
- Phone calls and emails taking up references, particularly from customers and also on the senior management.
- Team building sessions, for example, meeting up over lunch or in the pub, so everyone can get to know and trust each other.
- Regular management updates on current trading.

Step Four – The term sheet and heads of agreement

Private investors take different approaches to making formal offers of investment. Some follow the venture capitalist strategy of preparing a term sheet that details the terms of their offer; others might do it via a letter or email. Some will just want to agree the terms verbally. It will be up to you and the people in whom you are investing to choose a system that works for you all.

Once you have agreed the major terms of the deal, it is normal to put these into a document called the Heads of Agreement. If you have not done a deal before, ask your lawyers to become involved at this point (unless they already are).

Everyone then signs the Heads of Agreement and then the lawyers go away to prepare the paperwork. They will update or prepare lots of documents based on the Heads of Agreement, including:

- The company's memorandum and articles of association.
- The Shareholder Agreement including warranties and indemnities and tag along and drag along rights.
- The disclosure letter (this is the letter where the entrepreneurs declare all the things which, if they did not tell you, you could sue them over!).

- Share certificates.
- The capitalization table (which sets out who owns what in the business pre- and post- the investment).
- The papers for shareholder and board meetings.
- Employee and directors' contracts.

The fine detail of all these documents is too extensive to record here, but there are two key areas that do need mentioning.

Warranties and indemnities

As a new investor in a business you need to be sure that you have been told everything you need to know so that you are able to make your investment with confidence. Meanwhile you are planning to invest in a business where (probably) they are really desperate to get their hands on your money.

Luckily for you, the investment market has found an ideal way to address any conflict there may be between these two positions. That is the preparation of a document (or a section of the Shareholders Agreement) in which the existing management, founders and shareholders warrant (i.e. promise) that they have told you everything they know or suspect might be relevant to you in making your investment decision. And I mean everything: just wait until you see you first set of warranties and the all-inclusive way the paragraphs are written.

However, a simple declaration that you have told someone everything is not worth anything unless the person signing it will really suffer if they lie. So you need to include a financial penalty to be paid to you if you later discover that they did not tell you the full truth.

An indemnity will only have teeth if this penalty is big. It needs to be at least as big as the sum of money you are investing in the business. A typical indemnity will be worded so that if the warranties are breached, the individuals concerned (not the company) will have to pay you hard cash in compensation. They may even have to pay you this cash if one of their colleagues has breached a warranty, even if they did not.

Normally sensible limits are put onto the warranties and indemnities. For example, there will usually be a time limit for which the warranties are valid and another time limit for when you can bring a claim against a breach. You will also find that the level of indemnity paid out will depend on the extent of the breach. Clearly it would not be in anyone's interest to have a fight that makes the entrepreneur bankrupt, just because he or she failed to mention that the business had run out of tea bags on a Friday night!

In order to give the entrepreneurs and their cohorts a last minute get out of jail free card, one of the documents that gets signed as part of the deal is a Disclosure Letter. This is prepared by the lawyers representing the entrepreneur and lists anything and everything they know about the risks and liabilities facing the business and provides relevant supporting documentation. Anything that has been declared in the Disclosure Letter falls outside the warranties and indemnities and you will not later be able to sue under the warranties on any of this information.

Therefore, pay very close attention to the warranties, indemnities and the Disclosure Letter before you sign the deal.

Tag along and drag along rights

Under UK law, minority shareholders in a private company have very few rights and it is very expensive and time-consuming to sue a company, its directors or fellow shareholders if you do believe you have been treated badly.

One of the biggest risks as a small investor is that all the other shareholders do something, such as selling out to someone else, without including you in the deal. You may even find out about it after the event when it is too late to do anything about it.

Likewise, if you are a majority investor in a business, it can be very annoying if there is a smaller shareholder who does something to frustrate an action (for example, the sale of the company) because they have minority rights. They may even sell their shares to someone you actively do not want as a fellow shareholder in the business.

The private investment community noticed this long ago and has created a neat solution to these dilemmas. These are known as tag along and drag along rights. In summary, these rights, which are included in the Shareholders Agreement, enable the majority investors to force minority shareholders to follow their lead in important areas such as the sale of the business. Equally they give minority shareholders exactly the same rights and terms as the majority investor in these important areas.

Once you have signed up to the tag along and drag along rights, which you must do, you will therefore be bound much more closely with your fellow investors, however big or small they are.

Step Five – Closing the deal

Sometimes the deal gets signed at a meeting where everyone is present, but it is more usual for a final flurry of emails between everyone with various people signing documents and then sending them in to the lawyer or lead investor.

In terms of handing over the cash usually the investors will put the money into a client account held by a lawyer with an instruction to transfer the funds to the company once all the paperwork has been signed. However, some people are happy to write a cheque direct to the company or transfer the funds via their bank.

Whichever way you end up closing the deal, try to have a celebration drink with the entrepreneurs and your fellow investors. Why? Because the hard work really only starts after the investment has been made!

Ten top tips for negotiating the best deal

1 You are one of the biggest new investors, even in a pre-packaged deal, you could consider asking for a financial benefit such as a discount on the cost of the shares or the commissions payable. Note: bear in mind that if you do negotiate these preferable terms, it may upset the other investors in this round of investment.

2 If the deal is not pre-packaged, expect to spend a lot of time on negotiations and reading and commenting upon legal agreements.

3 Make sure you invest at the best possible valuation but remember that the best valuation is not always the lowest.

4 Structure the deal terms to optimize your cash returns.

5 You may be able to get good tax breaks if you invest under the Enterprise Investment Scheme.

6 Decide what role you want to play in the negotiations and after the deal has closed before you start negotiating.

7 Remember that the best outcome is a win:win for all concerned, not you winning at the expense of someone else losing.

8 Insist on a formal planned process, based on a pre-agreed timetable, for conducting the negotiations.

9 There are key points in any negotiation. One of the most important is the time you make a formal bid to buy shares in the company. However this bid may end up being anything from a conversation over a pint of beer to a formal letter, known as a term sheet.

10 Employ a good lawyer to represent you in the legal negotiations, but still make sure you read all the documents yourself and that all the routes to protecting your investment (such as warranties, indemnities and tag along and drag along rights) are included.

CHAPTER 23

The hard work starts now

Depending on what you have agreed to in the negotiations, your role in your investee company will be very different. Here is what to expect depending on the type of investor you are going to be.

Types of investor

Passive investor

Typically the Dragons are not passive investors and work with the teams they back to help things happen by offering advice, contacts or technical expertise. However sometimes they are passive investors in a deal. The best example is probably Richard Farleigh who has over fifty investments, many of which are passive.

If you are a passive investor, your job will be to sit and wait it out, though don't be surprised to be asked to invest more money sooner rather than later. You will have the right to attend shareholder meetings and companies should keep you informed about their successes, failures and plans for the future.

Don't be surprised if you get approached to open your address book and make introductions that will help the business to get more customers or to find better suppliers. Get ready to be a champion for the business too – tell everyone about the great business you have invested in to encourage them to do business with it.

You should also not be surprised if your passive status does not last! There are many cases of investors who have got dragged into a business either to help it grow or to sort out the problems it has fallen into.

Whatever happens, hopefully, one day, you will be sent a big cheque and can go and celebrate.

> **Case study: mentor investor**
>
> My involvement with the business in question began when I provided short-term finance to enable a planned TV advertising campaign to go ahead after another business angel had dropped out of the deal. I am now involved to the extent that I have made an equity investment, have been appointed finance director and travel to the business premises most weeks, and also do quite a lot of work for the business from home. Hardly the description of a mentor, however the business founder regularly speaks with me on the phone, on average five or six times a week. I believe that these conversations with him constitute 'mentoring'. He discusses his ideas, what he has achieved, what he perceives as problems, the strengths and weaknesses of his business. In return, I believe that I have learned a great deal about the real limiting factors that hamper growing businesses.

As a mentor you will find yourself acting as a safe and trusted confidant(e) of the management team who will share their hopes and disappointments with you. You will be able to advise and support the management as they make decisions about everything from employing people to executing their strategy. You may also be asked to help them in dealing with other shareholders. Don't be surprised if you find yourself in the office helping with everything from the financial projections, to writing pitch documents or even employee contracts and employee handbooks!

It would be reasonable to be paid the expenses, but do not expect to be paid for your time.

Being a mentor can be very time-consuming, so make space in your life, but it is also very rewarding. Hopefully, as a result of your support, the company will do even better than it would otherwise have done and you too will receive a big cheque and can go out and celebrate.

Investor director

If you become a director of the company, you will have the same legal duties as you have if you are the director of any other company. You will also be expected to attend and contribute to board meetings. Remember that as a director of a company, your duties are different from those as a shareholder. You will be as liable as the other directors if things go wrong. There is no defence in law in being a 'non-executive'. If nothing else, make sure that you have a good handle on the financial position of the company at all times. If things go wrong and you are found liable, you can be struck off as a director and this will prevent you from having other company directorships and many other posts for the relevant period.

Some investors keep their director's responsibilities to the legal minimum, whilst others will also take on similar tasks to the mentor angels. Clearly it will be a lot more interesting if you get involved.

Once involved, expect to be called upon frequently to work with the management team. You may be asked to go with them to sales pitches or help with negotiations with suppliers. You may also be asked to interview staff (and prepare their employment contracts!) or be there when they are sacked. Expect to have to review financial projections, help with borrowing money from the bank and even assist in a new round of fundraising which might see your shareholding significantly diluted. At all times you have to act in the best interests of the company, not of yourself as a shareholder.

It is reasonable to take a director's fee for the time you spend on company business, though often these fees will be accrued in a special account called the director's loan account and will only be paid when the company is generating surplus cash. It is also reasonable to claim expenses. If you get very involved in the management of the business you may also want a contract of employment and to be paid for the work you do. Discuss all this with the management and perhaps also with other key shareholders before you finalize anything.

With any luck by remaining very close to the company, you will maximize the opportunity for the business to be a great success. For companies that will be seeking venture capitalist investment in the future, it can be a very good thing to be a director of the company. If the venture capitalist decides that you are a crucial part of the team that will make the business a success, they are likely to try to strike a deal with you that keeps you enthusiastic and committed, so you are less likely to have your shareholding significantly diluted when they put their money in.

Taking a job

Earlier on in this book I included a case study about how Eileen Rutschmann made a private investment and ended up becoming CEO of www.iammoving.com.

So you can end up having a job at your new investee company. There are also times when investors use the opportunity to invest as a way of buying themselves an interesting and challenging job. They then become an employee of the company and will get on with the tasks they have been asked to complete. Sometimes the job will be part-time on paper, but be prepared to spend much more time than your contracted hours. It is a good idea to ensure that you not only have the founders on board when this happens, but that you also have the agreement of your other shareholders.

If it is the right thing to take a job as the best way to protect your investment, and if it is what you want to do, address the challenges and get on with it. However, before you jump in, work out if by taking the job it will have a negative impact on your other investments and your personal life. Before you accept the job, make sure that you have a proper contract and that your job description has been defined.

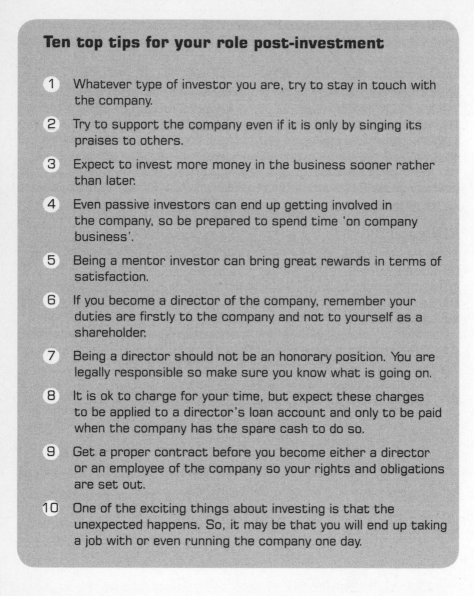

Ten top tips for your role post-investment

1. Whatever type of investor you are, try to stay in touch with the company.

2. Try to support the company even if it is only by singing its praises to others.

3. Expect to invest more money in the business sooner rather than later.

4. Even passive investors can end up getting involved in the company, so be prepared to spend time 'on company business'.

5. Being a mentor investor can bring great rewards in terms of satisfaction.

6. If you become a director of the company, remember your duties are firstly to the company and not to yourself as a shareholder.

7. Being a director should not be an honorary position. You are legally responsible so make sure you know what is going on.

8. It is ok to charge for your time, but expect these charges to be applied to a director's loan account and only to be paid when the company has the spare cash to do so.

9. Get a proper contract before you become either a director or an employee of the company so your rights and obligations are set out.

10. One of the exciting things about investing is that the unexpected happens. So, it may be that you will end up taking a job with or even running the company one day.

CHAPTER 24

Making money

Earlier in this section, I talked about some of the reasons to become an investor. You will have noticed that I did not put making money at the top of the list, but it is still the key reason why you are doing it. So here are some things to think about in terms of making a profit out of your investment.

Timescales

Private investing is a patient person's game. There are companies like last.fm which are amazingly successful and sell out in a couple of years giving their angels massive financial rewards, but for every one of those is The Body Shop and its equivalent where the angel investor holds shares for 10, 20 or even 30 years before they sell out. And those are the successful ones!

Time is very important in angel investing. Set out below is a chart which has kindly been passed to me by an early stage venture capital fund called The Capital Fund. It is an IRR (internal rate of return) calculator and shows very clearly how time affects the returns you make.

Most entrepreneurs will tell you that they have a timescale of three to five years before they will get you an exit for your shares. As far as I know, although this is a common prediction, there is no hard evidence that it is the timescale you should expect.

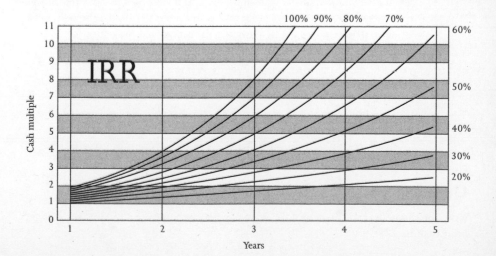

Investors tell me that it is more realistic to expect for a seven to 10 year timescale and then be delighted if you exit earlier.

Businesses with really amazing unique technology may sell much earlier than you expect because a much bigger company decides that they need to acquire it early, almost at any price, because of the threat or opportunity it represents. Other companies that grab significant market share are also likely to sell quickly.

The trouble with an early sale is that you will always wonder whether, if you had hung on for longer, you would have been able to sell for even more money.

When you are making an investment, think realistically about the timescales. A deal that seems attractive because you expect to exit in three years, may not look so attractive if your money is going to be tied up for 10 years and it may be that you need to get better terms when you invest, or even invest less money, to reduce the risks. It took the Dragons years to build their own businesses, whether it was Deborah Meaden who spent well over a decade building up Weststar Holidays or Peter Jones who founded Phones International Group in 1998.

Private investment theory

Books and books have been written about the investment theories surrounding business investing, but particularly what profits you are likely to make by investing in this way. Academics have made their careers on writing theses on these subjects. In summary, though, the conclusions are pretty consistent. They are as follows:

- Investing in young businesses is incredibly risky because the companies you back are unproven.
- All the statistical research suggests that there are no definite characteristics of early stage businesses or entrepreneurs that will guarantee that a large successful business will result from the investment.
- You need to invest in around 25 companies to have a statistical chance of one of them definitely returning you 10 x or more in cash, BUT
- If you do invest in this many, around 50% will make you a positive return and your overall return each year is likely to be between 17% and 27%, which is a lot more than you will get by putting your money into a savings account.

Therefore, as an investor you really have two choices.

- Become a portfolio investor and back as many (presumably good) opportunities as you come across, or
- Invest in just a few where you can add real value yourself by working closely with the management team to make the business a great success and to try like Ian McGlinn to make sure that you get a 10x return or even more.

Getting your cash back

Now the theoretical stuff is out of the way, let's get back to business. How do you get your cash back?

There are lots of ways you can get some or most of your cash back before you finally exit from your investment, but one of two things need to occur before you will have any chance of this happening. Either the company has to generate enough free cash (i.e. surplus cash above that which it needs to continue running and growing the company) or there has to be someone who is prepared to buy out your investment.

Before we go into any detail, it is worth discussing for a minute the theory of equity investing. Essentially the value of a business is made up of three things:

- what it is worth today
- the value that will be created from its ongoing growth and profitability
- the additional premium someone might be prepared to pay on top of those amounts in order to own it for themselves.

All that value belongs to the shareholders who own the business now and they have a choice of whether to try to take some or all of that value out today or to keep it in the company until some point in the future.

Putting it simply, if you take money out now, for example, through a dividend, that value is lost to the company forever. If you do take that cash therefore there is an opportunity cost because it might be that if you left it in the company, it could be used to generate even more value.

As an investor you have to balance that risk with the benefit of taking that cash for yourself and investing it in something else which may give even bigger returns than if you left it where it is. But you also have to weigh up the risk of the company keeping the money and failing to make good use of it, possibly with the result that you will never see it again.

Investors are pretty pragmatic people and, as a rule, tend to prefer to take the cash back where they can because they are well aware that no-one can definitely predict the future and every extra day you wait until the cash comes back, the lower your return will potentially be. In any case, there is probably another great deal waiting around the corner for your money!

So what are the routes to getting your cash back?

Dividends

Did you know that the shareholders in Cobra Beer have already had over 2x the money they invested back from dividends paid by the company? And they still have their shares in the business which are growing in value.

If Cobra Beer can do it, other companies should be able to do as well, especially those with rapidly growing sales and strong profits.

As an investor, keep an eye on how much cash the business is generating and encourage the management as soon as possible to consider paying some of it to the shareholders as a dividend. The only reason to discourage the payment of a dividend is if you hold EIS qualifying shares, because any dividends you receive will be taxed as usual, whereas if the cash is left in the company and therefore it gets more valuable, when you sell the shares, the Capital Gains you will make will be tax free.

Loan repayments

A good way of getting some money back is to lend the company money and set up a schedule for interest payments and for capital repayments. If you have lent the company money or invested in loan stock (which is effectively the same thing), think about the interest rate you charge on the loan. If you can get a higher interest rate than you would get if you put the money elsewhere, the sums you are paid will effectively be giving you a profit on your investment. It is your reward for lending money to a particularly risky proposition!

Try to ensure that the company both can and does repay the capital sum you gave them as a loan. Although you will not make a profit on this money, you will at least have it back to spend on other things.

Selling your shares

Dragon investments are by their nature difficult to sell easily. They are in private companies and usually represent a minority stake. More often than not their value will decrease before increasing, as the company spends the money you have given it and then waits for the results of this investment. You are unlikely to be able or even to be allowed to sell your shares unless all the other shareholders are allowed to do so as well.

Selling when the company raises more money

If a company raises more money, it is likely that the new investors will not be interested in buying your shares, especially if they are a venture capitalist. They want to invest in the company itself, not to reward you. The more likely effect will be that your own shareholding shrinks in (inverse) proportion to the new money being invested if you do not invest more money yourself. This scenario is magnified in the event of a 'down-round' when the new investors invest at a lower valuation than you invested earlier on.

A few enlightened venture capitalists are beginning to see that this is not the way forward because it traps private investor money in businesses. They understand that if these investors get their money returned to them, preferably at a profit, they will then go off and invest in more young companies, which hopefully the venture capitalists can also invest in one day. So a small tip for you is that if your investee does want to raise more money, point them towards a 'modern' thinking venture capitalist.

If by any chance one or more venture capitalists come knocking on their door, ask them to get the venture capitalist to make their offer (in their term sheet) include some sort of exit for you as the private investor.

Selling shares to fellow investors or others before the 'big' exit

The other day I received a letter from a fellow shareholder in a company where I have a dragon investment. In it he offered to sell me his shares for the same price in which he had invested. Unfortunately the price he had paid (he invested long after me) was about three times what I paid for my shares, so I was not interested. However, I might have been if he had offered them to me for less than I paid! At the meeting the following week I talked to a couple of people who also invested in this company. They had received the same letter, and like me, their response was the same. The moral of this story is that you are very unlikely to find buyers for your shares from amongst your fellow investors.

It is just possible that you will be able to sell your shares even if it is a minority stake to a third party who has a strategic reason for becoming a shareholder in the business. This happened at the US company CraigsList www.craigslist.com. The founders had given a 28.4% shareholding to one of their team and then fell out with him. That individual then went off and sold the shares to eBay who wanted to have a bargaining chip in a business which has become a global free advertising phenomenon. So if you really want to sell your shares, don't care what others might think, and are not restricted by the agreements you signed when you invested, it may be worth talking to some of the big commercial players in the sector in which your business operates or if you are feeling really evil, their competitors! Just beware. CraigsList and eBay are currently locked in a legal battle resulting from claims by eBay that CraigsList has treated it unfairly as a shareholder.

Selling your shares back to the founders

You may have more chance to sell your shares back to the founders of the business, especially if you have fallen out. Remember that the time you are most likely to want to sell will be when things are not going well. This will be just the time when the founders really have their backs up against the wall and are probably living off baked beans, so even if they do agree to buy them you are unlikely to get a really good price for them. If you want to sell to them for other reasons, for example, you need the money for something else, it may be worth agreeing a deal whereby you help them to buy back the shares. For example, you could offer to guarantee a loan with a bank which they use to buy the shares or you could sell them in small lots over a period of time.

Floating the business

It is common for entrepreneurs to tell you that they will get you your exit by floating the business on a stock market either here in the UK or sometimes abroad. If they achieve this it is a good result, but it is not the best one unless you are allowed to sell your shares in the flotation. Unfortunately, if you are a big shareholder in the business it is likely the advisers to the flotation will ask that you do not sell your shares at all or only in part at the flotation so that the new investors are given confidence that you still have faith in the company and are not jumping ship at the first opportunity.

It is common practice that you will not be able to sell the shares for at least three to six months and possibly even for a year, so even though on paper you may have made a fantastic profit you will not get your hands on any money until the shares are sold. During this 'lock-in' period the value of the shares will be dependent not only on how the company performs, but also on the stock market's perception of its value. If the stock market crashes, probably the value of your shares will go down, although if it performs well, you may find that the value rises equally sharply.

So fingers crossed, and with any luck, soon you will be able to cash in the shares and celebrate.

Getting the big exit in a trade sale

The ideal scenario, from an investor perspective, is that a trade buyer appears and wants to buy the whole company.

This is your big chance, but do you remember that reference in the previous chapter to drag along and tag along rights? You may find that, even though there is an offer on the table that you want to accept, your fellow shareholders do not agree with you. Equally you may think the offer is poor and you do not want to sell, but find that they do. If the drag along and tag along rights have been written correctly, you will probably not be able to force or stop the sale unless the majority of the other shareholders agree with you. Remember that although this may be very irritating, at least having drag along and tag along rights will mean that the other shareholders cannot sell out for cash themselves and leave you behind as the unwanted but powerless minority shareholder in another business.

The other issue in a trade sale is that sometimes a buyer will offer to sell you shares in themselves in exchange for your shareholding. So you may get your exit from one company only to find you have a smaller stake in another one. If this is the case, make sure that you can sell the new shares you have been given for cash as soon as possible.

How the government can help you make a profit on the sale of your shares

In the Appendix you will find a summary of the Enterprise Investment Scheme. Read this as it will explain to you how you can get the UK government to help you to make a profit on your investment.

There are lots of rules surrounding EIS, but, if your investee company qualifies for the Scheme (and stays qualifying for three years), there are three facts you really need to know. All of these will help you, by default, to make a profit out of your investment:

* You can claim 20% Income Tax relief in your tax return on any investment you make in the company, and
* You can roll over any Capital Gains Tax you are due to pay HM Revenue & Customs if you invest it in the company, and
* If you hold your shares for three years or more, when you do sell them, you will pay no Capital Gains Tax on the profit you make.

Selling the assets of the business and closing down the company

Sometimes you will gain the profit on your investment, not by selling the company, but by selling the assets within it and then extracting the cash from it and closing it down.

The most common asset to sell is the business that is trading from the company. Some buyers like to purchase the assets and relevant liabilities of a business, rather than the company, for one or both of two reasons.

- They know exactly what they are buying and do not have to take on the unquantifiable risk that they buy a company with a hidden liability or exposure within it. For example, they may be worried that there is some unidentified problem that means the company will be sued at some point in the future.
- It is more tax efficient for them to buy the assets and liabilities rather than the company.

As an investor, this exit route carries risks with it because the cash raised from the sale will go in the first instance to the company and not to the shareholders. The shareholders then have to extract the cash from the company usually via an extraordinary dividend. If this takes place, investors will not be able to benefit from EIS relief for starters. They will also continue to be investors in a cash rich shell which, as mentioned above, may have an unforeseen liability. Ultimately, and especially if you are a passive investor, you will not have much say in how a sale is negotiated, but it is worth talking to the company's management and their advisers about how they will get your money to you if this does happen.

A sale of one or more separate assets of the business

It may be that there is an asset in the business which builds a distinct value of its own. This could be a property or a patent. Sometimes this asset can be sold for cash and the money can then also be paid out as a dividend. Once again talk to tax experts about how to ensure that this is done as tax effectively as possible.

Closing down the company and distributing the net cash and assets to the shareholders

One day, it may be right for a company to be wound up and the assets (after all the liabilities have been cleared) to be shared amongst the shareholders. If this does happen there will probably be a horse trade amongst the investors about who takes which assets. Cash is easy to divide, but there may be more difficult discussions about the other assets. If this does happen, you will have to take a view on how to ensure that you optimize your own position, and talk to both your accountant and your lawyer for advice.

Make sure that the company is wound up correctly and that all the paperwork is completed. You do not want to find yourself still invested in something that everyone else has walked away from with only the taxman chasing you for some unpaid VAT.

Fees and earnings

Lastly, it is worth mentioning fees and earnings. No-one worth their salt values their time at less than it is worth. Investors are notorious for giving their valuable time to their investee companies for free or at a much reduced charge. They do this because they believe, rightly, that in doing so they will make the company stronger and more valuable and their shareholding will benefit accordingly.

The Dragons always make this point on TV and use it as one of the best reasons why entrepreneurs should take their money.

However, there are always some people who will try to make an additional 'profit' out of their investment by charging over the odds for their time. Clearly, it would be fraud to charge for time not spent on company business, so they will not have done that. If you are someone who seeks to make a profit out of their investment by charging over the odds, all I can say is good luck to you, but don't be surprised if you are soon spotted by the other members of the team and by the other investors. Remember also that the 'extra' money you take will no longer be in the company and available for investment in its future growth and therefore in the value of your shareholding will be affected.

Top Tips for making a profit out of your investment

1　Dragon investing is a patient man's game. Expect to be invested for about 7–10 years, even if the entrepreneur tells you it will only be for 3.

2　All the research proves that private investing is very risky. You will need to apply rules to your investment strategy to reduce these risks.

3　Roughly 1 in 25 deals give investors 10x their money back or more.

4　Roughly half of deals return no money to their investors or just pence in the pound.

5　You are most likely to make a profit on your investment if everyone else is too, especially the entrepreneur.

6　There are lots of different ways to get your money back and make a profit on your investment, ranging from dividend pay-outs to asset sales or even the well-known route – selling the business to someone else!

7　If your investee company floats on a stock market you may still not be able to sell your shares for several months.

8　Selling early may be selling too cheap or it may be the last chance you get. It's your call!

9　Earning fees or salary in return for working for the company is not the same as getting a financial return on your investment.

CHAPTER 25

When St George beats the dragon

As covered in the last chapter, around half of the deals invested in by them lose investors some or all of their money. Hopefully you will never invest in a deal that does go wrong, but just in case you do, here is an explanation of the things that do go wrong and what you might be able to do about it.

Investments go wrong for a wide variety of reasons. These are some of them.

- The market opportunity is not there or someone else gets there first so the business in which you are invested cannot create a profitable and large enough business for itself.
- Disaster strikes, for example, the factory burns down and the business cannot recover.
- The management team is not up to the job.
- Another disaster hits the management. Angels have told me stories of suicides, thefts and more which have brought teams to their knees.
- The business model is or goes wrong, for example, the costs of production do not leave any room for profits.
- The technology behind your company becomes obsolete or do not get to market because it is not scalable.
- General economic conditions move against the company, for example, recession.
- The company over-trades and cannot meet its bills.
- The shareholders fall out and bring the management of the company to a standstill.

Hopefully, the due diligence you will have done will have highlighted the obvious risks in the business, but no due diligence exercise is ever perfect and in the excitement of making an angel investment, it is very easy only to hear the good news and miss the bad. If this happens to you, you will only be one in a long line many investors of all types (including venture capitalists) that have faced the same thing, so do not beat yourself up about it. Instead make a decision about what you are going to do now, based on the facts you know.

The first sign that something is going wrong

Usually the first sign you will have that things have gone wrong is either when everything goes dangerously quiet, or alternatively you suddenly start hearing unexpected things. You may also start hearing stories or rumours from new or unexpected sources.

This is the time to start planning what you are going to do next and it may be a long time before someone actually steps forward to tell you anything coherent.

Once you are worried that something is going wrong, the first thing is to gather information so you have some facts upon which to make a sensible decision. It is around now that you will probably be very grateful that you have stayed friends with the management team and with your fellow investors.

What to do next

Once you have understood what is wrong you can decide what you personally are going to do about it. The answer may not be to step in and get involved for lots of reasons.

- Your investment may not be large enough in monetary terms to be worth saving.
- You may not have the time or the will power to get involved.
- By getting involved you may be exposing yourself to a liability or even litigation to which you are not currently exposed.

Seriously consider doing what many of the great US venture capitalists do, which is just to drop the deal completely. **Do absolutely nothing.** The worst case then will be that you lose your money, but you may just find that someone else steps up to the table to sort it all out and you will end up as a shareholder in a reformed and successful company.

Alternatively if you are already involved and cannot responsibly walk away consider the following scenarios.

Disaster scenarios

Disaster scenario 1: The market opportunity is not there or disappears

Usually you will be investing in a business when nothing is yet proved. Even Reggae Reggae sauce was not certain to be a success just because Levi Roots had managed to sell a few bottles of it at the Notting Hill Carnival. So, it is no surprise that many businesses will turn out not to be as good as was expected.

Funnily enough, one of the biggest risks is whether the company has been correctly funded. If it is over-funded, there is a risk that too much money will be wasted in proving that the opportunity is not there, but if it is under-funded there may be too little money available to make the investment needed at the right time.

This is where it is invaluable to have other investors who have a deep understanding of the business opportunity and can provide advice to the management and the other shareholders on what money should and should not be spent. If you do not have the experience, try to appoint a few industry experts to the board of directors or ask them to act as expert consultants to the business. With any luck if you do this early enough you will not get any nasty surprises.

Take the competitive environment very seriously. Make sure that someone is keeping a close eye on the market generally and is watching what the competition is doing. Do not be scared of competitors, they will help build the market in which your investee company is operating, but do try to anticipate their moves. Also remember that the noisiest competitors are not necessarily the most dangerous. It's the quiet ones to look out for!

If the competition really does seem to be overwhelming your business, you will all have to decide whether to change tack or give up. If you do decide to give up, try to manage the wind-down in an orderly way.

Disaster scenario 2: Commercial disasters that are nothing to do with the business model

Businesses should have a disaster recovery plan, which aims to deal with the commercial disasters. Hopefully, your investee business will have one, even if it is still sitting in the heads of the key shareholders, the directors or the management team. Find out if there is a plan and assess it to see if it can or should be adopted. Also look to see if you can add value to the plan by giving advice or lending resources, even if it means handing over your spare room to act as a temporary head office!

Disaster scenario 3: Something goes wrong with the management

Very often deals go wrong because the management team, for whatever reason, is not able to do the job it is expected to. These are some of the real stories that investors have told me where things have gone wrong with the management team.

Suicide or accidental death of the entrepreneur

Building and running a business from scratch, which is what entrepreneurs do, is an incredibly stressful activity and regrettably it is not unknown for entrepreneurs to commit suicide. Investors also tell me tales of entrepreneurs being killed in accidents.

This is why it is extremely important to take out key may insurance on each of the key people in the management team and not just the founder. Whilst a finance director might be replaceable the technical director might not be if they are the scientists who knows all the secrets. It is also why you should make sure that all the company's trade and commercial secrets are recorded on paper (or computer) so that other people can access them if necessary.

If you have been closely involved in the business, this type of disaster may affect you personally as well as be a disaster for the company. The most important action to take will be to support the remaining members of the team and as soon as possible reallocate tasks, if possible, to keep the business running. After that you should start looking for someone who can replace the founder, bearing in mind that the best person may not be a replica of the person who has gone.

The management team has an irresolvable row

With a team of lively, intelligent, strong-minded people, it would be amazing if conflict did not arise. Sometimes this will reveal irresolvable differences and the team will never be able to work together again. If this situation occurs, try not to take sides. The situation will need a neutral mediator to help manage the change process that will probably see some team members depart and new people brought in to replace them. This neutral mediator may not be you!

The management team fails

Sometimes there are good businesses, but the wrong team is managing them. The founder may be a brilliant innovator, but not a good business person. Depending on what has gone wrong, it may be necessary to move people into new roles or, sometimes, get them to walk away from the business. The shareholder agreement should have anticipated this with good and bad leaver clauses which set out what will be done.

Someone commits fraud

One of the best stories circulating around the investor world is from a now-famous private investor, who, as a young entrepreneur faced the challenge of his own investor running off with all the money! It is much more common for the entrepreneur either deliberately or unconsciously to commit fraud. This is a criminal offence and you should take legal advice about what to do next.

The management team falls out with some or all of the shareholders

Potentially this is a real disaster for you as it is very hard for shareholders to do anything about the management team without resorting to a legal process which will be lengthy and expensive or just closing down the business which will not be popular. It can happen to anyone, just read this case study from Rachel Elnaugh.

Case study: Grails

Rachel Elnaugh's first investment on *Dragons' Den* was in Grails, the bespoke tailoring service for women. Run by ex-corporate executive Tracey Graily it was actually a brilliant concept for a business. However, the logistics behind creating bespoke suits are horrifically complicated and the business was beset with operational problems. Rachel undertook the investment in partnership with co-Dragon Doug Richard and between them they ended up injecting a total of £110,000 into the business. However, much of this money was immediately sucked into paying off existing debt.

'In fact it took Tracey about 110 days to go through the entire £110,000. It was our own fault of course,' said Rachel Elnaugh. 'Firstly our due diligence should have been better, and secondly we should have retained signing control of the money, only allowing it to be spent on specific "value-add" projects. Of course Tracey

> believed that the Dragons would never let her business fail, but when she came back to us asking for more money, we declined to offer any additional support. It was apparent that we would be throwing good money after bad and to be honest we felt quite let down by the way Tracey had blown the opportunity to spend our original investment wisely. It was easier for Doug and I just to take the hit, reclaim the 60% tax rebate that comes with failed EIS investments and move on.'

If you do follow the legal process the business is quite likely to collapse anyway. Once again, if this happens try to find a neutral mediator to resolve the situation. Alternatively, just sit back. Sometimes the management team is right and will return one day leading an incredibly successful business and will announce that they have sold the business for a fortune. I know of one situation where this happened, so don't despair!

Disaster scenario 4: The business model is wrong

With any luck the due diligence exercise before you invested will have examined the business model and worked out what its weaknesses were. If the business model is not working, change it and try another tack! If you have more than three goes, maybe you will have to change the management team or change the business altogether.

Disaster scenario 5: The technology does not work or becomes obsolete

This is a real possibility and a real risk. Probably the only answer will be to try to salvage what you can and either turn the business into a consultancy or close it down. Remember what I said earlier on – in this situation it may not be in your best interests to get involved in these decisions.

Disaster scenario 6: The economy falters

As I am writing this book, the television is full of stories about the worrying economic climate in the UK and what the effects on business may be. You might think that a weak economy is a bad thing for a small, fast-growing business. It can be, especially if the business does not have tight cost controls in place. But there is also plenty of evidence that small, lean companies thrive in a weak economy, whilst their large fatter competitors falter. As an investor, you will now be very reliant on the skills of the management and the directors of the company. Expect to hear news of slower sales, higher costs and redundancies, but do not give up hope. This may be just the opportunity your company needs to steal a march over others.

Disaster scenario 7: The company is overtrading

Fast growing companies have an amazing capacity to absorb cash and can easily find themselves overtrading. When the economy is booming this is not usually a problem because they can either easily win new business or raise more money from the bank to cope with cash flow problems. There are lots of interpretations of overtrading, but in this context it usually means that the business has taken on sales commitments that it cannot fulfill because it does not have enough money to meet cost of the orders and pay all its other bills. A business can also be overtrading because it will have to pay for things soon, but does not expect its own invoices to be paid for several weeks or months.

Economic conditions like the effects being felt in the UK due to the credit crunch can make life difficult. Technically if a company cannot meet its liabilities and if it does not have the financial support of its shareholders it must declare itself insolvent and go into administration or declare itself bankrupt.

It is quite possible that the problems the company is facing are temporary and it will probably have given the management team the fright of their lives. As an investor you may find that your job is to help them manage their way out of their financial mess. Therefore, don't be surprised to be asked to invest more money!

Disaster scenario 8: You fall out with your fellow dragons

The trouble with any row is that it tends to have unforeseen consequences. Investors fall out with each other, especially when they have unequal investments in a business and their interests are not aligned. You must look after your own interests first, but sometimes those interests will be best served by co-operating with your other investors, not trying to win at their expense. The private investment world is still a small one and investors' memories are long. What you do now will be remembered and may be shared with others. Get it wrong and you may find that new, even better, deals are not offered to you in the future.

At all costs avoid involving the management team in your row. This will be hard as the temptation will be to try to build your supporters around you. But the more you do incite the row, the more likely you are to face a big adverse response. The most likely outcome will be that it will damage the value of your investment.

So, if a fall-out is unavoidable, at least try to keep formal channels of communication in respect of the company in which you are invested open (even if it is via your lawyer!) and do not antagonize the situation by making new aggressive moves unless you absolutely have to.

And after disaster there is hope!

Do you know? It is actually a badge of honour to have had a failed investment and survived to tell the story. Treat it as a rather expensive, personally tailored MBA in dragon investment. If Peter Jones can fail, end up sleeping on the floor of his office because he has nowhere else to live and then pick himself up and build a global telecommunications business, just think. The next person who appears in front of you looking for investment might just have the same drive and determination, but you will be given a chance to share in the riches.

Anyway, in all likelihood, once you have recovered from the shock or fury from losing your money, you will find that there are compensations.

You will have joined the club of 'blooded' investors and you will soon find yourself boring your family and friends stupid with tales of the shocking things you experienced.

And a failed deal also gives you more lessons in investing than a successful one, so you will know better for next time, when there is a next time. And there will be one! Angel investing is addictive. I look forward to seeing you the next time around!

Ten top tips for dealing with disasters

1 Disasters come in all sorts of disguises. Don't ignore your gut instinct if you think anything is not right.

2 Make sure that the obvious things to prevent disasters are sorted out, like up-to-date insurance and proper IT back-up systems.

3 Stay informed so that, if possible, you know when disaster is looming.

4 Have back-up and alternative plans in place for the obvious disasters which might occur.

5 Once you know a disaster has hit, gather your facts before doing anything.

6 Decide early on whether you would be better off, both financially and in terms of time and effort, in just walking away rather than trying to solve it.

7 Seek professional advice especially when it comes to areas like employment and financial problems.

8 Try not to incite a disaster or to antagonize one, however tempting. After all, you left those tactics in the school playground didn't you?

9 Don't be surprised if you are asked to provide more money to help the business buy its way out of the disaster.

10 There is no shame in honest failure. Sometimes it is the best thing to accept defeat and learn from it.

Final thoughts

Chris Blishen, an angel investor, kindly read this book for me in its final draft to check whether I had done a thorough job. After he read it, he said to me that he could now see that the best investments he had made had tended to follow a thorough investment process along the lines described in this book. I hope that you, like Chris, find enough information and advice to make some great deals yourself in the future. Please let me know if you do by emailing me at Modwenna@angelnews.co.uk. And if, in the past, you have some faced, and overcome, some truly disastrous deals and are willing to share what you learned, feel free to send me the details too. Perhaps one day, they will be able to be incorporated into an updated edition of this book.

Lastly, if you are already an angel investor, carry on – entrepreneurs out there need you. If you are new to investing, start investing as soon as you are confident. There is nothing like angel investing for interest, enjoyment, creativity, giving something back and, sometimes, making a large fortune!

PART 4

Appendices

APPENDIX 1

Some famous companies and the individuals who have backed them

The Body Shop

Dame Anita Roddick founded The Body Shop in the 1970s using ingredients that she had brought back from her travels or already had stored in her garage. Her first shop opened on 27th March 1974 in Brighton only stocking 15 products and was financed by Ian McGlinn, who invested less then £5,000 (around £25,000 in today's money) in return for 50% of the company. Speaking to a reporter, Anita described him as the 'perfect sleeping partner. He has never woken up.' Now the company has over 2,000 stores in more than 50 countries. In March 2006, The Body Shop agreed to a £652.3 million takeover by L'Oréal with the Roddicks and Ian McGlinn each making around £130 million from the sale. Anita Roddick sadly died in September 2007.

Facebook

Mark Zuckerberg founded Facebook in February 2004 while a student at Harvard University. The company was first funded by Peter Thiel in June 2005 with an initial investment of $500,000. This was followed a year later by $12.7 million in venture capital from Accel Partners, and then $27.5 million more from Greylock Partners. Facebook now has more than 80 million active users worldwide. Peter Thiel now reportedly owns 7% of Facebook, which, at Facebook's current valuation of $15bn, would be worth more than $1bn. In October 2007 Microsoft paid $240 million for a 1.6% stake, valuing Facebook at $15 billion.

Google

Google was co-founded by Larry Page and Sergey Brin as an online search engine while both were students at Stanford University and quickly spread to information seekers around the globe. Andy Bechtolsheim and David Cheriton were two of the first investors in Google, investing $100,000 in September 1998. In August 2004 Google succeeded in raising $1.67 billion from public floatation making it worth $23 billion. Google is still growing with 19,156 full-time employees as of March 2008 and is widely recognized as the world's largest search engine.

Innocent Drinks

Innocent Drinks was co-founded by Richard Reed, Adam Balon and Jon Wright while at Cambridge University in 1999. The company's primary business is producing smoothies and flavoured spring water. Maurice Pinto first invested after the trio formally presented to his venture capital fund. While the fund turned them down, Mr Pinto invested £250,000 of his own money. Innocent now has a 71% share of the £169m UK smoothie market and the company sells two million smoothies per week.

Apple

Apple was co-founded by Steve Jobs and Steve Wozniak in 1976. Capital was raised by selling the duo's prized possessions including a Volkswagen minibus and programmable HP calculator. They succeeded in raising $1,300 to launch the enterprise and built their first machines in Steve Jobs' family garage in 1976. In 1977 the company secured $600,000 venture funding under the management of Mike Markkula, a former Intel executive, who signed on as Apple's chairman. Apple Computer went public in 1980, making its founders multi-millionaires; Steve Jobs became chairman while Markkula took on the role of president. Apple is now worth $158.66 billion.

Last.fm

Last.fm was founded in 2002 by Felix Miller, Martin Stiksel, Michael Breidenbruecker and Thomas Willomitzer. The company is a UK-based Internet radio and music community website. In 2004 the company received the first round of angel funding from investor banker Peter Gardner. A second round was led by Stefan Glaenzer who invested a 'few hundred thousand' in 2004, also buying out Michael Breidenbruecker as a shareholder. In 2006 the company received the first round of venture capital funding from European investors Index Ventures. The company was bought by US media giant CBS for €280 million in May 2007, resulting in the original founders gaining $30 million each. The company now claims over 21 million active users based in more than 200 countries with more than 80 staff members.

Glasses Direct

James Murray Wells founded Glasses Direct in 2004. He started the company using £1,000 from his student loan. After two months of trading David Magliano invested £750,000 in return for a significant minority stake. David Magliano has continued to be very supportive in further rounds of investment. Glasses Direct is the first company to sells glasses online for a fraction of the price of a high-street shop. In 2007 venture capitalists Highland Capital Partners and Index Ventures also invested in the company together providing £3 million of funding. Al Gosling (CEO Extreme Group) has also invested for a minority stake in the business. In 2005 the company had a turnover of £1 million and employed 17 staff. The company is aiming to be worth £1 billion in the future.

APPENDIX 2

Twenty key questions business angels should ask and entrepreneurs should answer

1. What does your business do?

2. How many countries does and will your business operate in?

3. Who currently owns shares in your business?

4. Are they investing in this fundraising round? If not, why not?

5. Tell us about your management team.

6. What will you do to fill the gaps in your management team?

7. Who are your customers now and who will your customers be in the future?

8. Who are your suppliers and what will you do if they can no longer supply you?

9. What intellectual property protection do you have?

10. What is your business model?

11. What is your financial model?

12. What are your profit and cash flow projections for the next twelve months, three years and five years?

13. What do you need the investment for?

14. Will you need to raise more money for the business? If so, when, how much and what type of investment will you seek?

15. What is the valuation of your business?

16. How can you justify that valuation?

17. What are your long-term hopes for the business?

18. What are your long-term plans personally?

19. How do you plan to exit from the business?

20. When do you expect to exit from the business?

APPENDIX 3

ENTERPRISE INVESTMENT SCHEME (EIS) an outline by Vantis plc.

The notes below are a general outline only and professional advice should be taken in relation to specific investments and the applicability of the scheme to them.

What is the EIS Scheme?

EIS, and its predecessor the Business Expansion Scheme, were designed to encourage individuals to invest their own money in shares in small start-up trading companies, which by their nature tend to be high risk investments. Provided the shares are held in a qualifying trading company for three years then Income Tax relief is given on the initial investment, and there is no Capital Gains Tax on the sale of the shares.

Key benefits of the EIS Scheme

These are the key benefits of the Scheme.

- Income Tax relief at 20% for an individual for qualifying investments of up to £500,000 in any tax year from 2008/09 (previously £400,000).
- Equates to a tax refund of up to £100,000 for higher rate tax payers.
- Minimum investment of £500 in a qualifying company.
- Provided Income Tax relief has not been withdrawn, then full Capital Gains Tax relief on sale of shares after three year qualifying period.
- Can be used to defer Capital Gains on any assets made by individuals and trustees.
- If EIS shares are disposed of at any time at a loss (after taking into account income tax relief), such loss can be set against the individual's capital gains or his income in the year of disposal or the previous year. For gains offset against income tax, the net effect is to limit the investment exposure to 48p in the £1 for a 40% tax payer if the shares become totally worthless. Alternatively the losses can be offset against Capital Gains Tax at the prevailing rate — 18% from tax year.

Qualifying company for EIS purposes

These are the rules about which companies qualify for the EIS Scheme.

- Unquoted UK Trading Company.
- Alternative Investment Market (AIM) counts as unquoted for EIS.

- Trading – excluded trades include dealing trades, banking and financial services, leasing, property development, agriculture and forestry, hotels and nursing homes, legal and accountancy.
- Qualifying Business Activity – trading, preparing to trade, or carrying out research and development for intending trade.
- Gross assets less than £7 million before issue of EIS shares, and less than £8 million after issue.
- Standalone company or holding company of trading group – all subsidiaries must be 51% owned, and EIS activity subsidiaries must be 90% owned.

Investor qualifications

These are the rules which investors need to comply with to qualify under the Scheme.

- Individual subject to UK Income Tax/Capital Gains Tax.
- Must not be connected with the company for a period beginning two years before the issue of the EIS shares, and ending three years after the start of the qualifying period (does not apply for deferral relief).
- Connected means alone or with associates owning more than 30% of the company.

How to apply for EIS Status

This is what you have to do to apply for EIS Status.

- The company makes the application for qualifying EIS company status.
- A provisional application is made to The Small Company Enterprise Centre in Cardiff. The SCEC can be contacted at Centre for Research and Intelligence (CRI), Ty Glas, Llanishen, Cardiff CF14 5ZG (telephone 029 2032 7400; fax 029 2032 7398; email enterprise.centre@hmrc.gsi.gov.uk).
- HMRC will ask further questions if necessary, and provide their provisional views on whether the company will qualify for EIS status.
- When the company commences activity it makes a formal application on Form EIS 1 to be accepted. If HMRC are satisfied that all is in order they will issue Form EIS 2 to the company, which in turn enables the company to issue Forms EIS 3 to the investors.
- The company must have been trading or carrying out other qualifying activity for a period of at least 4 months before it can submit Form EIS 1, and has two years from the later of that date or two years from the end of the accounting period in which the shares were issued to submit the form.

Elephant traps!

The rules around the Scheme are very complicated and are easy to break. Here are some mistakes that companies and investors often make which result in the Scheme being withdrawn.

- Withdrawal of EIS status for any reason will result in HMRC reclaiming any tax relief given to the investors, along with interest on the tax reclaimed.

- Loans to the company by the investor prior to the EIS claim may result in a connection between the investor and the company and so relief being denied.
- The EIS shares must be ordinary plain vanilla and not carry any preferential rights to income or capital.
- The shares must be fully paid on issue and there must be minimal time delay between receipt of investment monies and shares being issued.
- EIS monies must be used for qualifying business activities, and this must be demonstrable to HMRC.
- At least 80% of the EIS money must be used within 12 months of the issue of the shares, or 12 months from the start of trading if later, and the remainder within a further 12 months.
- There are complex rules in relation to directors of companies.

Conclusion

At the time this book was published, HM Government was undertaking a review of the EIS Scheme. Therefore it is worth talking to your accountant about possible changes to the rules that may be implemented following the review. If you want to know more about the Scheme it is worth looking at the website of the Enterprise Investment Scheme Association www.eisa.org.uk.

APPENDIX 4

Business angel networks

The following pages provide a list of UK business angel networks and their contact details, divided by region.

South	Contact	Address	Address	Address	Address	Post code	Phone no.	Website	Email
Equus Capital	Nigel Johnson	St John's Innovation Centre	Cowley Road		Cambridge	CB4 0WS	01223 421228	www.equuscapital.co.uk	nigeljohnsonsimonharris@equuscapital.co.uk
Finance South East Limited	Paul Coleman	Riverside House	4 Meadows Business Park	Station Approach	Blackwater	GU17 9AB	01276 608510	www.financesoutheast.com	Paul.Coleman@financesoutheast.com
Kingston Business Angels	Christopher Fogg	3 Kingsmill Business Park		Chapel Mill Road	Kingston-Upon-Thames	KT1 3GZ	0208 5452875	www.kingstoninnovation.org	angels@kingstoninnovation.org
London Business Angels	Sarah Rowe	New City Court	20 St Thomas Street		London	SE1 9RS	020 70892327	www.lbangels.co.uk	info@lbangels.co.uk
SWAIN	Nicola Prosser	Argentum	510 Bristol Business House		Bristol	BS16 1EJ	08700 606560	www.swain.org.uk	enquiries@swain.org.uk
Thames Valley Investment Network	Nicki Hattingh	Crowthorne Enterprise Centre	T Wing Crowthorne Business Estate		Crowthorne	RG45 6AW	01344 753365	www.tvin.co.uk	Nicki@tvin.co.uk
Xénos	Leanna Davies	Oakleigh House			Cardiff	CF10 3DQ	029 2033 8144	www.xenos.co.uk	info@xenos.co.uk

Midlands	Contact	Address	Address	Address	Address	Post code	Phone no.	Website	Email
Central England Business Angels		The Venture Centre	Sir William Lyons Road	Coventry	West Midlands	CV4 7EZ	02476 323233	www.centralenglandbusinessangels.angelgroups.net	info@cebangels.com
Silverstone Investment Network	Eileen Modral	Silverstone Circuit	Silverstone		Northamptonshire	NN12 8GX	01327 856156	www.silverstoneinvest.co.uk	e.modral@oxin.co.uk
Minerva Business Angel Network	Harry Stott	The Venture Centre	Sir William Lyons Road	Coventry	West Midlands	CV4 7EZ	024 7632 3123	www.minerva.uk.net	capital@uwsp.co.uk

North	Contact	Address	Address	Address	Address	Post code	Phone no.	Website	Email
Entrust	Sarah Thorpe	Portman House	Portland Road		Newcastle Upon Tyne	NE2 1AQ	0191 2444000	www.entrust.co.uk	enquire@entrust.co.uk
Northwest Business Angels	Ruth Hollis	Northwest Development Agency	PO Box 37	Centre Park	Warrington	WA1 1XB	01925 400302	www.nwbusinessangels.co.uk	angels@nwda.co.uk
Yorkshire Association of Business Angels	Barbara Greaves	1 Hornbeam House	Hornbeam Park	Hookstone Road	Harrogate	HG2 8QT	01423 810 149	www.yaba.org.uk	admin@yaba.org.uk

(Continued)

National	Contact	Address	Address	Address	Address	Post code	Phone no.	Website	Email
Advantage Business Angels	Patricia Sutton	Edgbaston House	3 Duchess Place		Birmingham	B16 8NH	0121 4567940	www. advantagebusinessangels. com	pat.sutton@abangels.com
Beer & Partners	Rod Beer	Masters Yard	South Street	Dorking	Surrey	RH4 2ES	08701 633033	www.beerandpartners. com	rbeer@beerandpartners. com
Envestors	Oliver Woolley	1 Lancaster Place			London	WC2E 7ED	020 7240 0202	www.envestors.co.uk	funding@envestors.co.uk
E-Synergy	Cheryle Hart	6-7 New Bridge Street			London	EC4V 6AB	0207 5833503	www.e-synergy.com	c.hart@e-synergy.com
Great Eastern Investment Forum	Arabella Wright	Richmond House	16/20 Regent Street		Cambridge	CB2 1DB	01223 720316	www.geif.co.uk	arabella.wright@nwbrown. co.uk
Octopus Ventures Ltd	Alex Macpherson	8 Angel Court			London	EC2R 7HP	020 7710 2800	www.octopusventures. com	info@octopusventures.com
Oxford Early Investments	Eileen Modral	Oxford Centre for Innovation	Mill Street		Oxford	OX2 0JX	01865 811120	www.oxei.co.uk	e.modral@oxin.co.uk
Oxfordshire Investment Opportunity Network	Eileen Modral	Oxford Centre for Innovation	Mill Street		Oxford	OX2 0JX	01865 811143	www.oion.co.uk	e.modral@oxin.co.uk

GLOSSARY OF TERMS

Business angel – A business angel is a wealthy individual who invests in exciting young unquoted businesses in return for a share in the ownership of the company.

Capitalization table (cap table) – A spreadsheet listing all shareholders and holders of options and any other securities, along with the number of shares, options and convertible securities held.

Cold approach – When you ask for investment from someone you do not already know and they have not asked you to approach them.

Company director – A legal post in which a person is a director of a company. The post carries legal obligations and responsibilities for how the company is run. All directors, even if called non-executive directors, have equal responsibility and liability as each other. It is possible to have the title 'director' without being a legal director of a company.

Current trading – How the business is performing in terms of sales and profits now as opposed to in the past or in the future. Current trading may be assessed on a daily, weekly or monthly basis depending on what type of business it is.

Disclosure letter – A letter given by the founders, and maybe other key members of the management team, and the company to the investors setting out exceptions to the representations and warranties.

Drag along/tag along – A mechanism ensuring that if a specified percentage of shareholders agree to sell their shares, they can compel the others to sell ensuring that a prospective purchaser can acquire 100% of a company.

Due diligence – The process of researching a business and its management prior to deciding whether to proceed with an investment in a company.

Elevator pitch – A one to five minute verbal pitch made by an entrepreneur explaining what his or her business does and why it would make a good investment opportunity.

Gatekeeper – The individual who assesses business plans on behalf of investors. They may or may not be an investor. Usually it is a term used to describe the managers of a business angel network.

Gearing – The ratio of debt to equity capital. If a balance sheet shows five million of total assets and debt of four million, the gearing is 80%. A very highly geared business is living dangerously. As in a car, high gearing can produce dashing performance – but leads to problems when you have to climb a steep hill.

Heads of Agreement – The document which lists all the terms of the deal as agreed by the entrepreneur and the potential investors. The lawyers use this to prepare the Shareholders Agreement and all other documentation in preparation for the investment being made.

Intellectual property (IP) – Legal term used to describe the patents, licences, copyrights, trademarks and designs owned by a company.

Lead investor – An investor (who may be an angel or a VC) who leads the investment negotiations on behalf of other investors and (probably) who co-ordinates the investment process. Post the investment, the lead investor will represent the other shareholders' interests and may act as a non-executive director at the company.

Lifestyle business – A business run to maximize the benefits to the owner who probably also manages the business. It is often used as a term of insult about businesses that ask for investment but which are believed by potential investors to have no hope of ever giving them their money back.

Liquidity event – When shareholders in a business are able to release their investment for cash.

Loan principal – The capital sum lent by someone to a company. The lender may be a bank or a new investor. Loan principal has to be paid in addition to the interest charged by the lender on the loan.

Non–disclosure agreement or NDA – A legally binding document signed by potential investors in which they agree not to use any of the information they receive or find out whilst researching the investment opportunity, against the company they are researching. A key element of an NDA is the agreement by the potential investor that all information will be kept confidential.

Options/Share options – Share options can be issued to managers or sometimes institutions. They confer the right to acquire shares at a specified price at or after a future date, and they can be performance related. The release of share options will normally dilute the value of other shares in issue.

Personal guarantee – The promise made by an entrepreneur which obligates him/her to personally repay debts his/her corporation defaults on.

Post–money valuation – The value of a privately held company immediately after the most recent round of financing. This value is calculated by multiplying the company's total (fully diluted) number of shares by the share price of the latest financing.

Pre–money valuation – The value of a privately held company prior to the most recent round of financing.

Ratchet – A structure whereby the eventual equity allocations between the groups of shareholders depend on the future performance of the company. This allows management shareholders to increase their stake if the company performs particularly well.

Retainer – A regular (usually monthly) fee paid by a company to an adviser to assist them with the business's development and/or fundraising.

Sales pipeline – The lists of potential customers who are likely to buy services or products from the business in the future. Usually the sales pipeline is broken down into likely customers who will buy in the next three, six and twelve months. The amount of sales that may be generated by each customer is recorded against their names and then a probability is applied e.g. 50% chance of making that sale. Revenue projections for the financial forecasts should be based on the sales pipeline. The best pipelines are rolling and are updated all the time.

Shareholder register – The document held by the company that records all the shareholders in the business and the number of shares they own. A copy of this register is also held at Companies House in the UK.

Shareholders Agreement – Also known as an Investment Agreement. This is a summary of the main terms of the investment into the company. Typically it will describe the amounts and types of shares to be issued and the specific rights of the investors such as veto rights and information rights.

Syndicate – An arrangement whereby a group of investors come together to invest in an investment proposition which they would not be prepared to consider individually whether because of risk or amount of funding required. The syndicate is usually headed by a lead investor.

Term sheet – A document summarizing the details of a potential investment offered by the investor which serves as the start for negotiations for the Shareholders Agreement.

Venture Capital or VC – Venture Capital is money invested in privately owned businesses, i.e. those that are not quoted on the London Stock Exchange. This money is usually invested from a fund managed by a team of fund managers, know as Venture Capitalists. The money for the fund comes from private individuals and institutional investors such as pension funds. The Venture Capitalists are expected to invest the money so that they make large profits for the investors in the fund. The Venture Capitalists usually charge fees both from the fund investors for managing the fund and from the companies in which the fund invests.

Warranties – Also known as representations. These are the terms in a Shareholders Agreement whereby usually the founders and key managers and (subject to local company law) the company give undertakings in respect of the past and present operating condition of a company. Examples include operating in a legal fashion, no bad debts, ownership of assets. Breach of warranty gives the investors the right to claim damages and, if it is sufficiently fundamental, may enable the investors to terminate the contract.